THE CYCLIST'S TRAINING BIBLE

THIRD EDITION

Joe Friel

VELO press

Boulder, Colorado

The Cyclist's Training Bible, Third Edition
Copyright © 2003 Joe Friel

Distributed in the United States and Canada by Publishers Group West.

International Standard Book Number: 1-931382-21-2

Library of Congress Cataloging-in-Publication Data
Friel, Joe.
    The cyclist's training bible / Joe Friel.—3rd ed.
        p. cm.
    Includes bibliographical references and index.
    ISBN 1-931382-21-2
     1. Cycling—Training. I. Title.

GV1048.F75 2003
796.6'07—dc21

2002044600

VeloPress®
1830 North 55th Street
Boulder, Colorado 80301–2700 USA
303/440-0601 • Fax 303/444-6788 • E-mail velopress@insideinc.com

To purchase additional copies of this book or other VeloPress® books, call 800/234-8356 or visit us on the Web at velopress.com.

Cover and interior design: Christopher Cox and Shennon Murray
Interior production: Kate Keady Hoffhine
Interior photos: Anne Krause, pages 50, 132, and 227

To Dirk:
my friend, my training partner,
my mentor, my pupil,
my son.

CONTENTS

VI

FOREWORD

Dr. Tudor O. Bompa is considered the "father of periodization." He consults with national Olympic organizations and sports federations throughout the world on the development of training programs for elite athletes.

In 1963, while on the faculty of the Romanian Institute of Sport, I was asked to coach one of the country's young and promising javelin throwers. As I looked at the "traditional" training programs at the time, I came to realize that something was missing in the way athletes were trained. Everyone followed the "ancient" program of preparatory, non-specific training during the winter, followed by the competitive phase during the summer and a transition during the fall. Later on, the Russians even called this "periodization." One of the missing links, the change I introduced, refined the sequence and type of strength and endurance training performed for each training period so that athletes ultimately would reach higher levels of strength and endurance. Later, I called this the "periodization of strength" and the "periodization of endurance."

From the 1960s on, Romanian coaches, as well as other Eastern European training specialists, adopted my principles of periodization and dominated world and Olympic competition for many years in many sports. Today, these systems, along with periodization of training for young athletes, are used by most top athletes in Europe and are gaining popularity in the United States as well.

In *The Cyclist's Training Bible*, Joe Friel has carefully provided the competitive road cyclist with all of the tools necessary to design and employ a periodization program following the principles I have laid down. He didn't come to this level of expertise by accident. I have spent time with Joe and know him as a very knowledgeable and masterful coach and teacher who is an authority on periodization. Unlike many other training specialists, Joe has spent many years trying different types of periodization and training schedules to determine what works best for cyclists and other endurance athletes. If he were in Eastern Europe, he would be called a "master coach."

The Cyclist's Training Bible is perhaps the most comprehensive and scientific book ever written on training for road cycling, and yet it is also practical and easy to follow. This book will have you systematically training just as world-class cyclists do. If you scrupulously follow the guidelines presented here, I'm confident your racing performance will dramatically improve.

Tudor O. Bompa, Ph.D.
July 1996

ACKNOWLEDGMENTS

There are many people who have contributed to this book in some way over the years since I first sat down to write it in 1995 and in its two revisions. At the risk of leaving someone out, here is a list of those who have helped me produce the concepts and, ultimately, the most recent version you now hold in your hands: Bob Anderson, Gale Bernhardt, Dr. Tudor Bompa, Ross Brownson, Dr. Loren Cordain, Bob Dunihue, Gear Fisher, Greg Haase, Jennifer Koslo, Gerhard Pawelka, Chad Matteson, Charles Pelkey, Jill Redding, Mark Saunders, Ulrich and Beate Schoberer, Rob Sleamaker, Amy Sorrells, Oliver Starr, Bill Strickland, and Todd Telander.

I want to especially thank the many cyclists with whom I have worked during my twenty-some years as a coach. They were often my "lab rats" as new ideas for training came to me, or they asked the right questions at the right times. Chief among them was my son, Dirk Friel, who throughout a long and successful career as a pro cyclist continually gave me feedback on what did and didn't work for him.

My wife, Joyce, whose unconditional support and love as I pursued my dream for more than two decades, contibuted immeasurably to making this book a reality.

PROLOGUE

In 1995 this book started out as my personal challenge. It was my first book and I expected it to sell a thousand copies or so. My intent was not to sell a lot of books, but rather to record for my own edification how to train for bike racing. Having been a teacher, I knew that the best way to ensure that you really understood a subject was to teach it to someone else. That's what *The Cyclist's Training Bible* was all about originally.

Seven years after conceiving the idea for a training book, I am contacted daily by curious riders from around the world with challenging questions; two other books have sprung directly from it (*The Triathlete's Training Bible* and *The Mountain Biker's Training Bible*); a Web site (www.TrainingBible.com) has been launched that makes the tools described here accessible to all; and I have spoken to thousands of athletes about the concepts described here. I am overwhelmed by its success.

This is the third edition of *The Cyclist's Training Bible* and there have been many revisions. There is not a single chapter that was left unaltered and many were significantly changed. The reasons for these changes have to do with the accumulated advances in science that provided a greater understanding of issues and with my personal growth. Over the years I have continually tried slight changes in the training of the many athletes I've coached. Some of these produced variations in what I have found to work. Other changes to this edition sprung from the many questions asked by athletes. Athletes are as eager to understand how best to train for peak performance today as they were in the early 1990s when the concepts of this book were developing. They continue to support my methods and to offer suggestions. It's been an awe-inspiring journey.

While much about this book has changed for the third edition, there is one constant as described in the original prologue: "I offer this book with the hope that it will make you a better racer and that one day you will return the favor by teaching me something you learned along the course."

Joe Friel
Scottsdale, Arizona

INTRODUCTION

How should I schedule hard workouts? How is it best to train during the weeks of my most important races? How many miles do I need before starting speed work? Is it okay to ride the same day I lift? How long should my recovery rides be? What can I do to climb better?

These are a few of the questions I hear from cyclists nearly every day. The athletes who ask these questions are intelligent and curious people—much like you, I'll bet. They have been riding and racing for three or more years, seeing substantial improvements in fitness merely from putting in the miles and competing in races. In the first two years, the competition was fun and they finished well in races. But now they've upgraded and things are different. They can no longer expect to improve by just riding a lot and begin to train harder only to find out they have more questions than answers.

The purpose of this book is to provide options for solving training questions in order to help you achieve racing success. The answers aren't always as simple and straightforward as you might like them to be. While the science of training has come a long way in the last thirty years, training is still very much an art.

The answers to most training queries I receive almost always start with: "It depends." It depends on what you have been doing prior to this time. It depends on how much time you have to train. It depends on what your strengths and weaknesses are. It depends on when your most important races happen. It depends on your age. It depends on how long you've been seriously training.

I'm not trying to be evasive, but I want to make sure you understand that there usually is more than one way to solve a training problem. If you asked ten coaches to answer the questions that started this introduction, you'd get ten different answers. All could be right, as there's "more than one way to skin a cat" or train a cyclist. My aim in this book is to assist you in answering your own questions. To that end, *The Cyclist's Training Bible* builds on ideas and concepts presented in each chapter. Following the chapter-by-chapter progression will help you understand the "whys" of my training methods.

In Part I, the self-trained cyclist's need for commitment and a common sense training philosophy are detailed. Chapter 1 describes what it takes for success in cycling, other than physical talent. Chapter 2 proposes a way of thinking about training that more than likely runs counter to your tendencies. I hope the 10 Commandments of Training cause you to occasionally stop reading and reflect on how to train intelligently.

Part II lays the scientific foundation for the remainder of the book by describing generally accepted concepts that guide the training process in Chapter 3. Chapter 4 takes the most critical aspect of training, intensity management, and teaches you how to do it. With the ready availability of powermeters since the first edition of this book there is a revolution going on in how we perceive and monitor the intensity of training. Be prepared to rethink what you know about this important topic.

Part III addresses the idea of training with a purpose and offers a framework for accomplishing that purpose. Chapter 5 shows you how to test your strengths and weaknesses, while Chapter 6 tells you what the results mean in terms of racing.

The heart of *The Cyclist's Training Bible* is Part IV. Here, I take you through the same process I use in designing a year-long training plan for an athlete. Chapter 7 provides an overview to the planning process. Chapter 8 describes the step-by-step procedures of planning in a workbook format. By the end of this chapter, you will have determined where you're going in the race season and how you will get there. Chapter 9 puts the cap on the process by showing you how to schedule workouts for the season and, more specifically, on a week-to-week and daily basis. It also suggests workouts. If you're doing a stage race during the season, be sure to read Chapter 10 before completing your Annual Training Plan. Chapter 11 offers examples of other cyclists' Annual Training Plans with discussions of the thinking behind their design. You may find in Chapters 8 and 9 that skipping forward to this chapter for examples is helpful in designing your plan.

Part V addresses several other aspects of training that affect the annual plan. The importance of strength training for cycling and how to follow a periodized plan is explained along with illustrations of exercises in Chapter 12. Chapter 13 shows how stretching can benefit cycling performance. Training concerns specific to women, masters, and juniors are detailed in Chapter 14. If you are in one of these special groups, it may help you to read this chapter before beginning the planning process in Chapter 8. The importance of keeping a training diary is the topic of Chapter 15. A sample journal is provided that complements the weekly scheduling described in Chapter 9. The discussion of diet in Chapter 16 presents a different way of thinking about eating. Also included is information about supplements and ergogenic aids. Chapter 17 provides guidance for how to deal with training problems common to cyclists—overtraining, burnout, illness, and injury. Chapter 18 discusses the most important, but most neglected, aspect of training—recovery.

Before beginning, I want to offer this note of caution: This book is primarily meant for cyclists who have been training and racing for some time. If you are new to the sport or considering starting to train, you should first have a medical examination. This is particularly important for those over age 35 who have been inactive. Much of what is suggested here is strenuous and designed for those with highly established levels of fitness and riding experience.

While I believe this book will help most cyclists improve, I do not pretend that it will make everyone a champion. It takes something more than just inspiration and guidance for that. No training program is perfect for everyone. Consider my ways of training critically and take from this book what will benefit you now. I hope you will use it as a training reference for years to come.

As you can see, *The Cyclist's Training Bible* is quite methodical. I hope that you don't feel as some do that analyzing the process of training detracts from the fun of riding and racing. I don't believe it does. Being on a bike is most enjoyable when every starting line is a challenge and every finish line is jubilantly crossed with arms held high. Let's start.

PART ONE

THE SELF-TRAINED CYCLIST

Hints on Bicycle Racing
by Norman Hill
As it appeared in Review of *Cycling Magazine*, 1943

In training or conditioning for bike racing, one must remember that for best results it must be considered as a full-time job, and the entire mode of living must be directed toward one objective, namely, the best possible health, which is the basis of all athletic ability.

Another important fact to remember is that adoption of a correct training program will not produce overnight results but must be followed religiously for a period of time. In fact, athletic champions are seldom, if ever, developed with less than several years of constant training and experience.

The correct conditioning program can and will improve anyone's ability but cannot, of course, guarantee that everyone will become a champion, as there are hereditary factors plus an element of luck to be considered. A correct training program can be likened to proper care of a car, the proper care insuring maximum efficiency, performance, and endurance.

1

COMMITMENT

At the base of the climb, which was 12 kilometers long, I started to look around and saw Ullrich, Pantani, Virenque, Riis, Escartin, and Jimenez—all in the top 10 of the general classification—and then me. I was hanging. I was there with these guys for the first time.
—BOBBY JULICH, commenting on the moment in the 1997 Tour de France when he realized he was a contender

Talk is cheap. It's easy to have big dreams and set high goals before the racing starts. But the true test of a commitment to better racing results is not in the talking, but in the doing. It doesn't start with the first race of the season—it's all the things you do today to get stronger, faster, and more enduring. Real commitment means 365 days a year and 24 hours a day.

Talk to the best riders you know. Ask them about commitment. Once you probe past all of the "aw, shucks" stuff, you'll discover how big a role cycling plays in their lives. The better they are, the more you'll hear about life revolving around the sport. The most common remark will be that each day is arranged around training. It's a rare champion who fits in workouts randomly.

Racing to your potential cannot be an on-again, off-again endeavor. It's a full-time commitment—a passion. Excellence requires living, breathing, eating, and sleeping cycling every day. Literally.

The greater the commitment, the more life is centered around the basic three factors of training—eating, sleeping, and working out. Eating fuels the body for training and speeds recovery by replacing depleted energy and nutrient stores. Sleeping and working out have a synergistic effect on fitness: Each can cause the release of growth hormone from the pituitary gland. Growth hormone speeds recovery, rebuilds muscles, and breaks down body fat. By training twice daily and taking a nap, the dedicated rider gets four hits of growth hormone daily resulting in higher levels of fitness sooner.

In the final analysis, greater fitness is what we're all after. It's the product of three ingredients: stress, rest, and fuel. Table 1.1 illustrates how training, sleeping, and eating can be built into your day.

	TWO WORKOUTS DAILY		ONE WORKOUT DAILY	
	WORK DAY	NO-WORK DAY	WORK DAY	NO-WORK DAY
6:00 AM	AWAKE	AWAKE	AWAKE	AWAKE
:30	WORKOUT 1	EAT	WORKOUT	EAT
7:00	|	STRETCH	|	STRETCH
:30	|	PERSONAL	|	PERSONAL
8:00	EAT	|	EAT	|
:30	SHOWER	WORKOUT 1	SHOWER	WORKOUT
9:00	WORK	|	WORK	|
:30	|	|	|	|
10:00	|	|	|	|
:30	|	EAT	|	|
11:00	|	SHOWER	|	|
:30	EAT	NAP	|	EAT
12:00 PM	NAP	STRETCH	EAT	SHOWER
:30	WORK	PERSONAL	NAP	NAP
1:00	|	EAT	WORK	PERSONAL
:30	|	PERSONAL	|	|
2:00	|	|	|	|
:30	|	WORKOUT 2	|	|
3:00	EAT	|	|	|
:30	WORK	|	EAT	EAT
4:00	|	|	WORK	PERSONAL
:30	|	EAT	|	|
5:00	END WORK	SHOWER	END WORK	|
:30	WORKOUT 2	NAP	PERSONAL	|
6:00	|	STRETCH	|	|
:30	EAT	PERSONAL	EAT	EAT
7:00	SHOWER	|	PERSONAL	PERSONAL
:30	PERSONAL	EAT	|	|
8:00	|	PERSONAL	|	|
:30	EAT	|	|	|
9:00	TO BED	TO BED	TO BED	TO BED

Table 1.1
Suggested Daily Routines

This kind of commitment may not be for you. In fact, there comes a point at which each of us has to check our "want to" against our "have to." Jobs, families, and other responsibilities can't be forsaken for sport. Even the pros must consider other aspects of life. Those elements that contribute to making you a great cyclist may detract from your being a great employee, mother, father, or spouse. Realistically, there have to be limits to passion; otherwise we'd soon alienate everyone who wasn't equally zealous and be reduced to slobbering zombies.

Change

What can you do to improve your fitness and race performances? The first thing is to make small changes in your life. Balance can be hard to achieve, but remolding daily activities by 10 percent in the direction of better cycling doesn't take much and can bring noticeable improvement. How about committing to hitting the sack thirty minutes earlier each night so that you're more rested? Another small daily change that could bring better results is healthier eating. Could you cut out 10 percent of the junk food every day, replacing it with wholesome foods? What you put in your mouth is the stuff the body uses to completely rebuild and replace each muscle cell every six months. Do you want muscles made from potato chips, Twinkies, and pop; or from fruits, vegetables, and lean meat? What can you change?

The Cyclist's Training Bible can help you make some small changes that will bring big results. But what are the most important changes needed for success? What makes a champion a champion?

Attributes of Champions

Successful athletes and coaches ask two questions in their quest for peak athletic performance:

- What does science say?
- How do champions train?

Much of this book is based on answers to the first question, but the second is no less important. Often the top athletes are ahead of science when it comes to knowing what works and what doesn't. Exercise scientists become interested in some aspect of training because it seems to work for some athletes. Their studies are designed to determine why it's beneficial.

If we eliminate their individual abilities and boil the remainder down to the most basic elements, what is left are the attributes that bring success to the champions. I believe there are six such attributes: ability, motivation, opportunity, mission, support system, and direction.

Ability

Genetics have a lot to do with achievement in sport. There are some obvious examples: Tall basketball players, huge sumo wrestlers, small jockeys, and long-armed swimmers are but a few. Such athletes were born with at least one of the physical traits necessary to succeed in their chosen sport.

What are the physical traits common to most of those who are at the pinnacle of cycling? The most obvious are strong, powerful legs and a high aerobic capacity (VO_2max). There are other physical traits that aren't quite as obvious. In order to climb hills, muscular power is another key trait. We can't see power in a rider in the same way we can see body mass or long arms. There are other physiological traits that define ability in cycling, including lactate threshold and economy (see Chapter 3 for details). These are somewhat determined by genetics, but they may also be improved by training.

So how much natural ability do you have? How close are you to reaching your potential? No one can say for sure. The best indicator may be how you've done in the sport in the past relative to your training. Good results combined with mediocre training usually indicate untapped potential. Excellent training with poor results is also revealing of potential.

If you are new to the sport with less than three years of racing, your results may not tell you much about your ability and potential. In the first three years there are a lot of changes happening at the cellular level—changes that will eventually reveal a rider's ability. This means that even if someone new to the sport is successful, he or she may not continue to dominate. Other beginners may eventually catch up to and surpass the most successful novices. This is often due to the different rates at which the human body responds to training.

Some people are "fast responders" and others are "slow responders." Fast responders gain fitness quickly because, for some unknown reason, their cells are capable of changing rapidly. Others take much longer, perhaps years, to realize the same gains. The problem for slow responders is that they often give up before reaping the benefits of training. Figure 1.1 illustrates the response curve.

Motivation

The highly motivated cyclist has a passion for the sport. Passion is generally evident in how much time is devoted to riding, caring for the bike, reading books and magazines about cycling, associating with other riders, and simply thinking about the sport.

Those who are passionate about the sport also frequently have a well-developed work ethic. They believe that hard training is what produces good results. Up to a point that is a valuable trait to have, as success does indeed demand consistency in training. The problem is that the combination of passion for cycling and a strong work

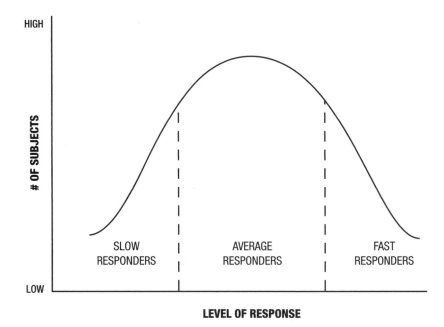

Figure 1.1

Theoretical bell-shaped curve indicating level of response to a given training stimulus

ethic sometimes leads to obsessive-compulsive training. These riders just can't stop riding. If they do, their sense of guilt can become overwhelming. For such athletes, training interruptions—such as injuries, business trips, or vacations—are emotionally devastating. This is because their training pattern may be disrupted, but their obsessive motivation is still intact.

This obsessive-compulsive trait is most common in riders who are new to the sport. They believe that they discovered the sport too late in life and need to catch up with others by training a lot. They also fear that if they stop training for even a few days that they may revert back to their former, unfit selves. No wonder overtraining is rampant among those in their first three years of racing.

Regardless of when in life you started or how burning your desire is to be good, it's critical that you view excellence in athletics as a journey, not a destination. You will never arrive at the point where you are fully satisfied with your performance. That's the nature of highly motivated people. So obsessive-compulsive training in order to achieve racing nirvana—where you can finally back off—is not going to happen. Once you realize this and take a long-term approach to training, your breakdowns from overtraining, burnout, and illness will diminish, allowing you to achieve training with greater consistency and better race performances. You will also experience less mental anguish and frustration when the inevitable setbacks occur.

Cycling is a life-long sport to be enjoyed for what it brings to your life—superb fitness, excellent health, enjoyable times, and good friends. It is not an opponent to be subdued and conquered.

Opportunity

The chances are great that the best potential athlete in the world is an overweight, sedentary smoker. Right now, sitting in front of a television somewhere is this person born to be the world champion in cycling and to dominate the sport as no one ever has. At birth he was blessed with a huge aerobic capacity and all of the other physiological ingredients necessary for success. The problem is that he never had the opportunity to discover his ability, even though the motivation may have been there at one time. Maybe he was born into poverty and forced to work at an early age to help feed the family. Maybe he lives in a war-ravaged corner of the world where staying alive is the number one priority. Or perhaps cycling just never caught his attention and he instead found success in soccer or piano playing. We'll never know what he could have been because the opportunity never presented itself.

The lack of opportunity need not be so extreme to hold back your growth as a cyclist, however. If any of the following are missing, your opportunity to realize full potential may be compromised:

- A network of roads to ride on
- Terrain variety—flats and hills
- Adequate nutrition
- Good equipment
- Coaching
- Training partners
- Weight-room equipment
- Time to train
- Available races
- A low-stress environment
- Supportive family and friends

This list could go on and on—there are many environmental elements that contribute to your overall opportunity to achieve your potential in cycling. The greater your desire to excel, the more important it becomes to mold your lifestyle and environment to match your aspirations.

Mission

When you think of champions such as Merckx, Hinault, LeMond, or Armstrong, what comes to mind? More than likely, it is winning the Tour de France. Why do you think of that? Probably because these athletes had a passion for winning the Tour that was, and is, evident for all to see. Their motivation to succeed was exceptional. They were willing to make any sacrifice, to ride any number of miles, to do any workouts deemed beneficial to achieving the goal. Approaching the peaks of their careers, riding was highly important in their lives. Everything else became just the details of life.

What you can learn from these champions is that motivation and dedication are paramount to achieving your dreams: The greater the dreams, the bigger the mission. Neither this book nor anyone else can help you choose dreams and become more dedicated. Only you can do that. I can tell you, however, that without passion, without a mission, you'll always be just another rider in the peloton.

Support System

The greatest rider with the biggest dreams will never become a champion without a support system—others who also believe in the mission and are committed to it. Surrounding champions are family, friends, teammates, directors, coaches, soigneurs, and mechanics, all of whom are there to help the champion attain his or her dream. The rider becomes immersed in the we-can-do-it attitude. The mission is no longer singular—it becomes a group effort. Once this is achieved, success is 90 percent assured.

Do you have a support system? Do those around you even know what your goals, let alone your dreams, are? Is there a mentor or close friend with whom to share your challenges and vision? Again, this book can't help you develop a support system. Only you can do that. Support systems start with you offering to help others, perhaps teammates, attain their highest goals. Support is contagious. Give yours to someone else.

Direction

Champions don't train aimlessly. They also don't blindly follow another rider's training plan. They understand that the difference between winning and losing is often as slight as a cat's whisker. They know their training can't be haphazard or left to chance. Merely having a detailed plan provides confidence. It's the final, and smallest, piece in the quest for the dream. Without a plan, the champion never makes it to the victory stand.

This is where *The Cyclist's Training Bible* can help you. While this book offers the reader individualized, results-oriented, and scientific methods, following its program won't guarantee success. But if you already have some ability, the opportunity has presented itself, a mission is well-defined, and the support system is in place, you're practically there. This just may be the final and decisive element.

SMART TRAINING

You can't train luck.
—EDDIE BORYSEWICZ,
renowned Polish-American cycling coach

Why is it that some start their cycling career with little sign of physical talent and years later reach the pinnacle of the sport as elite amateurs or pros? Why are there others who excel at an early age, fizzle, and eventually drop out of the sport before realizing their full potential?

Those who persevere probably had talent all along, but it wasn't immediately evident. More than likely, the young athlete had a parent, coach, or mentor concerned about the long term. They probably wanted to see their protégé in full bloom, so they brought the athlete along slowly and deliberately.

The successful athlete's workouts may not have been the most scientific, but a sensible training philosophy was established early in his or her career. In contrast, the young cyclist who failed to make it as a senior may have been driven too hard by a parent or coach whose intentions were good, but whose techniques left something to be desired.

When I begin to train athletes, I start by getting to know them fairly well—but it still takes weeks to determine exactly how they should train. There are many individual factors to consider in developing an effective training program. A few of these factors are:

- Years of experience in the sport
- Age and maturational level
- How training has progressed in the long term
- Most recent training program
- Personal strengths and weaknesses
- Local terrain and weather conditions

- Schedule of important races
- Details of the most important races: duration, terrain, competition, previous results
- Recent and current health status
- Lifestyle stress (work and family issues, for example)

The list could go on and on. There are simply too many unknowns for me or anyone else to advise you on how best to prepare for competition. After all, right now no one knows you as well as you do. Only you can make such decisions. All that is needed are the tools. That's why I wrote *The Cyclist's Training Bible*—so that you might do a better job of self-coaching.

Systematic Training

This book is about systematic and methodical training. Some riders think of that as boring and would rather work out spontaneously. They prefer to train by the seats of their pants—no planning, no forethought, and minimal structure. I won't deny that it is possible to become a good rider without a highly structured system and method. I have known many who have been successful with such an approach. But I've also noticed that when these same athletes decide to compete at the highest levels, they nearly always increase the structure of their training. Structured systems and methods are critical for achieving peak performance. It won't happen haphazardly.

But it should also be pointed out that the system and methods described in this book are not the only ones that will produce peak racing performance. There are many systems that work; there are as many as there are coaches and elite athletes. There is no one "right" way—no system that will guarantee success for everyone.

There are also no secrets. You won't find any magic workouts, miracle diet supplements, or all-purpose periodization schemes. Everything in this book is already known and used by at least some cyclists. No coach, athlete, or scientist has a winning secret—at least not one that is legal. Many have developed effective systems, however. Effective training systems are marked by comprehensively integrated components. They are not merely collections of workouts. All of the parts of effective programs fit together neatly, like the pieces of a complex jigsaw puzzle. Furthermore, there is an underlying philosophy that ties the parts together. All aspects of a sound program are based on this philosophy.

The Overtraining Phenomenon

Is there a relationship between fatigue and speed? Are there studies showing that if a rider gets really tired in training and does that often enough, he or she will get faster? Does starting workouts with chronically tired legs somehow improve power and other aspects of race fitness?

I pose these questions because so many athletes tell me that there's no improvement unless they feel at least a little sluggish all the time. But when I ask these same athletes why they train the answer is always, "To get faster for racing." Chronic fatigue is a strange way to get faster.

Recently I did a Web search of the sports science journals to see if any research has found a positive relationship between fatigue and athletic performance. Of the 2,036 studies I came across on these subjects, not a single one showed that an athlete performed better if he or she got tired often enough.

All of this leads me to believe that athletes who keep themselves chronically tired and leg weary must be making a mistake. Either that or they have a training secret. But I doubt it. More than likely the reason for their excessive training is a combination of an overly developed work ethic and obsessive-compulsive behavior.

In fact, there are a few athletes I have been unable to train for this reason. When I allow them to rest in order to go into a hard workout fresh, they interpret the lack of fatigue as a loss of fitness and become paranoid. After a few episodes of their putting in "extra" intervals, miles, hours, and workouts, we part company. My purpose in coaching is not to help otherwise well-intentioned athletes keep their addiction going. I'd like to see them race faster, not just be more tired.

On the other hand, I have trained many athletes in a variety of sports on a program of less training than they were accustomed to. It's amazing to see what they can accomplish once they fully commit to their actual training purpose—to get faster. When riders go into hard workouts feeling fresh and snappy the speeds and power produced are exceptional. As a result, the muscles, nervous system, cardiovascular system, and energy systems are all optimally stressed. Once they have a few more days of recovery to allow for adaptation, we do it again. And guess what—they are even faster.

Philosophy

The philosophy of training proposed in *The Cyclist's Training Bible* may seem unusual. I have found, however, that if it is followed, serious athletes improve. Here is my training philosophy: *An athlete should do the least amount of properly timed, specific training that brings continual improvement.*

The idea of limiting training is a scary thought for some. Many cyclists have become accustomed to overtraining that it seems a normal state. These racers are no less addicted than drug users. As is the case with a drug addict, the chronically overtrained athlete is not getting any better but still can't convince himself or herself to change.

Read the philosophy statement again. Notice that it doesn't say "train with the least amount of miles." Another way to state it might be "use your training time wisely." For those of us with full-time jobs, spouses, children, a home to maintain, and other responsibilities, using training time wisely is more than a philosophy; it's a necessity.

What this means is that there are times when it's right to do higher volume training, but not necessarily the highest possible. This is usually in the Base (general preparation) period of training. There are also times when high volume is not wise, but faster, more race-specific training is right. These are the Build and Peak (specific preparation) periods. (Periods are explained in Chapter 7.)

While it seems so simple, there are many who can't seem to get it right. They put in lots of miles when they should be trying to get faster. And when they should be building a base of general fitness, they're going fast—usually in group hammer sessions.

So what do you use to gauge your progress—how tired you are or how fast you are? If it's the former you're doomed to a career of less-than-stellar racing. Once you figure out that fatigue gets in the way of getting faster and you make the necessary changes, you'll be flying.

The 10 Commandments of Training

To help you better understand this training philosophy I have broken it down into the "10 Commandments of Training." By incorporating each of these guidelines into your thinking and training, you'll be following this philosophy and getting a better return on your time invested. Your results will also improve regardless of your age or experience.

Commandment 1—Train Moderately

Your body has limits when it comes to endurance, speed, and strength. Don't try too often to find them. Instead, train within those limits most of the time. Finish most workouts feeling like you could have done more. It may mean stopping a session earlier than planned. That's okay. Do not always try to finish exhausted.

Muscles will only contract forcefully a certain number of times before they refuse to pull hard again. When glycogen, the body's storage form of carbohydrate energy, begins to run low, no amount of willpower can fuel the body. Slowing down is the only option. If such limits are approached frequently and over a long enough period of time, the body's ability to adapt is exceeded, recovery is greatly delayed, and training consistency is interrupted.

The biggest mistake of most athletes is to make the easy days too hard, so when it comes time for a hard training day, they can't go hard enough. This leads to mediocre training, fitness, and performance. The higher your fitness level, the greater the difference between the intensities of hard and easy days.

Many cyclists also think that pushing hard all the time will make them tough. They believe that willpower and strength of character can overcome nature and speed up their body's cellular changes. Don't try it—more hard training is seldom the answer. An organism adapts best when stresses are slightly increased. That's why you've often heard the admonition to increase training volume by no more than 10 percent from week to week. Even this may be high for some.

By progressing carefully, especially with intensity, you'll gradually get stronger and there will be time and energy for other pursuits in life. An athlete who enjoys training will get far more benefits from it than one who is always on the edge of overtraining.

The self-coached cyclist must learn to think objectively and unemotionally. It should be as if you are two people—one is the rider and the other is the coach. The coach must be in charge. When the rider says, "Do more," the coach should question whether that's wise. Doubt is a good enough reason to discontinue the session. When in doubt—leave it out.

Do every workout conservatively, but with a cocky attitude. When the coach stops the hill repeats at just the right time, and the rider says, "I could have done more," stopping is not a loss—it's a victory.

Commandment 2—Train Consistently

The human body thrives on routine. Develop a training pattern that stays mostly the same from week to week—regular activity brings positive change. This does not mean do the same workout every day, week after week. Variety also promotes growth. Later in this book you'll see that there are actually slight changes being made throughout the training year. Some of the changes are seemingly minor. You may not even be aware of them, as when an extra hour is added to the training week during the base-building period.

Breaks in consistency usually result from not following the Moderation Commandment. Overdoing a workout or week of training is likely to cause excessive fatigue, illness, burnout, or injury. Fitness is not stagnant—you're either getting better or getting worse all the time. Frequently missing workouts mean a loss of fitness. This doesn't mean, however, you should work out when ill. There are times when breaks are necessary. For example, what choice do you typically make when you:

- Feel tired, but have a hard workout planned?
- Are afraid of losing fitness while taking time off even though you feel wasted?
- Believe your competition is putting in more training time than you?
- Feel like your training partners are riding too fast?
- Sense there is only one interval left in you?
- Think you could do more, but aren't sure?

- Have a "bad" race?
- Seem to have hit a plateau or even lost fitness?

If your personal philosophy is "more is better," you will answer these questions differently than if it is "do the least amount of properly timed, specific training that brings continual improvement." Do you see the difference?

This is not to say that you shouldn't do hard workouts or that it isn't necessary to push the limits on occasion and experience fatigue as a result. It's obvious that if coming close to your riding potential is your goal, then you must often face and conquer training challenges. The problem arises when you don't know when to back off, when to rest, and when to do less than planned. The inevitable consequences of "more is better" are burnout, overtraining, illness, and injury. Extended or frequent downtime due to such problems inevitably results in a loss of fitness and the need to rebuild by returning to previous, lower levels of training. Riders who experience these problems with some regularity seldom achieve their potential in the sport.

Training consistently, not extremely, is the route to the highest possible fitness and your ultimate racing performances. The key to consistency is moderation and rest. That may not be what you want to hear about in a book on training, but read on to better understand how consistency will make you faster.

Commandment 3—Get Adequate Rest

It's during rest that the body adapts to the stresses of training and grows stronger. Without rest there's no improvement. As the stress of training increases, the need for rest also accumulates. Most cyclists pay lip service to this commandment; they understand it intellectually, but not emotionally. It is the most widely violated guideline. You will not improve without adequate rest.

What's the first aspect of daily life most athletes cut back on when they are pressed for time and feel the need to fit in a workout? The answer is sleep. They get up earlier or go to bed later in order to wedge more into each day.

The problem with this way of "creating" time is that it compromises recovery and adaptation. It's during rest, especially sleep, when the body mends and grows stronger. While we sleep, human growth hormone is released in spurts. If our time spent snoozing is shortened, it takes us longer to recover and our consistency in training suffers. Glycogen stores aren't fully replenished between workouts, leading to decayed endurance performance over several days. Damaged cells take longer to heal, raising the risk of injury and illness. If the training workload remains high despite decreased sleep time, overtraining becomes a real threat. Burnout is waiting just around the corner. Most athletes need seven to ten hours of sleep daily. Professionals, with few other

AND TO ALL A GOOD NIGHT

Quality of sleep may be improved by:
- Going to bed at a regular time every night, including the night before races
- Darkening the room in the last hour before bedtime and narrowing your focus by reading or engaging in light conversation
- Sleeping in a dark, well-ventilated room that is 60 to 64 degrees Fahrenheit (16 to 18 degrees Celsius)
- Taking a warm bath before bed
- Progressively contracting and relaxing muscles to induce total body relaxation
- Avoiding stimulants such as coffee and tea in the last several hours before going to bed
- Restricting alcohol (which interferes with sleep patterns) prior to retiring

demands on their time than training, usually include naps to get their daily dose. The rest of us need to get to bed early every night. The younger you are, the more rest you need. Junior riders should be sleeping nine to ten hours daily.

Refer back to Table 1.1, Suggested Daily Routines, to determine a daily schedule that will ensure you get adequate rest every day. Until you establish a schedule, you're not really training—you're playing on a bike.

Commandment 4—Train with a Plan

This is fundamental to improvement in almost any endeavor of life, yet few self-trained athletes do it. Sometimes I find riders who use a sound plan from a magazine, but as soon as a new issue comes out, they abandon the old plan and take up a new one. Most people will improve if they follow a plan—any plan. It can be of poor design, yet still work. Just don't change it.

This book is all about planning. In Part IV you will learn about annual training plans and weekly scheduling routines. This is the section you will come back to year after year as you plan for the next season.

Realize that all plans can be changed. Yours will not be chiseled into stone. It takes some flexibility to cope with the many factors that will get in your way. These may include a bad cold, overtime at work, unexpected travel, or a visit from Aunt Jeanne. I have yet to coach an athlete who didn't have something interfere with the plan. Expect it, but don't be upset. Roll with the punches and change the plan to fit the new situation.

Commandment 5—Train with Groups Infrequently

There's a real advantage to working out with others—sometimes. Pack riding develops handling skills, provides experience with race dynamics, and makes the time go faster. But all too often, the group will cause you to ride fast when you would be best served by a slow, easy recovery ride. At other times, you will need to go longer or shorter than what the group decides to ride. Group workouts too often degenerate into unstructured races at the most inopportune times.

For the winter base-building period, find a group that rides at a comfortable pace. During the spring intensity-building period, ride with a group that will challenge you to ride fast, just as when racing. Smart and structured group rides are hard to find. You may need to create your own. Stay away from big packs that take over the road and are unsafe. You want to get faster, not get killed. Use groups when they can help you. Otherwise, avoid them.

Commandment 6—Plan to Peak

Your season plan should bring you to your peak for the most important events. I call these "A" races. The "B" races are important, too, but you will not taper and peak for these, just rest for three to four days before. "C" races are tune-ups to get you ready for the A and B races. A smart rider will use these low-priority races for experience, or to practice pacing, or as a time trial to gauge fitness. If all races are A-level priority, don't expect much for season results.

This book will show you how to peak for A races two or more times in a season. Each peak may last for up to a couple of weeks. You will still race between peaks, but the emphasis will be on re-establishing endurance, force, and speed skills to prepare for the next peak.

Commandment 7—Improve Weaknesses

What do riders with great endurance, but not much speed, do the most of? You guessed it—endurance work. What do good climbers like to do? Not surprisingly, they like to train in the hills. Most cyclists spend too much time working on what they're already good at. What's your weakest area? Ask your training partners if you don't know. I'll bet they do. Then spend more time on that area. *The Cyclist's Training Bible* will help identify your weaknesses and teach you how to improve them. Understanding your "limiters" is critical to your success in racing. Pay close attention whenever you run across that term here.

Commandment 8—Trust Your Training

Few of us trust our training when it comes time to race. There's a great fear as the big race approaches that we haven't done enough, so we train right up to race day. I've seen people the day before an important race go out for a long ride or compete in a hard race because they think it will help. It takes 10 to 21 days of reduced workload for the human body to be fully ready to race, depending on how long and hard the training has been. Cut back before the big races, and you'll do better. Trust me.

Commandment 9—Listen to Your Body

In the early 1990s after the fall of the Berlin Wall, I attended a talk by the former head of the East German Sports Institute. After conceding that East German athletes had indeed used illegal drugs, which he felt was a minor aspect of their remarkable success, he went on to explain what he saw as the real reason for their great number of Olympic medals. He described how elite athletes lived regulated lives in dormitories. Every morning, each athlete met with a group of experts—an event coach, a physiologist, a doctor or nurse, and a sports psychologist, for example. The group checked the athlete's readiness to train that day and made adjustments as necessary to the schedule. In effect, they were listening to what the athlete's body was saying. The athlete trained only to the level they could tolerate that day. Nothing more.

It would be nice if each of us could afford such attention. We can't, so we must learn to listen to our bodies for ourselves. If you listen to what the body is saying, you'll train smarter and get faster. Cyclists who train smart always beat athletes who train hard. *The Cyclist's Training Bible* will teach you how to hear what your body is saying every day—and train smart.

Commandment 10—Commit to Goals

If you want to race farther, faster, and stronger this season you need to train differently and may even need to make changes in your lifestyle. What could be holding you back? Is it too little sleep? Maybe you need to go to bed earlier. Or perhaps you eat too much junk food. You may benefit from putting in more time in the weight room during the winter to build greater force. Maybe your training partners are holding you back.

After you set your goals in a later chapter, take a look at them and determine how they relate to your lifestyle and training. Determine that if change is needed, you can do it. Only you can control how well you race. It's time to put up.

Striving for peak performance is a 24-hour-a-day, 365-day-a-year task. Racing at the highest possible level demands a full-time commitment that is not just training-related. The higher the goals, the more life must revolve around eating, sleeping, and working out. Eating nutritious food fuels the body for training and helps speed recovery by replenishing depleted energy and nutrient stores and by providing the building blocks for a stronger body. Sleeping and working out have a synergistic effect on fitness.

Every day you have lifestyle choices to make about diet, sleep, and other physical and mental activities. The decisions you make, often without even thinking, will impact how well you ride.

A fully committed rider is a student of the sport. Read everything you can get your hands on. Talk with coaches, trainers, athletes, mechanics, race officials, salespeople, and anyone else who may have a unique perspective. Ask questions, but be a bit skeptical. If you're to grow as an athlete, change is necessary. Other knowledgeable people are often the sources for this change.

Training to improve includes keeping a training log. Record workout details, perceptions of effort, stress signals, race results and analyses, signs of increasing or decreasing fitness, equipment changes, and anything else that describes your daily experience. It may all prove helpful down the road. Most athletes also find that keeping a log provides them with a sharper training focus and more rapid growth toward their goals.

Each of us has a comfortable level of commitment. There are times when we need to check our "want to" against our "have to." Jobs, families, and other responsibilities cannot be forsaken just to ride a bike. Passion must be restrained or we'll quickly alienate others who aren't equally zealous—we will become "cycling bums."

PART TWO

FROM LAB TO ROAD

HISTORICAL PERSPECTIVES

Training Tips at Random
by Fred Kugler
As it appeared in *Bicycling Magazine*, April 1946

A stunt that we have often used in road training is to walk rapidly for about a half a mile but carrying the bicycle with your arm cocked so the bicycle's cross bar is just off your shoulder. This tends to throw your shoulders back and stretches your chest and lungs, developing your grip, wrists, and arms. Change arms in carrying at will, but at no time during your set distance for this exercise let the bike touch the ground or your shoulder. If in a group, it can be made interesting by seeing who can carry their bicycle the farthest, or race to a given point under the above rules. Do this at the beginning or end of a ride, or just before or after a rest stop.

If interest is dull during a training ride, try this. The man in front sticks in ten hard kicks (counting on one foot only), then swings out and drops back to last place, and the next fellow sticks in his ten hard kicks, drops back, etc. You will soon find the going quite tough, that is if each rider really puts in ten good hard kicks.

THE SCIENCE OF TRAINING

Having all the sports science knowledge in the world, having all the best coaches, having all the best equipment, will that win a gold medal for you? No. But not having all that can lose it for you.
—CHRIS CARMICHAEL

It was not until the 1960s that the study of exercise as a science became widespread, and not until the 1970s before it began to significantly change the way serious cyclists trained. In the 1980s, exercise science made a quantum leap. We learned more about the human athlete in those ten years than in the previous eighty.

The earliest scientists learned more from studying the methods of top athletes than they did from independent study in their ivory towers. That is still the case today; the people in white lab coats seek an explanation for why some athletes succeed and others do not.

Even in the early days, riders learned through trial and error that they couldn't develop both maximal endurance and maximal power simultaneously. Coaches and athletes found that by first establishing an aerobic endurance base and later by adding faster riding, they could come into top form at the right time. This method of training was often imposed on them by the weather. Winter made long, easy rides a necessity, while summer favored faster riding.

Since those leather shoe and wool jersey days, we've learned a lot from the best athletes, coaches, and scientists. It's been a long and winding road. The entire range of training elements, including nutrition, recovery, strength, mental skills, fitness measurement, and workouts, has been explored and greatly refined. Still, many athletes continue to train as if it were 1912. They go out the door day after day with no plan, deciding as the ride develops what they will do. Some are successful despite their backward ways. Could they do better? Probably. Will you improve if you adopt a more scientific way of training as described in this book? I believe you will.

I hope to help you reach toward your potential by taking advantage of the most recent training knowledge available. This knowledge has been gleaned from research studies, from the training methods of top cyclists and coaches, and from athletes and coaches in other sports such as swimming, running, rowing, and triathlon. Some of it is proven beyond doubt, but much is still theory. You need to determine how everything applies to you and your training. Even well-established and proven practices may not be applicable given your unique set of circumstances. Some things may not work for you although they do for others.

Before getting scientific, I want to explain a few basics about training for cycling. These may be so elementary that they seem evident, but I'll describe them just in case.

No one starts out at the top. Many of those who get there make it because they are more patient than others. Training has a cumulative effect from year to year. If done correctly, a cyclist should see improvement over time. Don't expect miracles overnight.

Physical and psychological breaks from training are normal and necessary. No one can improve at an uninterrupted pace forever. If you don't build rest and recovery into your training plan, your body will force you to. It doesn't matter how mentally strong you are: You need frequent breaks from training.

If you're new to cycling, the most important thing you can do is ride consistently and steadily for a year. Don't be concerned about all of the detail stuff this book will describe until you've put at least one season under your belt. Then you can begin to plug in the finer elements of training.

Physiology and Fitness

How can we measure physical fitness? Science has discovered three of its most basic components—aerobic capacity, lactate threshold, and economy. The top riders have excellent values for all three of these physiological traits.

Aerobic Capacity

Aerobic capacity is a measure of the amount of oxygen the body can consume during all-out endurance exercise. It is also referred to as VO_2max—the maximal volume of oxygen your body can process to produce movement. VO_2max can be measured in the lab during a "graded" test in which the athlete, wearing a device that measures oxygen uptake, increases the intensity of exercise every few minutes until exhaustion. VO_2max is expressed in terms of milliliters of oxygen used per kilogram of body weight per minute (ml/kg/min). World-class male riders usually produce numbers in the 70- to 80-ml/kg/min range. By comparison, normally active male college students typically test in the range of 40- to 50-ml/kg/min. On average, women's aerobic capacities are about 10 percent lower than men's.

Aerobic capacity is largely determined by genetics and is limited by such physiological factors as heart size, heart rate, heart stroke volume, blood hemoglobin content, aerobic enzyme concentrations, mitochondrial density, and muscle fiber type. It is, however, trainable to a certain extent. Typically, in otherwise well-trained athletes, it takes six to eight weeks of high-intensity training to significantly elevate VO_2max peak values.

As we get older, aerobic capacity usually drops by as much as 1 percent per year after age 25 in sedentary people. For those who train seriously, especially by regularly including high-intensity workouts, the loss will be far smaller and may not occur until they are well into their thirties or even later.

Lactate Threshold

Aerobic capacity is not a good predictor of endurance performance. If all of the riders in a race category were tested for aerobic capacity, the race finishing results would not necessarily correlate to their VO_2max test values. The athletes with the highest VO_2max values would not necessarily finish high in the rankings. But the highest value of VO_2max that one can maintain for an extended period of time is a good predictor of racing capacity. This sustainable high value is a reflection of the lactate threshold.

Lactate threshold, sometimes called "anaerobic threshold," is the level of exercise intensity above which lactate begins to rapidly accumulate in the blood. At this point metabolism rapidly shifts from dependence on the combustion of fat and oxygen in the production of energy to dependence on glycogen—the storage form of carbohydrates. The higher this threshold is as a percentage of VO_2max, the faster the athlete can ride for an extended period of time, as in a race. Once lactate threshold reaches a high enough level, there is no option but to slow down in order to clear it from the blood.

Sedentary individuals experience lactate thresholds at 40 to 50 percent of VO_2max. In trained athletes, the lactate threshold typically occurs at 80 to 90 percent of VO_2max. So it is obvious that if two riders have the same aerobic capacity, but rider A's lactate threshold is 90 percent and B's is 80 percent, then A should be able to maintain a higher average velocity and has quite a physiological advantage in a head-to-head endurance race (unless rider B is smart enough to protect himself from the wind and has a great sprint).

Compared with aerobic capacity, lactate threshold is highly trainable. Much of the training detailed in this book is intended to elevate the lactate threshold.

Economy

Compared with recreational riders, elite cyclists use less oxygen to hold a given, steady, submaximal velocity. The elite riders are using less energy to produce the same power output. This is similar to automobile fuel efficiency ratings that tell prospective buyers which cars are gas guzzlers. Using less fuel to produce the same amount of power is an obvious advantage in competition.

Studies reveal that an endurance athlete's economy improves if he or she:

- Has a high percentage of slow-twitch muscle fibers (largely genetic)
- Has a low body mass (weight to height relationship)
- Has low psychological stress
- Uses light and aerodynamic equipment that fits properly
- Limits body frontal area exposed to the wind at higher velocities
- Eliminates useless and energy-wasting movements

Fatigue negatively impacts economy as muscles that are not normally called upon are recruited to carry the load. That's just one reason why it's critical to go into important races well rested. Near the end of a race, when economy deteriorates due to fatigue, you may sense that your pedaling and technical handling skills are "getting sloppy." The longer the race is, the more critical economy becomes in determining the outcome.

Just as with lactate threshold, economy is highly trainable. Not only does it improve by increasing all aspects of endurance, but it also rises as you refine bike skills. This is why I emphasize drill work for pedaling in the winter training months and a commitment to improving skills year-round.

Perspective

The preceding discussion probably makes it sound as if fitness can be easily quantified, and, perhaps, used to predict or even produce top athletes. Fortunately, that's not the case. The best scientists in the world can take a group of the most fit cyclists into a state-of-the-art lab, test, poke, prod, measure, and analyze them, then predict how they will do in a race—and fail miserably. Labs are not the real world of racing, where many variables beyond the ken of science escape quantification.

Training Stress

There are five terms used repeatedly in this book that relate to the stresses applied in training; it is important to understand these terms. By carefully changing workout *frequency*, *duration*, and *intensity* throughout the season, the body's comfortable state is disturbed, forcing it to adapt with the positive changes we call "fitness." This manipulation has to do with *volume* and *workload*. Let's briefly examine each of these terms.

Frequency

This refers to how often training sessions are done. Novice riders may work out three to five times a week and experience a rapid change in fitness, perhaps in the range of 10- to 20-percent improvement in a short period of time. Experienced cyclists train with greater frequency, often doing two workouts a day at certain times of the year. An Olympic hopeful might work out twelve to fifteen times in a week, but such high frequency may only produce a 1-percent gain in fitness, since these athletes are already so close to their potential.

Studies have found that training three to five times a week brings the greatest gain for the time invested, and that additional workouts have diminishing returns. If you are trying to realize your racing potential, however, those small gains are worth it since the competition will be quite close in ability.

Should a novice try to train at the same high level as the more experienced rider, he or she may actually see a decrease in fitness due to overtraining. If the experienced rider trains for a substantial length of time at the novice's low level, there will also be a loss of fitness because of undertraining—the stress frequency is too low.

The frequency at which you work out is dependent on what your body is currently adapted to. For example, even if you're an experienced rider but have not trained for several weeks, it's best to start with a lower frequency and gradually increase it.

Duration

Training sessions may vary considerably in length. Some last several hours in order to improve aerobic endurance. Others are short to allow for higher efforts or to promote recovery. Just as with frequency, workout duration is determined by experience level, with seasoned riders doing the longest sessions. Duration may be measured in time or in distance covered. *The Cyclist's Training Bible* bases training sessions on time.

The appropriate time for long rides is largely determined by the anticipated duration of your races. Typically, the longest workouts are about the same duration as the longest race the athlete will compete in or slightly longer. Early in the season, the higher-intensity workouts are done on lower-duration days, but as the racing season approaches, harder workouts incorporate both long duration and high intensity. This prepares the body for the stresses of racing.

Intensity, Volume, and Workload

Frequency and duration are easy to quantify, so athletes often refer to them in describing their training program. They may, for example, say that they rode seven times last week for a total of fourteen hours. This actually only describes a portion of their training—the portion called "volume." Volume is the combination of frequency and duration and it does, indeed, provide an idea of what an athlete's training is like. But volume is an incomplete description of the stress of training.

A better summary of one's training is "workload," defined as the combination of volume and intensity. By also knowing how hard the rider trained—how much effort or power went into each workout—the stress magnitude is more completely defined. The problem for the average rider is that it's difficult to quantify intensity in the same way that frequency and duration are quantified. One way to do this is to assign an average exertion level to each training session when it is completed, using a 1 to 10 scale with 1 being extremely easy and 10 an all-out race effort. By multiplying the number of minutes of the session by the exertion level, the workload is adequately quantified.

For example, let's say you rode for sixty minutes including a warm-up, several high-intensity hill repeats, and a cool-down. Assume that you assigned an average effort level of 7 to this entire session. Your workload might then be expressed as 420 (7 x 60).

To determine weekly workload, which includes frequency, add up the daily workload values. By comparing the workloads for a number of weeks, you can see how the stress experienced by the body changes.

Training intensity is the stressor that athletes most often get wrong. They ride a little too intensely when they should be taking it easy and, as a consequence, are slightly tired when a high-intensity workout is needed. All training therefore shifts toward mediocrity as the easy rides become too hard and the hard rides too easy. For most cyclists, getting the intensity right is the key to moving up to the next level of performance. Chapter 4 offers greater detail on this complex issue.

Volume versus Intensity

Which is more important—volume or intensity? Given the finite amounts of physical resources available to the rider, should he or she get in as many miles as possible, or ride fewer miles with high intensity?

The answers to such questions depend on the rider's level of experience in the sport. Those new to cycling will improve rapidly merely by riding frequently and with relatively high durations. As the rider becomes more experienced—and fit—increases in volume have less and less impact on performance and variations in training intensity become critical.

Fatigue

Were it not for fatigue we would all be champions. How quickly and to what extent we experience fatigue is a great determiner of our fitness level—it is a primary reason for training. The fittest athletes are those who can best resist its slowing effects.

There are several causes of fatigue, but the ones the cyclist is most concerned with are:

- Lactate accumulation
- Glycogen depletion
- Muscle failure

A sound training program improves fitness by stressing the body's systems associated with these causes of fatigue. Let's briefly examine each.

Lactate Accumulation

Energy for pedaling the bike comes largely from two sources—fat and carbohydrates. The body's storage form of carbohydrates is called "glycogen." As glycogen is broken down to produce energy, lactic acid appears in the working muscle cells. The lactic acid gradually seeps out of the cells and into the surrounding body fluids, where it is picked up in the bloodstream. As it leaves the cells, hydrogen ions are released and the resulting salt is called "lactate." If the concentration of lactate becomes great enough, its acidic nature reduces the ability of the muscle cells to contract, causing the rider to slow down.

Lactate is always present in the blood as the body uses carbohydrates along with fat for fuel at all levels of exertion—including the exertion involved in reading this page. But during exercise, as the use of glycogen increases, there is a concurrent rise in blood lactate levels. At low levels the body has no trouble removing and buffering the acid. But as the intensity of exercise shifts from aerobic (light breathing) to anaerobic (labored breathing), the lactate eventually reaches so great a level that the body is no longer able to remove it at the same rate it is produced. The resulting lactate accumulation causes short-term fatigue. The only way the rider can deal with it now is to slow down so lactate production is decreased and the body can catch up.

This type of fatigue occurs during brief but extremely high-intensity efforts such as long sprints, bridging to a break or climbing a hill. Thus, the way to improve your body's ability to clear and buffer lactate is by doing short-duration interval workouts that replicate these race conditions.

Depletion of Glycogen

Fat is the primary source of fuel for every ride you do, but as the intensity of the ride varies, the contribution of carbohydrates to the energy demand rises and falls considerably. Figure 3.1 illustrates this shift.

Carbohydrates are stored in the muscles and liver as glycogen and in the blood as glucose. A well-nourished athlete has about 1,500 to 2,000 kilocalories of glycogen

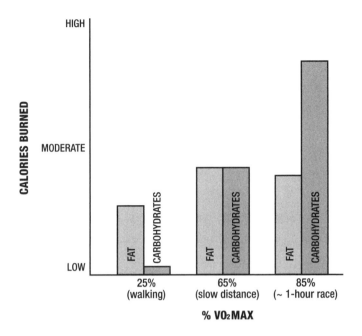

Figure 3.1
Relative contribution of fat and carbohydrate (glycogen and glucose) to exercise fuel at three levels of aerobic capacity (VO_2max).

Source: Adapted from J.A. Romijn et al. "Regulation of Endogenous Fat and Carbohydrate Metabolism in Relation to Exercise Intensity and Duration." *American Journal of Psysiology* 265 (1993): E380.

and glucose packed away, depending on body size and fitness level. That's not much energy. Most of this, about 75 percent, is in the muscles.

The problem is that when glycogen and glucose stores run low, exercise slows considerably, since the body must now rely primarily on fat for fuel, as shown in Figure 3.1. This is called "bonking."

A 2.5-hour race may have an energy cost of 3,000 kilocalories, with perhaps half of that coming from carbohydrate sources. If the rider starts with a low level of glycogen on board and these carbohydrate calories are not replaced during the race, he or she may be forced to abandon the race. The same sorry results may also occur if the rider pedals the bike uneconomically or if general aerobic fitness is poor.

Research reveals that a well-trained athlete is capable of storing greater amounts of carbohydrates while using it more sparingly than an untrained person. The diet you habitually eat also determines how much fuel is socked away and how rapidly it is used up. This is discussed in greater detail in Chapter 16.

Muscle Failure

Exactly what causes the cyclist's working muscles to fail to contract forcefully near the end of a long and grueling race is unknown. It is probably related to chemical failure at the point of connection between the nerve and the muscle, or by a protective mechanism in the central nervous system intended to prevent muscle damage.

High-intensity training may help to fortify the body against muscle failure by training the nervous system to recruit more muscles for endurance activity. Working out at high intensity, as when doing intervals, involves more fast-twitch muscles than riding long and slow, which favors slow-twitch muscles. Fast-twitch muscles are not called upon until the effort becomes so great that the slow-twitch muscles can no longer handle the effort. As fast twitchers are recruited to support the slow twitchers during what is basically an endurance activity, such as intervals, they begin to take on some of the slow-twitch characteristics. This is of great benefit to the endurance athlete.

Principles of Training

The principles upon which periodization training is based are individualization, progression, overload and specificity. Bear with me here as these may sound somewhat scientific and theoretical. Understanding the principles will make you a better cyclist—one capable of smart self-coaching.

Individualization

The capacity of an athlete to handle a given workload is unique. Each athlete can be considered an ecosystem influenced by three categories of factors—sociocultural, biological, and psychological. Each of these categories has the potential to impede or promote improvement.

Sociocultural factors such as lagging career progression, economic pressure, and poor interpersonal relationships often undercut how much time and energy, both mental and physical, is available for training. Examples of biological factors are allergies, use of drugs, and inadequate nutrition. These factors may restrict the individual's physical ability to train successfully. Psychological factors are perhaps the most overlooked, yet the most likely to compromise the benefits of training. Some examples are fear of failure, low self-esteem, and the unreasonable expectations of others.

In addition, some athletes are "fast responders" while others are "slow responders." This means that if you and a teammate do exactly the same training in precisely the same way, you probably won't reach a common level of fitness by a given race. Being a slow or fast responder is probably genetic—you may have inherited a body that changes at a given rate. Generally, four to eight weeks of a given type of training are necessary to show significant results. While you can't change how quickly your body responds, you can learn to design your training program around your unique characteristics.

The bottom line is that you cannot simply do what others are doing and expect to get the same benefits—or any benefits at all. What is an easy day for one rider may be race effort for another. Chapters 5 and 6 will address the issue of individualizing training to fit your unique set of abilities.

Progression

Have you ever done a workout so hard that you were sore for days afterward and did not have the energy to even ride easily? We've all done that. Such a workout violated the progression principle. The body didn't get stronger, it lost fitness. The workout caused you to waste two very precious resources: time and energy.

The workload must be gradually increased, with intermittent periods of rest and recovery, as the athlete focuses fitness for the most important races of the season. The stresses must be greater than the body is accustomed to handling. The workloads, especially the intensity component, are increased in small increments, usually of 5 to 15 percent. This allows the cyclist to avoid overtraining and injury, yet provides enough stress to allow adaptation to occur. Workload increases are largely individual matters, especially with regard to intensity. Chapters 5 and 6 will guide you through the maze of building race fitness progressively.

Overload

The object of training is to cause the body to positively change in order to better manage the physiological stresses of racing. In order to stress the body, it must be presented with a load that challenges its current state of fitness. Such a load will cause fatigue, followed by recovery and eventually a greater level of fitness known as "overcompensation (see Figure 3.2)."

Top-level performance is the result of years of well-planned overload resulting in adaptation. This optimum training repeatedly places measured stresses on the athlete. If the workloads are of the right magnitude, slightly more than the body can handle, adaptation occurs and fitness steadily improves.

It's important to note that overload happens during workouts, but adaptation occurs during rest. It is as if the potential for fitness is produced by training, but the realization of fitness occurs during subsequent rest. If you repeatedly short-change your rest, the body will not continue to improve. You'll actually lose fitness. This is

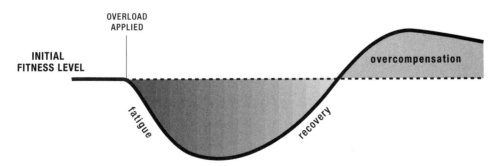

Figure 3.2
Overcompensation resulting from a training overload

called "overtraining." The biggest mistake I see self-coached athletes make is disregarding their need for rest. Smart athletes know when to abandon a workout early. They know when to do less instead of more. In short, they understand and listen to their bodies. You must learn to do the same. In Chapter 15, I'll teach you some techniques to help you refine this skill.

If the load of training is decreased for extended periods, the body adapts to lower levels of fitness. We call this "being out of shape." But once a rider has reached optimal fitness, it can be maintained with infrequent, but regular and judiciously spaced stress allowing for increased recovery between hard workouts.

Specificity

According to this principle, the stresses applied in training must be similar to the stresses expected in racing. Sometimes the workload must include long, steady distance. At others, brief bouts of high intensity are required to bring the needed changes. Riding slow all the time is just as wrong as always going hard. In Chapter 6, I'll teach you how to isolate the various stresses required in road races and show you how to blend them into a comprehensive program.

References

Bompa, T. "Physiological Intensity Values Employed to Plan Endurance Training." *New Studies in Athletics* 3, no. 4 (1988): 37–52.

Bompa, T. *Theory and Methodology of Training.* Dubuque, IA: Kendall/Hunt, 1983.

Bouchard, C., et al. "Aerobic Performance in Brothers, Dizygotic and Monozygotic Twins." *Medicine and Science in Sports and Exercise* 18 (1986): 639–646.

Brynteson, P., and W.E. Sinning. "The Effects of Training Frequencies on the Retention of Cardiovascular Fitness." *Medicine and Science in Sports* 5 (1973): 29–33.

Costill, D.L., et al. "Adaptations to Swimming Training: Influence of Training Volume." *Medicine and Science in Sports and Exercise* 23 (1991): 371–377.

Costill, D.L., et al. "Effects of Reduced Training on Muscular Power in Swimmers." *Physician and Sports Medicine* 17, no. 2 (1985): 94–101.

Coyle, E.F., et al. "Cycling Efficiency Is Related to the Percentage of Type I Muscle Fibers." *Medicine and Science in Sports and Exercise* 24 (1992): 782.

Coyle, E.F., et al. "Physiological and Biomechanical Factors Associated with Elite Endurance Cycling Performance." *Medicine and Science in Sports and Exercise* 23, no. 1 (1991): 93–107.

Coyle, E.F., et al. "Time Course of Loss of Adaptations after Stopping Prolonged Intense Endurance Training." *Journal of Applied Physiology* 57 (1984): 1857.

Daniels, J. "Training Distance Runners—A Primer." *Sports Science Exchange* 1, no. 11 (1989): 1–4.

Fitts, R.H., et al. "Effect of Swim-Exercise Training on Human Muscle Fiber Function." *Journal of Applied Physiology* 66 (1989): 465–475.

Gonzalez, H., and M.L. Hull. "Bivariate Optimization of Pedaling Rate and Crank-Arm Length in Cycling." *Journal of Biomechanics* 21, no. 10 (1988): 839–849.

Heil, D.P., et al. "Cardiorespiratory Responses to Seat-Tube Angle Variation during Steady-State Cycling." *Medicine and Science in Sports and Exercise* 27, no. 5 (1995): 730–735.

Hickson, R.C., et al. "Reduced Training Intensities and Loss of Aerobic Power, Endurance and Cardiac Growth." *Journal of Applied Physiology* 58 (1985): 492–499.

Hopkins, W.G. "Advances in Training for Endurance Athletes." *New Zealand Journal of Sports Medicine* 24, no. 3 (1996): 29–31.

Houmard, J.A., et al. "The Effects of Taper on Performance in Distance Runners." *Medicine and Science in Sports and Exercise* 26, no. 5 (1994): 624–631.

Houmard, J.A., et al. "Reduced Training Maintains Performance in Distance Runners." *International Journal of Sports Medicine* 11 (1990): 46–51.

Jacobs, I., et al. "Blood Lactate: Implications for Training and Sports Performance." *Sports Medicine* 3 (1986): 10–25.

Kearney, J.T. "Training the Olympic Athlete." *The Scientific American*, June 1996: 52–63.

Klissouras, V. "Adaptability of Genetic Variation." *Journal of Applied Physiology* 31 (1971): 338–344.

Loftin, M., and B. Warren. "Comparison of a Simulated 16.1-km Time Trial, VO_2 Max and Related Factors in Cyclists with Different Ventilatory Thresholds." *International Journal of Sports Medicine* 15, no. 8 (1994): 498–503.

MacLaren, C.P., et al. "A Review of Metabolic and Physiologic Factors in Fatigue." *Exercise and Sports Science Review* 17 (1989): 29.

Matveyev, L. *Fundamentals of Sports Training*. Moscow: Progress Publishing, 1981.

McArdle, W., F. Katch, and V. Katch. *Exercise Physiology*. Baltimore: Williams & Wilkins, 1996.

Neufer, P.D., et al. "Effects of Reduced Training on Muscular Strength and Endurance in Competitive Swimmers." *Medicine and Science in Sports and Exercise* 19 (1987): 486–490.

Nicholls, J.F., et al. "Relationship between Blood Lactate Response to Exercise and Endurance Performance in Competitive Female Masters Cyclists." *International Journal of Sports Medicine* 18 (1997): 458–463.

Poole, et al. "Determinants of Oxygen Uptake." *Sports Medicine* 24 (1996): 308–320.

Romijn, J.A., et al. "Regulation of Endogenous Fat and Carbohydrate Metabolism in Relation to Exercise Intensity and Duration." *American Journal of Physiology* 265: E380.

Tanaka, K., et al. "A Longitudinal Assessment of Anaerobic Threshold and Distance-Running Performance." *Medicine and Science in Sports and Exercise* 16, no. 3 (1984): 278–282.

Weltman, A. *The Blood Lactate Response to Exercise.* Champaign, IL: Human Kinetics, 1995.

Wenger, H.A., and G.J. Bell. "The Interactions of Intensity, Frequency and Duration of Exercise Training in Altering Cardiorespiratory Fitness." *Sports Medicine* 3, no. 5 (1986): 346–356.

Weston, A.R., et al. "Skeletal Muscle Buffering Capacity and Endurance Performance after High-Intensity Training by Well-Trained Cyclists." *European Journal of Applied Physiology* 75 (1997): 7–13.

Wilber, R. L., and R.J. Moffatt. "Physiological and Biochemical Consequences of Detraining in Aerobically Trained Individuals." *Journal of Strength Conditioning Research* 8 (1994): 110.

Wilmore, J., and D.L. Costill. *Training for Sport and Activity: The Physiological Basis of the Conditioning Process.* Champaign, IL: Human Kinetics, 1988.

Wilmore, J., and D.L. Costill. *Physiology of Sport and Exercise.* Champaign, IL: Human Kinetics, 1994.

Wyatt, F.B., et al. "Metabolic Threshold Defined by Disproportionate Increases in Physiological Parameters: A Meta-Analytic Review." *Medicine and Science in Sports and Exercise* 29, no. 5 (1997): S1342.

INTENSITY

Every time I suffer I'm a better man because of it.
—LANCE ARMSTRONG

Recreational cyclists generally believe that the more miles they ride the better they will race, regardless of what they do with those miles. To some extent they are right, as there does seem to be a threshold of miles or hours that a given athlete must ride in order to boost fitness to a sufficient level to race well. But once beyond that threshold, adding more miles has less benefit than increasing the intensity. It's not *how many* miles, but *what you do* with the miles that counts most.

Of the three elements of training—frequency, duration, and intensity—the most important element to get right is intensity. Oddly enough, this is the part cyclists all too often get wrong. Most train too intensely when they should be going easy. Then when it's time to go fast they are a little too tired to push their limits. As a result, all of their training becomes moderate. They race the same way: Stay with the pack until it's time to put the hammer down. Then they're off the back wondering how they got there.

In the context of this chapter, intensity refers to the effort or power output that closely simulates that of the A-priority events for which you are training. For a road race or criterium this may be a wide variety of intensities including steady efforts near lactate threshold while in a fast-traveling group, aerobic capacity intensities for several minutes while chasing down a break, or an all-out intensity for sprinting. For a time trial, century ride, or ultra-marathon the intensity will be much more narrowly defined. The intensity necessary to produce peak fitness must be well defined in order to create a sound training program.

Developing peak fitness is like building a house. The most important part of the house is its foundation. Without a solid foundation the house will settle, walls will crack, and it will have little value. If the foundation is constructed well, the house will be solid and last a long time. The same can be said of training to race. A solid foundation built on a base of easy miles is necessary before the finish work—intervals, hill repeats, and fast group rides—is added. But once the foundation is well established, workouts that mimic the intensities expected in the race pay dividends. Do these same intense workouts too soon and your house will shift and crack.

Another training comparison that has stood the test of time is that of a pyramid. The broader the base of the pyramid (easy aerobic training), the higher the peak will be (fast racing speed).

The bottom line is that high-intensity training needs to be undertaken with thought and planning in order to peak at the right times of the year. Too much, too soon and you won't be able to maintain the fitness. Too little, too late and you're off the back.

Learn to apply the intensity concepts in this chapter and you'll avoid overtraining and undertraining; your racing fitness will be high when the time is right.

Measuring Intensity

What's going on inside a cyclist's body during a race or workout? How does a rider know to go faster or back off during a time trial? Is a workout too hard or too easy? How is it possible to finish with enough left for a sprint?

The answers to these and other questions come down to keeping close tabs on your use of energy. By measuring intensity and comparing the information with what you have learned about your body in training and racing, you can make decisions as new situations such as breakaways, head winds, and hills occur. Today's technology allows an athlete to measure intensity quickly and accurately.

The oldest, and still one of the best, gross indicators of intensity is perceived effort. An experienced cyclist is able to judge his or her intensity quite accurately by taking a subjective survey of the entire body at work. This is a skill honed by years of riding, making mistakes, and relearning as fitness changes.

Perceived exertion is quantifiable using the Borg Rating of Perceived Exertion Scale (see Table 4.1) and is frequently used by scientists to determine at what level an athlete is working. Some athletes are so good at using a Rating of Perceived Exertion (RPE) that in a laboratory graduated-effort test they can pinpoint their lactate threshold precisely just from feel.

There are two other ways of measuring intensity that are related more or less to specific systems of the body. Heart rate is closely aligned with monitoring of the cardiovascular system, while power measurement relates closely to the ability of the

PURPOSE	RATING	EXERTION
RECOVERY	6	
RECOVERY	7	VERY, VERY LIGHT
RECOVERY	8	
RECOVERY	9	VERY LIGHT
AEROBIC DEVELOPMENT	10	
AEROBIC DEVELOPMENT	11	FAIRLY LIGHT
AEROBIC DEVELOPMENT	12	
TEMPO DEVELOPMENT	13	SOMEWHAT HARD
TEMPO DEVELOPMENT	14	
SUBTHRESHOLD DEVELOPMENT	15	HARD
SUBTHRESHOLD DEVELOPMENT	16	
SUPERTHRESHOLD DEVELOPMENT	17	VERY HARD
AEROBIC CAPACITY DEVELOPMENT	18	
AEROBIC CAPACITY DEVELOPMENT	19	VERY, VERY HARD
AEROBIC CAPACITY DEVELOPMENT	20	

Table 4.1
Borg Rating of Perceived Exertion Scale

muscular system to drive the pedals. Let's see how these and other methods can be utilized in measuring training and racing intensity.

Systems

The body is made up of several interconnected and mutually beneficial systems, such as the energy production, cardiovascular, and nervous systems. Regardless of what method of intensity measurement is used, you're taking a peek into the body through a small systems window, but since the systems are linked, you can draw conclusions about the entire body once you have experience and knowledge. I'll help you with the knowledge part in this chapter; you'll need to acquire the experience by using what you learn here.

The systems we can presently use to peek into the body while out on the road and the measurable indicator of each are:

- Energy production system—lactate
- Muscular system—power
- Cardiovascular system—heart rate

Energy Production System

The metabolic system provides fuel to muscles in the form of carbohydrates, fat, and protein. Within the muscle, these fuels are converted to a usable energy form called adenosine triphosphate (ATP). This process happens either aerobically or anaerobically.

Aerobic energy production occurs while you are riding easily. It relies primarily on fat and to a lesser extent on carbohydrates for fuel and uses oxygen in the process of converting fuel to ATP. The slower you go, the greater the reliance on fat and the more carbohydrates are spared. As the pace of your ride increases, there is a gradual shifting away from fat and toward carbohydrate as the fuel of choice. At high efforts, around 15 to 17 RPE, oxygen delivery no longer keeps up with the demand, and you begin producing ATP anaerobically, meaning "without oxygen."

Anaerobic exercise relies heavily on carbohydrates for fuel. As carbohydrates are converted to ATP, a by-product called lactic acid is released into the muscle. This causes the familiar burning and heavy-legged sensations you've experienced while riding hard. As lactic acid seeps through the muscle cell walls into the bloodstream, it gives off a hydrogen molecule and becomes lactate. Lactate accumulates in the blood and can be measured by taking a sample from the finger or earlobe. The unit of measurement used in labs is millimoles per liter, expressed as mmol/L.

Since carbohydrates are in use during both of these types of energy production, to a lesser extent in aerobic and more so anaerobically, lactic acid is always being produced. Even while you are reading this book, your muscles are producing measurable amounts of lactic acid.

By measuring lactate, an athlete, or more than likely his or her coach, could determine—with some degree of accuracy depending on skill level and equipment used—several key aspects of fitness, such as:

- **Lactate threshold.** As previously described, this is the level of exertion at which metabolism shifts from aerobic to anaerobic marked by lactate being produced so rapidly that the body can't keep up with its removal. Lactate thus accumulates in the blood. I often explain lactate threshold using an analogy. If I slowly pour water into a paper cup that has a hole in the bottom the water will run out as fast as I pour it in. This is what happens to lactate in the blood at low levels of exertion. If I pour faster, there comes a point when the water begins to accumulate despite the fact that some is still leaking out through the hole. This is similar to the lactate threshold point that is achieved at higher levels of exertion. Lactate threshold is an important concept that will be used throughout this book.
- **Training zones.** Training and racing intensities may be determined based on lactate levels (see Table 4.2).
- **Physiological improvement.** The faster a rider can go or the more power that can be generated without accumulating high levels of lactate, the better his or her racing fitness.
- **Economy of pedaling.** The smoother one pedals, the less effort he or she uses, and therefore, the less lactate that accumulates in the rider's muscles.

- **Equipment selection.** Optimal crank arm lengths, saddle heights, and handlebar adjustments create a greater pedaling economy, which then produces low levels of lactate in the rider's muscles.
- **Recovery interval.** Reduced levels of lactate indicate that a cyclist is ready for the next work interval in a workout.

RPE	PURPOSE	LACTATE (mmol/L)
<10	RECOVERY	<2
10–12	AEROBIC	2–3
13–17	THRESHOLD	3–5
18–19	AEROBIC CAPACITY	5–12
20+	ANAEROBIC CAPACITY	12–20

Table 4.2
Lactate Zones

The key piece in achieving all of these benefits is the ability to accurately measure lactate in a "field" setting (using an indoor trainer or track) rather than a lab—in other words, inexpensively. Until recently, the only way to measure lactate was in a lab using an analyzer such as the YSI 2300, the accepted standard in the United States. Its size, expense, and the need for electricity, however, make it impractical for field use.

In the past few years relatively inexpensive portable lactate analyzers have been introduced to the U.S. fitness market but these are not for the average rider's use. Using such a device requires extensive skill that comes only with the experience of sampling hundreds of athletes. The bottom line is that lactate sampling, while helpful, is not something for the rider to use, but rather a tool that may be used by his or her coach or a lab technician.

Muscular System

Power is a measure of work compared to time. It is expressed in units called "watts," named for James Watt, the inventor of the steam engine. In physics, power is described in a formula as:

$$\text{Power} = \frac{\text{work}}{\text{time}}$$

At the risk of oversimplification, in cycling "work" is essentially gear size and "time" is cadence. So if gear size is increased and cadence kept steady, power rises. Or, if cadence is increased (time per revolution of the crank is decreased) while using the same gear size, power also rises.

Several scientific studies have found that power is closely related to performance. If the average power output increases, race velocity also increases. The same cannot always be said for heart rate, as explained above; that is why power monitoring is such an excellent tool for bicycle training. It is the most effective way for the serious rider to monitor intensity.

The downside of power monitoring, as compared with heart rate, is equipment cost. In the early and middle 1990s, a powermeter cost about twenty times as much as a heart rate monitor. With the introduction of the Tune Power-Tap in 1999, however, the cost ratio was lowered to something approaching 4 to 1.

Power-based training begins with determining one's "critical power profile." This is a visual representation of the ability to produce power at various durations. Finding and graphing average power output for the critical power (CP) durations of 12 seconds and 1, 6, 12, 30, 60, 90, and 180 minutes produces a curve or profile such as those shown in Figure 4.1.

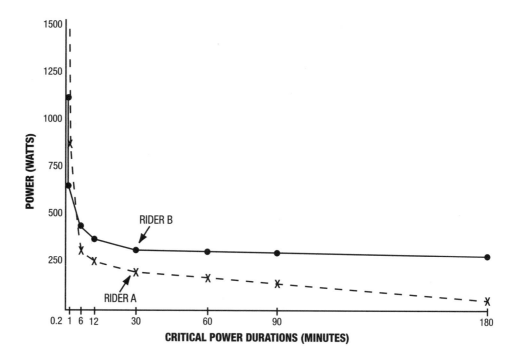

Figure 4.1

Critical profiles of two riders

Note that the profiles in Figure 4.1 are considerably different for the two riders. Rider A is capable of producing far greater power than Rider B for short durations. Although Rider B lacks short-duration power, the generally shallower slope indicates much greater endurance capability. In an all-out sprint near the finish line, Rider A has an advantage, but Rider B has the upper hand as the duration increases.

Once you've determined average power for each of the above durations (Chapter 5 describes how to do this), your CP training zones can be established. For the average power at each duration, add and subtract 5 percent to establish zones. For example, if your average power for six minutes is 360 watts, then CP6 is 342 to 378 watts (360 x 0.05 = 18, 360 − 18 = 342, 360 + 18 = 378).

Focusing your training on a given range of CP zones has the potential to produce fitness benefits that can be applied in certain race situations, as shown in Table 4.3.

DURATION	CP ZONES	FITNESS BENEFIT	RACE APPLICATION
12 SEC.	CP0.2	EXPLOSIVE POWER	Finishing sprint Short hill Start
1 MIN.	CP1	LACTATE CLEARANCE	Fast starts Short climbs
6 MIN.	CP6	VELOCITY AT VO$_2$MAX	Moderate duration climbs Short, high-intensity segments
12 MIN.	CP12	AEROBIC CAPACITY (VO$_2$MAX)	Fast starts
30 MIN.	CP30	LACTATE SUPERTHRESHOLD	Long steady efforts
60 MIN.	CP60	LACTATE THRESHOLD	Short duration race endurance
90 MIN.	CP90	SUBLACTATE THRESHOLD	Moderate duration race Endurance
180 MIN.	CP180	BASIC AEROBIC FUNCTION	Long duration race endurance

Table 4.3
Critical Power Zone Benefits and Race Applications

Cardiovascular System

In the early 1980s, the introduction of the portable heart rate monitor brought about a profound change in athletes' approaches to training. It is now a commonly used training device, second only to the handlebar computer in popularity.

From the time heart rate monitors first hit the market until about 1990 they were "gee whiz" toys—fun to play with, but the numbers didn't mean much. Now that nearly everyone has one, athletes are becoming more astute in their use. At criteriums, road races, and time trials around the country you can find most cyclists wearing them to regulate or monitor exertion.

A heart rate monitor is much like the tachometer in an automobile. Neither one tells how fast you're going, but rather how hard the engine is working. Just as a car can rev up the engine without moving and redline the tachometer, heart rate can zoom while you are running in place.

Knowing how hard the heart is working is important information that allows you to make decisions as a workout progresses. Sometimes motivation, or lack of it, gets in the way of rating your perceived exertion during high-quality training sessions.

Be aware that a low heart rate is not always a bad sign. In fact, a low workout heart rate relative to what experience has shown to be more common for you can be a good sign. Improving aerobic fitness typically produces a lower heart rate than when you were less fit. In the same way, a high heart rate is not always a good sign, either.

For a cyclist, knowing lactate threshold heart rate (LTHR) is as important as knowing frame size. But forget about trying to find maximum heart rate. Not only does this require great motivation—as in a gun to the head—but it's not as good an indicator as LT.

Heart rate training zones are best if based on LTHR, since the percentage of maximum at which one becomes anaerobic (lactate accumulates) is highly variable. For example, one cyclist may have a LTHR that is 85 percent of his maximum heart rate, while another goes anaerobic at 90 percent of max. If both riders train at 90 percent of max, one is deeply anaerobic and the other is at threshold. They are not experiencing the same workout or getting the same benefits. If, however, both train at 100 percent of LT or any other percentage of LT, they experience the exact same exertion level and reap the same benefits.

Finding LT requires scientific precision, but don't let that scare you away. It's actually a simple procedure. I'll describe how to do it in the next chapter. For this reason I prefer to first determine LTHR and then establish heart rate zones on either side of it.

One "easy" way of finding your lactate threshold heart rate is to time trial while wearing a monitor. The distance of the individual time trial (ITT) could be 5k, 10k, 8 miles, 10 miles, or 40k. The test can be done at an established race or as a workout you do alone. The average heart rate from this test will serve as a predictor of your LT. Since you will undoubtedly have higher motivation in a race than when doing this test alone, the results should be interpreted differently. Table 4.4 provides guidelines for determining LT heart rate from an ITT.

Example: A 10-mile individual time trial is done as a race when the athlete is rested and highly motivated. The average HR is 176. Divide 176 by 1.05 = 167 for LT. (See bold number 167 in table 4.6 for HR training zones.) Table 4.4 may also be used to determine HR to be used in an ITT. For example, a 40k ITT should be ridden at 100 percent of LT.

Table 4.4
Lactate Threshold Heart Rates based on Individual Time Trial

DISTANCE	AS RACE	AS WORKOUT
5K	110% OF LT	104% OF LT
10K	107% OF LT	102% OF LT
8–10 MILES	105% OF LT	101% OF LT
40K	100% OF LT	97% OF LT

Another simple test that can be done alone and has proven to provide a fairly accurate estimate of LTHR is to ride a thirty-minute time trial alone. Ten minutes into the time trial click the lap button on your heart rate monitor. The average heart rate for the last twenty minutes of your time trial is a reasonable estimate of LTHR. As with all of these tests, the more frequently you repeat the test, the more accurately you can estimate LTHR.

You may even be able to use your workouts to help confirm what was previously found in tests to be LTHR. Simply pay attention to your heart rate whenever you feel yourself initially becoming anaerobic. This level of intensity will be marked by burning sensations in your legs and the onset of heavy breathing.

Once you've found your LTHR, you can determine your heart rate training zones by using Table 4.5 or Table 4.6.

ZONE	RPE	PURPOSE	% OF LTHR
1	<10	RECOVERY	65–81%
2	10–12	AEROBIC	82–88%
3	13–14	TEMPO	89–93%
4	15–16	SUBTHRESHOLD	94–100%
5A	17	SUPERTHRESHOLD	101–102%
5B	18–19	AEROBIC CAPACITY	103–105%
5C	20+	ANAEROBIC CAPACITY	106%+

Table 4.5
Heart Rate Training Zones based on Lactate Threshold Heart Rate (LTHR)

Since we'll be referring to it frequently, I've numbered each heart rate zone. Zones 1 through 4 are each aerobic zones and zones 5A, 5B, and 5C are each anaerobic.

Heart rate varies with sport. If you're crosstraining in the winter by running, your lactate threshold heart rate will be different from cycling, as will all of your training zones. Because of this, you should either determine heart rate zones for each sport you crosstrain in or go only by RPE for other sports.

Race-Fit Systems

Coming into top racing form means optimizing the performance of each of the three systems. A cyclist with a great muscular system but poor energy and cardiovascular systems won't last long on the roads. It takes all three systems working together.

These systems must go through many changes during the training year for you to race effectively and attain your goals. The following is a partial list of changes that occur as a result of training.

THE CYCLIST'S TRAINING BIBLE

Table 4.6

Heart Rate Training Zones
Find your LT heart rate in the "Zone 5a" column (bold number). Read across from left to right for training zones.

ZONE 1 RECOVERY	ZONE 2 AEROBIC	ZONE 3 TEMPO	ZONE 4 SUB-THRESHOLD	ZONE 5A SUPER-THRESHOLD	ZONE 5B AEROBIC CAPACITY	ZONE 5C ANAEROBIC CAPACITY
90–108	109–122	123–128	129–136	**137**–140	141–145	146–150
91–109	110–123	124–129	130–137	**138**–141	142–146	147–151
91–109	110–124	125–130	131–138	**139**–142	143–147	148–152
92–110	111–125	126–130	131–139	**140**–143	144–147	148–153
92–111	112–125	126–131	132–140	**141**–144	145–148	149–154
93–112	113–126	127–132	133–141	**142**–145	146–149	150–155
94–112	113–127	128–133	134–142	**143**–145	146–150	151–156
94–113	114–128	129–134	135–143	**144**–147	148–151	152–157
95–114	115–129	130–135	136–144	**145**–148	149–152	153–158
95–115	116–130	131–136	137–145	**146**–149	150–154	155–159
97–116	117–131	132–137	138–146	**147**–150	151–155	156–161
97–117	118–132	133–138	139–147	**148**–151	152–156	157–162
98–118	119–133	134–139	140–148	**149**–152	153–157	158–163
98–119	120–134	135–140	141–149	**150**–153	154–158	159–164
99–120	121–134	135–141	142–150	**151**–154	155–159	160–165
100–121	122–135	136–142	143–151	**152**–155	156–160	161–166
100–122	123–136	137–142	143–152	**153**–156	157–161	162–167
101–123	124–137	138–143	144–153	**154**–157	158–162	163–168
101–124	125–138	139–144	145–154	**155**–158	159–163	164–169
102–125	126–138	139–145	146–155	**156**–159	160–164	165–170
103–126	127–140	141–146	147–156	**157**–160	161–165	166–171
104–127	128–141	142–147	148–157	**158**–161	162–167	168–173
104–128	129–142	143–148	149–158	**159**–162	163–168	169–174
105–129	130–143	144–148	149–159	**160**–163	164–169	170–175
106–129	130–143	144–150	151–160	**161**–164	165–170	171–176
106–130	131–144	145–151	152–161	**162**–165	166–171	172–177
107–131	132–145	146–152	153–162	**163**–166	167–172	173–178
107–132	133–146	147–153	154–163	**164**–167	168–173	174–179
108–133	134–147	148–154	155–164	**165**–168	169–174	175–180
109–134	135–148	149–154	155–165	**166**–169	170–175	176–181
109–135	136–149	150–155	156–166	**167**–170	171–176	177–182
110–136	137–150	151–156	157–167	**168**–171	172–177	178–183
111–137	138–151	152–157	158–168	**169**–172	173–178	179–185
112–138	139–151	152–158	159–169	**170**–173	174–179	180–186
112–139	140–152	153–160	161–170	**171**–174	175–180	181–187
113–140	141–153	154–160	161–171	**172**–175	176–181	182–188
113–141	142–154	155–161	162–172	**173**–176	177–182	183–189
114–142	143–155	156–162	163–173	**174**–177	178–183	184–190
115–143	144–156	157–163	164–174	**175**–178	179–184	185–191
115–144	145–157	158–164	165–175	**176**–179	180–185	186–192
116–145	146–158	159–165	166–176	**177**–180	181–186	187–193
116–146	147–159	160–166	167–177	**178**–181	182–187	188–194
117–147	148–160	161–166	167–178	**179**–182	183–188	189–195
118–148	149–160	161–167	168–179	**180**–183	184–190	191–197
119–149	150–161	162–168	169–180	**181**–184	185–191	192–198
119–150	151–162	163–170	171–181	**182**–185	186–192	193–199
120–151	152–163	164–171	172–182	**183**–186	187–193	194–200
121–152	153–164	165–172	173–183	**184**–187	188–194	195–201
121–153	154–165	166–172	173–184	**185**–188	191–195	196–202
122–154	155–166	167–173	174–185	**186**–189	190–196	197–203
122–155	156–167	168–174	175–186	**187**–190	191–197	198–204
123–156	157–168	169–175	176–187	**188**–191	192–198	199–205
124–157	158–169	170–176	177–188	**189**–192	193–199	200–206
124–158	159–170	171–177	178–189	**190**–193	194–200	201–207
125–159	160–170	171–178	179–190	**191**–194	195–201	202–208
125–160	161–171	172–178	179–191	**192**–195	196–202	203–209
126–161	162–172	173–179	180–192	**193**–196	197–203	204–210
127–162	163–173	174–180	181–193	**194**–197	198–204	205–211
127–163	164–174	175–181	182–194	**195**–198	199–205	206–212

Energy Production System

- Greater utilization of fat and sparing of glycogen
- Enhanced conversion of lactate to fuel
- Increased stores of glycogen and creatine phosphate
- Improved ability to extract oxygen from blood

Muscular System

- Increased force generation within a muscle fiber
- Enhanced recruitment of muscle fibers
- More economical movement patterns
- Enhanced endurance qualities

Cardiovascular System

- More blood pumped per heartbeat
- Greater capillarization of muscle fibers
- Increased blood volume
- Enhanced oxygen transportation to the muscles

DON'T BE A SLAVE TO YOUR HEART RATE MONITOR

Sidebar 4.1

Ten years ago hardly anyone had a heart rate monitor. Now almost everyone has one. Generally, I'm glad to see that trend, but there's a downside. It seems that we're becoming overly concerned with heart rate. Let me explain.

Before heart rate monitors, when an athlete started a hard workout such as intervals, he or she continually gauged how the session was going and may have decided to cut it short or to extend it. The usual basis for this pre–heart rate monitor decision was perceived exertion (PE). PE is based on a subjective reaction to breathing, lactate accumulation, fatigue, and other less-defined sensations during exercise. From this somewhat vague data the athlete would make decisions. What was good about this system was that it forced athletes to stay in tune with what their bodies were feeling. The downside was that it took experience to develop the skills to know what the sensations meant.

But now, with heart rate monitors, many athletes largely ignore their PE and focus solely on what their heart rates are. While it's effective to know your heart rate when training, it is not the only metric that should be monitored. In fact, doing so can really mess you up. Why is that so? Well, for one thing, heart rate is not giving you a complete picture of the body's workload, nor is it necessarily even giving you an accurate picture, since many factors—such as heat, diet, and stress, to name just a few—affect it.

Heart rate by itself does not tell you how well you're performing in a workout or a race, and yet many athletes try to draw conclusions from one number. For example, something I

Sidebar 4.1
continued

hear all the time is, "I couldn't get my heart rate up so I stopped the workout." Is a low heart rate bad? It could be, but then again, it might be good. One of the physiological side effects of improving aerobic fitness is an increased heart stroke volume—more blood is pumped per beat. That means a reduced heart rate for any submaximal level of exertion. So a low heart rate in a workout or race may be telling you that fitness is high and to keep going—not that you should stop.

In the same way, a high heart rate is not necessarily good, as most athletes typically conclude. "It was easy to get my heart rate up today" translates into "I'm in good shape." That's, again, not necessarily true. We could take a sedentary person off the street, put him on a bike, and force him to ride fast. Guess what? His heart rate would rise very easily. We might even be able to achieve a maximal pulse with very little power output. If his heart rate achieved the same max as that of a fit rider it would really tell us nothing about either one of them. You see, there is no difference between the maximal heart rate of a very fit athlete and that of an obese couch potato. The less fit you are, the easier it is to get heart rate up to max.

When testing athletes I have found that when they are in very good race shape their maximal heart rates appear to drop. I don't know exactly why that is. It may have something to do with their aerobic system adapting so well to endurance training that the muscular system is incapable of driving it any higher.

Another misuse of the heart rate monitor number is drawing conclusions about one's state of well-being. "My resting heart rate is high (or low) so I must be overtrained," is another common complaint I hear. It is not possible, however, to look at resting or exercising heart rates and draw such a conclusion. If it was, sports scientists would have stopped looking long ago for a way to gauge overtraining—something they have not been able to find.

Heart rate by itself tells you nothing about performance or well-being. It must be compared with something else to have meaning. For example, when it comes to cycling performance, comparing heart rate with power (for example, on a CompuTrainer or with a Power-Tap or SRM) is an excellent way to determine gains in fitness. If heart rate is low and power is normal to high, when compared with previous performances, then fitness is high. If heart rate is high and power is high then the athlete is probably still building fitness. This is a good way to gauge when the Base period should come to an end.

If heart rate is low and power is also low then the athlete may be experiencing fatigue, lifestyle stress, or even overtraining. There are other possibilities in this combination, so all we know is that something is not right.

Metrics other than power could also be used in conjunction with heart rate to help draw conclusions about the athlete's status. For example, what would low heart rate and high PE be telling you? This is saying that fitness and well-being are probably good. What would you say about high heart rate and low PE? Common sense would suggest that something isn't right. Think your way through the various possibilities.

The main point here is that heart rate alone tells you only one thing—you are still alive. Drawing conclusions only from what your monitor says on a given day is folly. Use the information that this miraculous training tool gives you, but don't rely on it alone.

Multisystem Training

RPE, heart rate, and power each offer unique benefits for the serious cyclist when it comes to monitoring intensity of a workout or race. RPE provides a subjective yet comprehensive view of what you are encountering when on the bike. Heart rate offers a window into the cardiovascular system and thus a glimpse of the workload the body is experiencing. A powermeter reports what the body is accomplishing. Power is a measure of performance rather than an indicator of the physiological stress experienced. Each is valuable in the training process.

Using all three is like seeing a picture in three dimensions instead of only one or two—training makes more sense. Whether or not a number is assigned, RPE should be an integral method of monitoring intensity in all workouts. This will pay dividends in races where closely observing heart rate and power is not possible. RPE is the "stake in the ground"—the supreme reference for all intensity monitoring. You must become good at using it. Heart rate is best used for steady-state training, particularly that done below the lactate threshold. It is especially effective during long, aerobic rides and for recovery workouts. Focus on power for intervals, hill training, sprint-power training, and all anaerobic workouts. I've seen significant improvement in race performance when riders have begun training with power. This is unquestionably the future of bicycle training. Mastering and appropriately applying each of these intensity monitoring systems has the potential to dramatically improve your training and, therefore, your racing.

Measuring Workload

Now that you have three systems for monitoring intensity, it's possible to quantify workload. Recall from the previous chapter that workload is the combination of frequency, duration, and intensity of training. Knowing workload allows you to keep track of and compare weekly training stress loads placed on the body. Such information is valuable for avoiding overtraining. It also helps in planning daily workouts if you know how much stress training is likely to produce. In turn, this allows you to determine how much and when recovery is needed. It also makes periodization of training more effective (see Chapter 7 for details on periodization).

The following are three workload-measuring methods, one based on each RPE, heart rate, and power.

RPE

At the end of a training session, assign an average workout RPE using the 6 to 20 scale. Then multiply this RPE value by the number of minutes in the session. For example, if a 60-minute session including intervals had an average RPE of 14, the workload for this day is 840 (60 x 14 = 840).

Heart Rate

Using a heart rate monitor with a time-by-zone function, it's possible to know how many minutes were spent in at least three zones (with a three-zone monitor, all five zones may be observed by switching zones during the ride). By multiplying each of the zone's numeric identifiers (Zone 3, for example) by the number of minutes spent in each zone and then adding them up, workload for a week or any other period of time may be determined.

For example, if you completed a 60-minute ride that included 20 minutes in Zone 1, 25 minutes in Zone 2, and 15 minutes in Zone 3, the cumulative workload is 115. Here's how that number was determined:

$$20 \times 1 = 20$$
$$25 \times 2 = 50$$
$$15 \times 3 = 45$$
$$\text{Total} \quad 115$$

Power

The Tune Power-Tap offers a quick way of monitoring workload—session kilojoules, recalled as "E" (for energy) and displayed in units called kilojoules (kJ) on the Power-Tap. This is a measure of energy expended. One kilocalorie (kcal or calorie) is equal to 4.184 kJ. Energy used in training is a nearly perfect way of expressing workload.

Cumulative Workload

Whichever method you use, record your daily workload in a training log. By totaling the daily workloads, a cumulative workload for the week is determined. This number serves as an indicator of how difficult the week was. By comparing it with past weeks, you can quickly see what is happening to the stress load. In general, the cumulative workload should increase as the year progresses from the start of training season in early winter until the spring races. This should not be a straight-line progression, however. It instead follows a wave-like pattern that allows the body to gradually adapt and grow stronger. Figure 4.2 shows how the cumulative weekly workload advances through one portion of the training year.

Unfortunately, there is no rule of thumb for determining what a given athlete's workload should be. It varies considerably with the individual, so experience is the best teacher. By comparing your weekly cumulative workloads with your training and racing performances, it's possible to plan optimal training patterns while avoiding overtraining. But always bear in mind that optimal workload is a moving target that is dependent on accumulated fitness, time of the training year, health, psy-

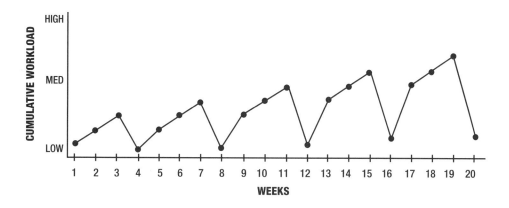

Figure 4.2
Example of weekly cumulative workload progression

chological stress and other variables. Cumulative workload history provides a better starting point for determining how you should train today and in the future than does merely guessing.

References

Baker, A. "Training Intensity." *Performance Conditioning for Cycling* 2, no. 1 (1995): 3.

Billat, V.L., et al. "A Comparison of Time to Exhaustion at VO$_2$ Max in Elite Cyclists, Kayak Paddlers, Swimmers, and Runners." *Ergonomics* 39, no. 2 (1996): 267–277.

Billat, V.L., et al. "Interval Training at VO$_2$ Max: Effects on Aerobic Performance and Overtraining Markers." *Medicine and Science in Sports and Exercise* 31, no. 1 (1999): 156–163.

Billat, V.L., and J.P. Koralsztein. "Significance of the Velocity at VO$_2$ Max and Time to Exhaustion at this Velocity." *Sports Medicine* 22, no. 2 (1996): 90–108.

Borg, G. *An Introduction to Borg's RPE Scale.* Ithaca, NY: Movement Publications, 1985.

Boulay, M.R., et al. "Monitoring High-Intensity Endurance Exercise with Heart Rate and Thresholds." *Medicine and Science in Sports and Exercise* 29, no. 1 (1997): 125–132.

Coyle, E.F., et al. "Physiological and Biomechanical Factors Associated with Elite Endurance Cycling Performance." *Medicine and Science in Sports and Exercise* 23, no. 1 (1991): 93–107.

Dunbar, C.C., et al. "The Validity of Regulating Exercise Intensity by Ratings of Perceived Exertion." *Medicine and Science in Sports and Exercise* 24 (1992): 94–99.

Friel, J. *CompuTrainer Workout Manual.* RacerMate, 1994.

Friel, J. *The Mountain Biker's Training Bible.* Boulder, CO: VeloPress, 2000.

Friel, J. *Training with Power.* Cambridge, MA: Tune Corp., 1999.

Gibbons, E.S. "The Significance of Anaerobic Threshold in Exercise Prescription." *Journal of Sports Medicine* 27 (1987): 357–361.

Goforth, H.W., et al. "Simultaneous Enhancement of Aerobic and Anaerobic Capacity." *Medicine and Science in Sports and Exercise* 26, no. 5 (1994): 171.

Hagberg, J.M. "Physiological Implications of the Lactate Threshold." *International Journal of Sports Medicine* 5 (1984): 106–109.

Herman, E.A., et al. "Exercise Endurance Time as a Function of Percent Maximal Power Production." *Medicine and Science in Sports and Exercise* 19, no. 5: 480–485.

Hopkins, S.R., et al. "The Laboratory Assessment of Endurance Performance in Cyclists." *Canadian Journal of Applied Physiology* 19, no. 3: 266–274.

Ivy, J.L., et al. "Muscle Respiratory Capacity and Fiber Type as Determinants of the Lactate Threshold." *Journal of Applied Physiology* 48 (1980): 523–527.

Jacobs, I. "Blood Lactate: Implications for Training and Sports Performance." *Sports Medicine* 3 (1986): 10–25.

Janssen, P.G.J.M. *Training, Lactate, Pulse Rate*. Polar Electro Oy, 1989.

Kindermann, W., et al. "The Significance of the Aerobic-Anaerobic Transition for the Determination of Workload Intensities during Endurance Training." *European Journal of Applied Physiology* 42 (1979): 25–34.

Lehmann, M., et al. "Training-Overtraining: Influence of a Defined Increase in Training Volume versus Training Intensity on Performance, Catecholomines and Some Metabolic Parameters in Experienced Middle- and Long-Distance Runners." *European Journal of Applied Physiology* 64, no. 2 (1992): 169–177.

Lindsay, F.H., et al. "Improved Athletic Performance in Highly Trained Cyclists after Interval Training." *Medicine and Science in Sports and Exercise* 28, no. 11 (1996): 1427–1434.

McArdle, W.D., F.I. Katch, and V.L. Katch. *Exercise Physiology*. Baltimore: Williams & Wilkins, 1996.

Myburgh, K.H., et al. "High-Intensity Training for 1 Month Improves Performance but Not Muscle Enzyme Activities in Highly Trained Cyclists." *Medicine and Science in Sports and Exercise* 27, no. 5 (1995): S370.

Niles, R. "Power as a Determinant of Endurance Performance." Unpublished study at Sonoma State University, 1991.

Pompcu, F.A., et al. "Prediction of Performance in the 5000m Run by Means of Laboratory and Field Tests in Male Distance Runners." *Medicine and Science in Sports and Exercise* 28, no. 5 (1996): S89.

Romijn, J.A., et al. "Regulation of Endogenous Fat and Carbohydrate Metabolism in Relation to Exercise Intensity and Duration." *American Journal of Physiology* 265 (1993): E380.

Skinner, J.S., et al. "The Transition from Aerobic to Anaerobic Metabolism." *Research Quarterly for Exercise and Sport* 51 (1980): 234–248.

Tanaka, K., et al. "A Longitudinal Assessment of Anaerobic Threshold and Distance-Running Performance." *Medicine and Science in Sports and Exercise* 16, no. 3 (1984): 278–282.

Weltman, A. *The Blood Lactate Response to Exercise.* Champaign, IL: Human Kinetics, 1995.

Weltman, A., et al. "Endurance Training Amplifies the Pulsatile Release of Growth Hormone: Effects of Training Intensity." *Journal of Applied Physiology* 72, no. 6 (1992): 2188–2196.

Wenger, H.A., and G.J. Bell. "The Interactions of Intensity, Frequency, and Duration of Exercise Training in Altering Cardiorespiratory Fitness." *Sports Medicine* 3, no. 5 (1986): 346–356.

Weston, A.R., et al. "Skeletal Muscle Buffering Capacity and Endurance Performance after High-Intensity Interval Training by Well-Trained Cyclists." *European Journal of Applied Physiology* 75 (1997): 7–13.

Wilmore, J., and D. Costill. *Physiology of Sport and Exercise.* Champaign, IL: Human Kinetics, 1994.

PART THREE

TRAINING WITH A PURPOSE

The Racing Cycle
by Willie Honeman
As it appeared in *Bicycling Magazine*, October 1946

The Novice, with rare exceptions, will find himself lacking in one or more of the following: (1) ABILITY TO REPEAT, in other words ride five or six times at one race meeting, (2) ABILITY TO CARRY A SPRINT, (3) ABILITY TO RIDE AROUND THE MAN IN FRONT, (4) NO ENDURANCE, (5) CONCERN ABOUT NERVOUSNESS, (6) DISCOURAGED UPON FAILURE TO PLACE.

An important point to keep in mind is that nothing can be accomplished by a rider in Racing if he does not try to improve on his Weak Points in Training. To ride around the Track or Road accepting pace (known as sitting in) at a slow speed and with no purpose will accomplish nothing toward the rider's preparation for a coming event.

TESTING

Motivation can't take you very far if
you don't have the legs.
—LANCE ARMSTRONG

What are my strengths as a cyclist? What aspects of performance should I focus on in training? Am I making progress toward my long-term goals? How can I improve my race results?

These are questions the serious bicycle racer must ask several times every year. For the novice cyclist, these questions are difficult to answer since there is so much self-discovery to come. Even for an experienced rider, the answers are not always easy. The problem is that athletes often "can't see the forest for the trees." Subjective self-evaluation is always difficult. Someone else's studied opinion—often a coach or a concerned teammate—is usually necessary to get at the answers to such questions. Because the purpose of this book is to make you your own coach, I'm going to show you how to determine what you need to emphasize in training and race preparation.

You may not like what you discover about yourself. Several years ago, a master rider asked me to coach him. He described how when it came to climbs he was unable to hang on with the peloton and was off the back early in most races. Although unhappy with the situation, he wasn't completely dejected. He had given it a lot of thought and decided that the problem was a lack of power. So over the course of the winter he took a plyometrics class with a trainer who worked with professional power athletes such as football players.

My new charge had attended workouts four times a week that winter and had been so committed to improving that he ended up with stress fractures in both feet. What he wanted to know was how could I help him improve his power.

The first thing I had him do was test power on his CompuTrainer. What we discovered was that he had tremendous power, despite inactivity due to the stress fractures. He easily ranked in the top 5 percent for maximum power generation of all the masters I had ever coached. We also found, however, that he couldn't sustain the power output for even a few seconds and that his anaerobic endurance was poor. Once he crossed the redline and became anaerobic on a short climb or a long, intense effort he quickly fatigued. Maximum power generation wasn't holding him back at all. I subsequently set up a program for him that would improve his anaerobic endurance and lactate tolerance. He went on to have a much-improved race season.

You also may have reached a conclusion about your strengths and weaknesses that is not true. By pursuing the wrong course of training, you're expending both time and energy and may still end up with very little to show for your trouble. It is not unusual at all for riders to concentrate on the wrong abilities in training. What is most common among cyclists is to focus primarily on strengths. Good climbers, for example, prefer to spend their training time climbing rather than working on time trialing that may be the cause of lackluster results in A-priority stage races.

I call these race-specific weaknesses "limiters." Knowing what limits your race performance is like finding the weak link in a chain. Once you strengthen this "link" your results immediately improve. But if all you work on is your strengths and the weak link remains weak, race performance stays much the same from year to year.

Of course, your limiters may never become strengths, but you must always be trying. The trick is to improve the limiters without letting the strengths deteriorate. That's what I want to teach you to do in the planning chapters of this book. For now, let's discover what your strengths and limiters are.

There are two general categories of assessment that should be done each year to see where your training needs to be focused during the Base and Build periods. Performance assessment is done on the bike and self-assessment is done with paper and pencil. There are three times during the season when it is quite beneficial to conduct an assessment:

- Near the end of the last Race period of the season, complete a performance assessment to establish a high-fitness baseline.
- At the start of the Base period, do both performance and self-assessment to determine what is needed for training in the coming months.
- At the end of the Base period, repeat the performance assessment to measure progress before starting the Build period.

I will cover these training periods in detail in Chapter 7.

By the end of this chapter, you'll score yourself in several performance-related areas. From this data you will be able to compare your capabilities to the specific demands of cycling and customize a training program specific to your needs.

Some athletes are not keen on testing and prefer to make decisions intuitively based on what they have discovered in races. That may work for some, but for most it often results in guessing and jumping to inaccurate conclusions based more on emotion than fact. By completing all of the assessments included here, you'll be on the road to training more effectively than you've ever done before. Imagine what that could mean for your next race season.

Performance Assessment

There are several tests that can be done to gauge your physiological improvement. It is best to use them comparatively. Establish a baseline in each of the tests that you decide to use and then retest at intervals throughout the year to see how your physical ability is changing. It is not necessary that you repeat all of the tests throughout the season. Focus on the ones that seem to best reflect what your limiters are. This may come down to one test of all of those described here. By regularly gauging your progress with it you can ensure that the training program is on track—or that it isn't.

When testing it is important that you eliminate as many variables from one test to the next as is possible. For example, the warm-up procedure needs to be the same. Some other elements that may affect the test include diet, hydration, level of fatigue, equipment, bike set-up, tire pressure, and time of day.

If at any time during a test you feel lightheaded or nauseous, stop immediately. You are not attempting to achieve a maximum heart rate on any of the tests described here, but it is necessary to attain a very high level of exertion.

Here are the tests broken down by category.

Sprint Power Test

Tests done on the bike are usually the best indicators of racing performance. With a powermeter, a CompuTrainer, or in a laboratory, measure your maximum power and average sustained power. The accompanying CompuTrainer Sprint Power Test describes how this is done with a CompuTrainer. With a powermeter, perform the test on the road in the same way. The course should be about 0.2 miles (352 yards or 322 meters) and either flat or slightly uphill. Mark the start and finish points so you can find them in the future for re-tests.

If you can conduct the test in a lab, the applicable protocol will probably be something called a "Wingate Power Test." The technician should be able to explain

Sidebar 5.1

SPRINT POWER TEST ON COMPUTRAINER

CompuTrainer Set-up

You will need one or two assistants to record information and possibly to spot for safety (there is a risk of the bike tipping over with a maximal effort). Set up and calibrate the equipment as described in the user's manual. Warm up for about ten minutes and calibrate the equipment. Select a course that is 0.2 miles long.

Test

1. Following your warm up, take two or three increasingly powerful practice starts of 8–12 seconds each to determine the best gear to start the test in. The start is with the rear wheel stopped. If rear wheel slips, tighten and recalibrate.
2. During the test you may stand or sit and shift gears at any time. If you are a large or powerful rider, you'll want a spotter on either side of the bike to prevent tipping. You may also bolt your CompuTrainer to a sheet of plywood to prevent tipping.
3. When ready to begin the test, stop your rear wheel and have an assistant press the button on the handlebar control unit to begin the test.
4. Sprint the 0.2-mile course as fast as you can. It will probably take 25–40 seconds.
5. At the completion of the test, record maximum watts and average watts.
6. Recover by spinning in a light gear and resistance for several minutes.

what the results mean. The technician will probably not be able to relate the information to other cyclists, however.

Once you've completed the power test, use Table 5.1 to help you decide what the results mean.

Don't be disheartened if your maximum is lower than expected. You need to realize that this is a weakness and if it is also a limiter (it prevents you from attaining better results in A-priority races) you must work on your ability to quickly generate force against the pedals if you're going to improve. A low average power is a warning to improve lactate tolerance. I will discuss how to improve both force and lactate tolerance in later chapters. If you score four or five for both, the quick application of

RANKING	SCORE	SENIOR MEN		SENIOR WOMEN	
		MAXIMUM	AVERAGE	MAXIMUM	AVERAGE
EXCELLENT	5	1,100+	750+	1,000+	675+
GOOD	4	950–1,099	665–749	850–999	600–674
AVERAGE	3	800–949	560–664	720–849	500–599
FAIR	2	650–799	455–559	585–719	410–499
POOR	1	<650	<455	<585	<410

Table 5.1
Power Ranges of Cyclists (watts)

force and lactate tolerance are among your strength areas. You're probably a very good sprinter in this case, and we'll need to keep looking for your weakness.

Average power output will vary more throughout the year than will maximum power. While testing in the winter, for example, you may find average power relatively lower than in the summer when race fitness is high. That's because you quickly lose the ability to tolerate lactate (winter) when the body is no longer experiencing it.

Graded Exercise Test

The graded exercise test can be done with a CompuTrainer or powermeter. Most laboratory testing facilities at hospitals, clinics, and universities also conduct a very sophisticated ergometer stress test that measures aerobic capacity and also determines lactate threshold. Some may even sample blood to determine lactate profiles as described in Chapter 4. Expect to pay dearly for a lab test.

One of the measures to be gleaned from the graded exercise test is your lactate threshold heart rate and power. In the scientific world, there are different definitions for the point at which lactate threshold is reached. I've found that labs frequently use the more conservative of these definitions. That conservative approach yields a low threshold heart rate and power level for a racer. If you're a master, the lab technicians may also be reluctant to allow you to continue the test until fatigue sets in, choosing instead to stop the test prematurely. They don't want you to die in their labs. Be sure to work out these issues before scheduling a lab test.

If you're new to racing or have coronary risk factors such as a history of heart disease in your family, high cholesterol, high blood pressure, a heart murmur or dizziness after exercise, then you should only conduct this test in a laboratory under the close supervision of a physician.

It is possible to conduct the graded exercise test using an indoor trainer or stationary bike. To use a trainer, you will need a handlebar computer sensor for the rear wheel. Power outputs will not be known, but you can measure speed instead. Accurate and reliable stationary bikes are hard to find for such precise measurement. Look for one that digitally displays power or speed. Do not use a health club bike that shows speed or power with a needle or sliding gauge. These are far too inaccurate.

If using a powermeter, use an indoor trainer of any type and follow the CompuTrainer protocol.

Lactate Threshold Test on Road

If you'll be training with either a heart rate monitor or a powermeter, this test will also give you a good indication of your lactate threshold relative to heart rate and power.

GRADED EXERCISE TEST ON COMPUTRAINER

CompuTrainer Set-up

You will need an assistant to record information. Set up and calibrate the equipment as described in the user's manual. Warm up for about ten minutes and calibrate the equipment. Select a flat course that is 8–10 miles (12–16 kilometers) long. You won't use all of it.

Test

1. Throughout the test, you will hold a predetermined power level (plus or minus 10 watts). Start at 100 watts and increase by 20 watts every minute until you can no longer continue. Stay seated throughout the test. Shift gears at any time.

2. At the end of each minute, tell your assistant how great your exertion is using the guide on the following page (place this where it can be seen):

6		14	
7	VERY, VERY LIGHT	15	HARD
8		16	
9	VERY LIGHT	17	VERY HARD
10		18	
11	FAIRLY LIGHT	19	VERY, VERY HARD
12		20	
13	SOMEWHAT HARD		

3. Your assistant will record your exertion rating and your heart rate at the end of the minute and instruct you to increase power to the next level.

4. The assistant will also listen closely to your breathing to detect when it becomes noticeably labored for the first time in the test. This point is defined as the VT or ventilatory threshold.

5. Continue until you can no longer hold the power level for at least fifteen seconds.

6. The data collected should look something like this:

Power	Heart Rate	Exertion	
100	110	9	
120	118	11	
140	125	12	
160	135	13	
180	142	14	
200	147	15	
220	153	17	VT
240	156	19	
260	159	20	

Sidebar 5.3

GRADED EXERCISE TEST ON STATIONARY BIKE

1. Test must be done with a stationary bike that accurately displays speed (or watts).
2. Select "manual" mode.
3. You will need an assistant to record information.
4. Warm up on equipment for 5 to 10 minutes.

Test

1. Throughout the test, you will hold a predetermined speed or power level. Start at 15 mph (or 100 watts) and increase by 1 mph (or 20 watts) every minute until you can no longer continue. Stay seated throughout the test. Shift gears at any time.
2. At the end of each minute, tell your assistant how great your exertion is using this guide (place this where it can be seen):

6		14	
7	VERY, VERY LIGHT	15	HARD
8		16	
9	VERY LIGHT	17	VERY HARD
10		18	
11	FAIRLY LIGHT	19	VERY, VERY HARD
12		20	
13	SOMEWHAT HARD		

3. Your assistant will record your exertion rating and your heart rate at the end of the minute and instruct you to increase speed (watts) to the next level.
4. The assistant will also listen closely to your breathing to detect when it becomes labored. This is the VT or ventilatory threshold.
5. Continue until you can no longer hold the speed (watts) for at least fifteen seconds.
6. The data collected should look something like this:

Speed	Watts	Heart Rate	Exertion	
15	100	110	9	
16	120	118	11	
17	140	125	12	
18	160	135	13	
19	180	142	14	
20	200	147	15	
21	220	153	17	VT
22	240	156	19	
23	260	159	20	

Most riders find this test to be far easier to conduct than either of the aforementioned lactate threshold tests.

It's simple. Merely complete a thirty-minute time trial on a flat to slightly uphill road course. This may also be done on an indoor trainer, although most riders find this harder than being on the road. If you want to determine or confirm your lactate threshold heart rate (LTHR), click the lap button on your heart rate monitor ten minutes into the time trial. Your average heart rate for the last twenty minutes is a good estimation of LTHR.

If you are training with power, your average power output for this test also functions as an approximation of lactate threshold power. It will also establish your CP30 zone as described in Chapter 4.

The more times you do this or any of the previously described tests, the more reliable your training zones will be.

Lactate Threshold Test Results

Testing for lactate threshold reveals two elements of your race fitness—power at lactate threshold and anaerobic endurance. It also locates your lactate threshold heart rate—a key element of your training when using a heart rate monitor. In order to derive the full benefit of a workout, you should regulate the intensity of that workout using lactate threshold heart rate as a guide to set zones as listed in Table 4.6.

Power at lactate threshold is a good indicator of performance and will allow you to train the muscular system with a powermeter or CompuTrainer. Anaerobic endurance is important in criteriums and during the sustained, high-intensity efforts of road races. Most race-fit athletes can last four or more minutes beyond their lactate threshold on the indoor trainer test for LT. If you're unable to achieve that, then anaerobic endurance is a weakness. This is nearly always the case with tests completed at the start of the winter Base period so don't be concerned if it is early in the season and you are unable to last long on the test.

RANKING	SCORE	TIME (min.)
EXCELLENT	5	> 5:00
GOOD	4	4:00–4:59
AVERAGE	3	3:00–3:59
FAIR	2	2:00–2:59
POOR	1	< 2:00

Table 5.2
Anaerobic Endurance Time indicates the athletes efforts from LT to end of test.

The lactate threshold test also serves as an excellent baseline of your fitness. By graphing the results from two or more serial tests, you can see the changes in your fitness throughout the year. Construct a graph by plotting heart rate on the vertical axis versus power on the horizontal axis. The Conconi Test, developed by Italian physiologist Francesco Conconi in the early 1980s, applied the method to Francesco Moser's training program in preparation for his attempt on the world hour record. The test relies on the establishment of the lactate threshold heart rate as the point at which the line on such a graph deflects or bends downward. I've found very few athletes who have an obvious deflection in their graph, so don't be concerned with looking for this in your test results.

Figure 5.1 illustrates the tracings of a lactate threshold test performed on two separate occasions. The first was conducted at the start of the Base period and second following twelve weeks of Base training. Notice that the tracing for Test 1 has shifted to the right and slightly down. This shows that the athlete has a lower heart rate at any given power level. That is one effective way of measuring progress. Another is that power has increased for every given heart rate. While the lactate threshold heart rate (indicated as LT) has not changed in twelve weeks, power has.

Critical Power Tests

If you have a powermeter, establishing power-based training zones will allow more complete use of the unit in training while also providing you with valuable comparison points for fitness throughout the season. If you also establish and periodically update a personal critical power profile as shown in Figure 4.1, you will have a visual representation of how performance is changing over time.

Figure 5.1
Graph of two graded
exercise tests

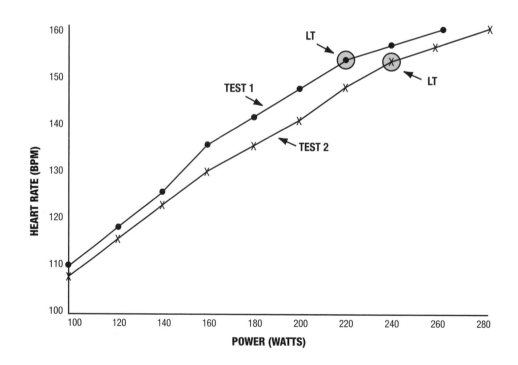

To establish a critical power profile you will need to complete five time trials, one each of 12 seconds and 1, 6, 12, and 30 minutes. Each test is a maximum effort for the entire duration. It's best to spread these out over several days. Once your profile is established you may want to update only certain critical power points along the curve in subsequent tests without completing the entire battery.

There is a learning curve associated with this testing. It's common to start out too fast on each time trial and then fade near the end. It may take two or three attempts over a few days or even a few weeks to get the pacing right. To reduce the need for such continued testing, it's best to start each time trial test at a lower power output than you think is appropriate. This will pay off with fewer test failures. Begin such testing in the early Base period with at least one other battery of follow-up tests completed before beginning the Build period. (These periods are explained in Chapter 7.)

The longer durations of 60, 90, and 180 minutes may be estimated from the profile graph by extending the slope of the CP12 to CP30 line. You may also get an estimation of the values for these extended data points with a little math. To estimate 60-minute power, subtract 5 percent from your 30-minute average power result. For an approximation of 90-minute power, subtract 2.5 percent from the 60-minute power. Subtracting 5 percent from the 90-minute power figure estimates 180-minute power.

Keep in mind that these power points beyond 30 minutes are estimates only and may well be inaccurate. That's acceptable since training with power is normally only recommended for shorter durations as when doing intervals, hill repeats, sprints, or tempo efforts. Long, steady rides are best done using heart rate or perceived exertion to regulate intensity.

Once all of these power data points are established you are ready to determine your critical power training zones as shown in Table 4.3.

Applying Test Results

Establishing a profile and completing selected tests is not enough—you must now determine what all of this data means for your training. Again, keep in mind that the results of these tests are only as good as the effort put into controlling the many variables discussed earlier. Sloppy testing provides no basis for measuring fitness. Also realize that there are many variables not completely under your control, such as weather. In addition, the changes in fitness can be so slight—2 percent or less—that field testing may not be sophisticated enough to detect them. Because of these confounding factors, it might appear in subsequent tests that fitness is slipping even though you sense an improvement. Your feelings and indications of fitness from workouts are valid—don't completely disregard them in an attempt to train "scientifically."

Sprint Power Test

The purpose of this test is to determine whether sprinting is a weakness or strength for you. Table 5.1 will help you determine that. Bear in mind that even if it is a weakness, it is not necessarily a limiter. If your race goals do not include events that often come down to a sprint for the line, then it is merely a weakness but not a limiter.

While it seems that good sprinters are born that way, this does not mean that your sprinting cannot improve. Good sprinters have several things in common. The first is that they have a tremendous ability to instantaneously recruit a large number of muscle fibers to initiate and finish the sprint. They also can generate tremendous force on the pedals due to a high level of total-body strength. And they can turn the pedals at a very high cadence. These are all characteristics that can be trained. Some will find such training produces quick and easy results, while others, who do not have the sprinter body type, will not realize as much gain.

Graded Exercise Test

As mentioned earlier, this test provides a snapshot of your aerobic fitness and helps to establish a lactate threshold heart rate. Both are applicable only to you. Comparing the heart rate data of this test with another rider's will be of little or no value. Comparing your present results with those of future tests is quite revealing, however. Figure 5.1 is a graph of an initial test (Test 1) and a follow-up test done several weeks later (Test 2).

In subsequent tests, improving aerobic fitness is evident if the slope of the line moves to the right and down, as shown by Test 2 in Figure 5.1. This indicates that for any given power level, heart rate has dropped. Or, to look at it another way, for any given heart rate, power is greater.

Now let's determine your lactate threshold (LT). It may be estimated from the test data by observing four indicators: rating of perceived exertion (RPE), ventilatory threshold (VT), time above LT, and power percentage. For the experienced rider, LT typically occurs when RPE is in the range of 15 to 17. A rough estimation of LT is made by noting the heart rates that fall in this RPE range. If you are new to cycling, you may find it awkward to assign an RPE. The more experience you gain on the bike at various intensities, the easier this task will become.

LT may also be estimated by your assistant's estimation of VT. If this falls in the range of RPE 15 to 17, it narrows the possibilities even more. Realize, however, that determining VT is quite difficult for the person who has never done it. Another way of determining LT is that a rider will typically not be able to continue for more than five minutes on this type of test once LT has been reached. So your LT is likely within the last five data points collected.

Power output may also be used to estimate LT for the experienced rider as it generally is found at about 85 percent of the maximum power achieved on the test. From these four indicators you should be able to closely estimate lactate threshold heart rate (LTHR). The more times you complete this test, the more refined the estimate of LT becomes.

Notice in Figure 5.1 that the lactate threshold heart rate has not changed from Test 1 to Test 2, although LT power has increased. This is typical of the results seen in experienced and generally well-conditioned riders during their base period. On the other hand, a novice, or someone who has had a long break from training, may expect to see the lactate threshold heart rate rise slightly in subsequent tests.

Lactate Threshold Test on the Road

This is a simple analysis. Your heart rate average for the last twenty minutes of the thirty-minute, all-out time trial done on the road as a workout is a close approximation of LTHR. If you compete in a time trial as a race, take 5 percent of your average heart rate and add it to the average to estimate LT. But if either of these is the only test done, it's a good idea to continue evaluating what you found your LTHR to be when on training rides. When riding steadily at this heart rate you should be aware of labored breathing and a feeling of burning tightness in the legs, and your RPE should be about 15 to 17. As with all testing, the more frequently this test is done the more refined the estimate becomes.

Critical Power Tests

The data gathered for the critical power tests should be graphed to produce a Power Profile as shown in Figure 5.2. The longer critical power durations may be estimated by extending the slope of the line for CP12 to CP30. This provides rough estimations that may be a bit low or high depending on your aerobic-anaerobic fitness balance. For example, in the early winter months your aerobic fitness is probably relatively better than your anaerobic fitness. As a result, CP12 may be lower than what would be found in the summer months, thus causing the extended slope of the line to be high on the right end. Follow-up tests done over the ensuing months of the winter and spring will help to correct this overestimation.

What should your Power Profile look like? This depends somewhat on the courses on which you race. A short-duration race contested on a course with short, steep hills favors a rider with high CP1 and CP6 power, whereas a longer race with rolling hills and long, steady climbs favors those with high CP12 and CP30 power. In theory, those power zones that are trained in most frequently will improve the most.

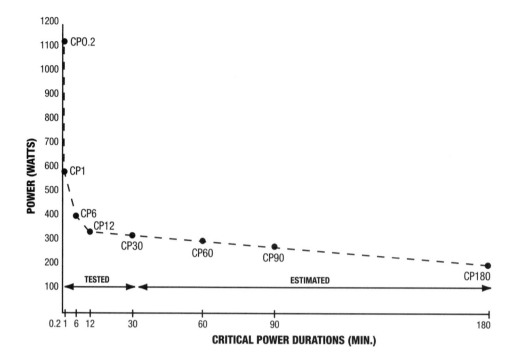

Figure 5.2

Power profiile for hypothetical rider

So comparing your Power Profile with course and race requirements of the most important races of the season provides guidance in determining exactly how to train. Chapter 6 provides greater detail on this.

Self-Assessment

By now you've collected a lot of data on yourself. All of this is of no value unless the information is used to improve training and racing. Completing the following three profiles—Proficiencies, Mental Skills, and Natural Abilities—will provide a start toward doing that. Chapter 6 will take this one step further by providing a system for improvement in weak areas.

If you have the equipment to conduct the performance assessment tests you now have a good idea of some of your areas of strength and weakness. Chances are, however, that you don't have access to sophisticated equipment. We can still get a pretty good understanding of your capabilities by asking the right questions and, of course, answering honestly. Even if you were able to do the performance testing, you should evaluate your proficiencies, mental skills, and natural abilities at the start of every training year. Before reading any further, complete the three profiles in Sidebars 5.4–5.6. Then I will explain your scores.

PROFICIENCIES PROFILE

Sidebar 5.4

Read each statement below and decide if you agree or disagree with it as it applies to you. Check the appropriate answer. If unsure, go with your initial feeling.

A=Agree   D=Disagree

A   D

___ ___ 1. I'm quite lean compared with others in my category.

___ ___ 2. I'm more muscular and have greater total body strength than most others in my category.

___ ___ 3. I'm usually capable of single-handedly bridging big gaps that take several minutes.

___ ___ 4. I'm capable of enduring relentless suffering for long periods of time, perhaps as long as an hour.

___ ___ 5. I can climb long hills out of the saddle with most others in my category.

___ ___ 6. I can do "wheelies," hop and jump my bike better than most.

___ ___ 7. I can spin at cadences in excess of 140 rpm with no difficulty.

___ ___ 8. I look forward to the climbs in races and hard group workouts.

___ ___ 9. I'm comfortable in an aerodynamic position: aero bars, elbows close, back flat.

___ ___ 10. I have a lot of fast-twitch muscle based on my instantaneous sprint speed, vertical jump, or other indicator.

___ ___ 11. While I suffer, I seldom "blow up" on climbs even when the tempo increases.

___ ___ 12. In a race, I can ride near my lactate threshold (heavy breathing) for long periods of time.

___ ___ 13. In a long individual time trial, with the exception of turnarounds and hills, I can stay seated the entire race.

___ ___ 14. In a pack sprint, I feel aggressive and physically capable of winning.

___ ___ 15. When standing on a climb, I feel light and nimble on the pedals.

Scoring: For each of the following sets of questions count the number of "Agree" answers you checked.

Question numbers		Score	
1, 5, 8, 11, 15	Number of "agrees" _____	Climbing	_____
2, 6, 7, 10, 14	Number of "agrees" _____	Sprinting	_____
3, 4, 9, 12, 13	Number of "agrees" _____	Time trial	_____

MENTAL SKILLS PROFILE

Sidebar 5.5

Read each statement below and choose an appropriate answer from these possibilities:

1=Never   2=Rarely   3=Sometimes   4=Frequently   5=Usually   6=Always

___ 1. I believe my potential as an athlete is excellent.

___ 2. I train consistently and eagerly.

___ 3. When things don't go well in a race, I remain positive.

___ 4. In hard races, I can imagine myself doing well.

THE CYCLIST'S TRAINING BIBLE

Sidebar 5.5
continued

___ 5. Before races, I remain positive and upbeat.

___ 6. I think of myself more as a success than as a failure.

___ 7. Before races, I am able to erase self-doubt.

___ 8. The morning of a race, I awake enthusiastically.

___ 9. I learn something from races when I don't do well.

___10. I can see myself handling tough race situations.

___11. I'm able to race close to my ability level.

___12. I can easily picture myself training and racing.

___13. Staying focused during long races is easy for me.

___14. I stay in tune with my exertion levels in races.

___15. I mentally rehearse skills and tactics before races.

___16. I'm good at concentrating as a race progresses.

___17. I make sacrifices to attain my goals.

___18. Before an important race, I can visualize doing well.

___19. I look forward to workouts.

___20. When I visualize myself racing, it almost feels real.

___21. I think of myself as a tough competitor.

___22. In races, I tune out distractions.

___23. I set high goals for myself.

___24. I like the challenge of a hard race.

___25. When the race gets hard, my concentration improves.

___26. In races, I am mentally tough.

___27. I can relax my muscles before races.

___28. I stay positive despite late starts or bad weather.

___29. My confidence stays high the week after a bad race.

___30. I strive to be the best athlete I can be.

Scoring: Add up the numerical answers you gave for each of the following sets of questions and rate the associated categories according to the scoring chart below.

Question numbers		Score	
2, 8, 17, 19, 23, 30	Total _____	Motivation	_____
1, 6, 11, 21, 26, 29	Total _____	Confidence	_____
3, 5, 9, 24, 27, 28	Total _____	Thought habits	_____
7, 13, 14, 16, 22, 25	Total _____	Focus	_____
4, 10, 12, 15, 18, 20	Total _____	Visualization	_____

Total	Ranking	Score
32–36	Excellent	5
27–31	Good	4
21–26	Average	3
16–20	Fair	2
6–15	Poor	1

NATURAL ABILITIES PROFILE

Sidebar 5.6

Read each statement below and decide if you agree or disagree with it as it applies to you. Check the appropriate answer. If unsure, go with your initial feeling.

A=Agree   D=Disagree

A   D

___ ___ 1. I prefer to ride in a bigger gear with a lower cadence than most of my training partners.

___ ___ 2. I race best in criteriums and short road races.

___ ___ 3. I'm good at sprints.

___ ___ 4. I'm stronger at the end of long workouts than my training partners.

___ ___ 5. I can squat and/or leg press more weight than most in my category.

___ ___ 6. I prefer long races.

___ ___ 7. I use longer crank arms than most others my height.

___ ___ 8. I get stronger as a stage race or high-volume training week progresses.

___ ___ 9. I comfortably use smaller gears with higher cadence than most others I train with.

___ ___ 10. I have always been physically quicker than most other people for any sport I've participated in.

___ ___ 11. In most sports, I've been able to finish stronger than most others.

___ ___ 12. I've always had more muscular strength than most others I've played sports with.

___ ___ 13. I climb best when seated.

___ ___ 14. I prefer workouts that are short but fast.

___ ___ 15. I'm confident of my endurance at the start of long races.

Scoring: For each of the following sets of questions, count the number of "agree" answers you checked and rate the categories accordingly.

Question numbers		Score	
1, 5, 7, 12, 13	Number of "agrees" ___	Strength	___
2, 3, 9, 10, 14	Number of "agrees" ___	Skill	___
4, 6, 8, 11, 15	Number of "agrees" ___	Endurance	___

Proficiencies

There are three proficiencies that determine success in cycling:

- Climbing
- Sprinting
- Time trialing

It's an unusual cyclist who scores a 4 or 5 on each of these. Body size and shape, aerobic capacity potential, and muscle type often determine which of these are your strength. Just because you are a good sprinter, however, doesn't mean that you should neglect climbing. What value is it to have a tremendous sprint but be unable to climb and so arrive at the finish well after winners? You must work to improve your limiters. Any proficiency in which you scored a three or less needs work if it is a race-specific weakness—a limiter. Just how much work you need depends on the types of races you plan to be doing. We'll explore that issue in the next chapter.

Mental Skills

Mental skills are the most neglected aspect of racing for serious cyclists at all levels. I've known talented riders who, except for their lack of confidence, were capable of winning or always placing well, but were seldom contenders. Their heads were holding them back.

More than likely, you scored a 4 or 5 in the area of motivation. I always see this in the athletes I coach. If you didn't, then it may be time to take a long look at why you train and race bicycles.

A highly motivated and physically talented rider who is confident, has positive thought habits, can stay focused during a race and has the ability to visualize success is practically unbeatable. A physically talented athlete without these mental qualities hopes to finish with the peloton. If you are weak in this area, other than working closely with a good sports psychologist, one of the best courses of action is to read a book by one of them. Here are some books I've found to be helpful in improving mental skills. Some may be difficult to find as they are out of print:

Bull, Stephen J. *Sport Psychology.* Crowood Press: 2000.

Elliott, Richard. "The Competitive Edge." TAFNEWS: 1991.

Jackson, Susan A., and Mihaly Csikszentmihalyi. *Flow in Sports.* Human Kinetics: 1999.

Loehr, James. *Mental Toughness Training for Sports.* Stephen Greene Press: 1982.

Loehr, James. *The New Mental Toughness Training for Sports.* Penguin Books: 1995.

Lynch, Jerry. *Creative Coaching.* Human Kinetics: 2001.

Lynch, Jerry. *Running Within.* Human Kinetics: 1999.

Lynch, Jerry. *Thinking Body, Dancing Mind.* Bantam Books: 1992.

Lynch, Jerry. *The Total Runner.* Prentice Hall: 1987.

Lynch, Jerry, and Chungliang Al Huang. *Working Without, Working Within.* Tarcher & Putnam: 1998.

Orlick, Terry. *Psyched to Win.* Leisure Press: 1992.

Orlick, Terry. *Psyching for Sport.* Leisure Press: 1986.

Ungerleider, Steven. *Mental Training for Peak Performance.* Rodale Sports: 1996.

Natural Abilities

Some were born to be cyclists. Their parents blessed them with the physiology necessary to excel on two wheels. Others were born to be soccer players or pianists. Many of us who are cyclists have chosen to race a bike regardless of our genetic luck. Passion for the sport means a lot and helps overcome many physiological shortcomings.

The right mix of three basic abilities determines success in any sport:

- **Endurance:** The ability to continue for a long time.
- **Strength:** The ability to generate force against a resistance.
- **Speed Skill:** The ability to make the movements of the sport at a required speed.

For example, an Olympic weight lifter must generate a tremendous amount of force, and needs a fair amount of skill and very little endurance. A pole vaulter needs tremendous skill, a moderate amount of strength, and little endurance. A marathon runner doesn't need much strength, only a little skill, but great endurance. Every sport is unique in terms of the mix of these three elements and, therefore, requires unique methods of training.

Road cycling puts a premium on endurance, but strength for climbing hills and skill for sprinting and pedaling correctly are also important elements of the formula. This unique combination of abilities is one of the reasons that cycling is such a difficult sport for which to train. A cyclist can't just put in a lot of miles to develop huge endurance and disregard strength and skill. It takes a mix of all three abilities to excel.

The Natural Abilities Profile you completed provides a snapshot of your individual capabilities for the three elements of fitness for cycling. A score of 4 or 5 for one of the abilities indicates a strength area. If all of your scores are 4 or 5 you undoubtedly have been a good athlete in many sports. A score of 3 or less indicates a weakness, one that may partly be due to heredity and partly to training. You can't change your genes, but you can change your training, if it's needed. That's what you'll find out in the next chapter.

Miscellaneous Factors

There is a fourth category for self-assessment included in the Cyclist Assessment at the end of this chapter—Miscellaneous Factors. Most of these are quite subjective, but try to rate them using the same 1-to-5 scale as for the other profiles. The following brief comments may help you to do this.

Nutrition. Could your nutrition improve? Do you eat a lot of junk food? On a scale of 1 to 5, how strict is your diet? If it is very strict with no junk food, circle 5. If nearly all you eat is junk food, circle 1.

Technical equipment knowledge. How well do you know your bike's inner workings? Could you repair or replace anything that may need it? If you're a certified mechanic, circle 5. If you're unable to repair even a flat tire, circle 1.

Race strategy. Before starting every race, do you have a master plan of what you will do under various circumstances? If so, mark 5. If you never give race strategy any thought and just react to what happens, circle 1.

Body composition. Power-to-weight ratio is extremely important in cycling. Evaluate your weight side of the ratio. Are you carrying excess flab that if removed would make you a better climber? Use the following scale:

Excess Weight	Rating
10 or more pounds	1
7–9 pounds	2
4–6 pounds	3
1–3 pounds	4
No excess weight	5

Support of family and friends. For those who are not fans of the sport, cyclists may seem somewhat strange. Those we are closest to have a tremendous effect on our psychological stress. How supportive of the time you spend training and racing are your family and friends? If they are 100 percent supportive, circle 5. If you have no support and are ridiculed by those who are close to you, or if they try to convince you not to devote so much time to riding, circle 1.

Years of racing experience. How many years have you been training and racing? Circle that number. If more than five years, still circle 5. Experience plays a significant role in high-level training and racing.

Tendency to overtrain. Do you come on strong about December—and are you ready to quit by June every year? If so, you're prone to overtraining—circle 1. Or do you frequently take rest breaks throughout the year and stay enthusiastic for training and racing right up until the last race on the calendar? If you're one of the few racers with such wisdom and patience, circle 5.

You've now evaluated yourself in several key areas. To compile the results mark your score for each on the Cyclist Assessment form (Sidebar 5.7). All of those with a score of 4 or 5 are strength areas. Scoring a 3 or less indicates a weakness. For each item, briefly comment on what you learned about yourself. Later on we'll come back to this form to help design your training plan for the year.

At the top and bottom of the Cyclist's Assessment, there are spaces for you to write in goals for the season and training objectives to help achieve them. Don't do anything with these sections yet. The next chapter takes a closer look at how to go about correcting some of the abilities that may be holding you back from better racing. In Chapter 7, the assessment will come together as you complete the last sections at the bottom of the form and begin the process of designing an annual training plan for better racing results.

CYCLIST ASSESSMENT

Sidebar 5.7

Season Goals

1. _____
2. _____
3. _____

	Score (5=Best, ?=Unsure)	Comments
Sprint Power Test		
Maximum power	? 1 2 3 4 5	_____
Average power	? 1 2 3 4 5	_____
Graded Exercise Test		
Lactate threshold power	? 1 2 3 4 5	_____
Anaerobic endurance	? 1 2 3 4 5	_____
Proficiencies Profile		
Climbing	? 1 2 3 4 5	_____
Sprinting	? 1 2 3 4 5	_____
Time trialing	? 1 2 3 4 5	_____

To improve weaknesses: _____

Mental Skills Profile		
Motivation	? 1 2 3 4 5	_____
Confidence	? 1 2 3 4 5	_____
Thought habits	? 1 2 3 4 5	_____
Focus	? 1 2 3 4 5	_____
Visualization	? 1 2 3 4 5	_____

To improve weaknesses: _____

Natural Abilities Profile

Endurance	? 1 2 3 4 5	_____
Strength	? 1 2 3 4 5	_____
Skill	? 1 2 3 4 5	_____

To improve weaknesses: _____

_____

Miscellaneous Factors

Nutrition	? 1 2 3 4 5	_____
Technical equipment knowledge	? 1 2 3 4 5	_____
Race strategy	? 1 2 3 4 5	_____
Body composition	? 1 2 3 4 5	_____
Support of family and friends	? 1 2 3 4 5	_____
Years of racing experience	? 1 2 3 4 5	_____
Tendency to overtrain	? 1 2 3 4 5	_____

Training objectives to achieve goals

1. _____
2. _____
3. _____
4. _____
5. _____

References

Bouchard, C., and G. Lortie. "Heredity and Endurance Performance." *Sports Medicine* 1 (1984): 38–64.

Costill, D. "Predicting Athletic Potential: The Value of Laboratory Testing." *Sports Medicine Digest* 11, no. 11 (1989): 7.

Daniels, J. "Physiological Characteristics of Champion Male Athletes." *Research Quarterly* 45 (1974): 342–348.

Droghetti, P., et al. "Non-Invasive Determination of the Anaerobic Threshold in Canoeing, Cycling, Cross-Country Skiing, Roller and Ice Skating, Rowing and Walking." *European Journal of Applied Physiology* 53 (1985): 299–303.

Francis, K.T., et al. "The Relationship between Anaerobic Threshold and Heart Rate Linearity during Cycle Ergometry." *European Journal of Applied Physiology* 59 (1989): 273–277.

Friel, J. *Training with Power*. Cambridge, MA: Tune, 1999.

Gibbons, E.S. "The Significance of Anaerobic Threshold in Exercise Prescription." *Journal of Sports Medicine* 27 (1999): 357–361.

Hagberg, J.M. "Physiological Implications of the Lactate Threshold." *International Journal of Sports Medicine* 5 (1984): 106–109.

Kuipers, H., et al. "Comparison of Heart Rate as a Non-Invasive Determination of Anaerobic Threshold with Lactate Threshold when Cycling." *European Journal of Applied Physiology* 58 (1988): 303–306.

Noakes, T.D. "Implications of Exercise Testing for Prediction of Athletic Performance: A Contemporary Perspective." *Medicine and Science in Sports and Exercise* 20, no. 4 (1988): 319–330.

Schneider, D.A., et al. "Ventilatory Thresholds and Maximal Oxygen Uptake during Cycling and Running in Biathletes." *Medicine and Science in Sports and Exercise* 22, no. 2 (1990): 257–264.

Sharkey, B. *Coaches Guide to Sport Physiology*. Champaign, IL: Human Kinetics, 1986.

Simon, J., et al. "Plasma Lactate and Ventilation Thresholds in Trained and Untrained Cyclists." *Journal of Applied Physiology* 60 (1986): 777–781.

Sleivert, G.G., and H.A. Wenger. "Physiological Predictors of Short-Course Biathlon Performance." *Medicine and Science in Sports and Exercise* 25, no. 7 (1993): 871–876.

Steed, J.C., et al. "Ratings of Perceived Exertion (RPE) as Markers of Blood Lactate Concentration during Rowing." *Medicine and Science in Sports and Exercise* 26 (1994): 797–803.

6 RACING ABILITIES

Things worth having are not easy to obtain.
Once obtained, those items must be treated
with care and respect or they slip away.
—GALE BERNHARDT, elite coach

You have identified your strengths and weaknesses. Based on this testing and previous race experience you should now have a good idea of what makes you the rider you are. As discussed in that chapter, there are many possibilities when it comes to this determination: physical, mental, nutritional, technical, strategic, and more. In this chapter, as with most in this book, we will focus on the physical aspects of training.

Back in the 1970s when I began to study training seriously from a scientific perspective, I was convinced that if I could find a diagram which illustrated what training was all about I'd have a better grasp of the subject. For years I played around with various drawings, always trying to find the one that made it clear. Could training be a straight-line continuum? Might a circle best explain what happens in training for competition? Or maybe it's a three-dimensional spiral that best shows what training is all about. Nothing seemed to work.

Then I discovered the writings of Dr. Tudor Bompa, a Romanian scientist-coach who has written extensively about periodization. In his work he uses a simple diagram to describe training. This was it! Once I got a handle on the components of his diagram, training became simple. His figure not only helped me to simplify the elements of training, it also provided a third dimension of time.

In this chapter I'll introduce you to the Bompa diagram, which now serves as the basis for all I do when training athletes. While it appears to be very simple, there are many subtle nuances that require some consideration. But once you have grasped the concepts, the process of training—and the answers to many of the questions about how to train—will be evident.

First, it's necessary that you first fully understand the concept of limiters that was touched on in Chapter 5. This is necessary because you must consider how the concepts of the diagram relate to your own strengths and weaknesses.

Limiters

There are aspects of your physical fitness that hold you back when it comes to race performance. We discovered some of these weaknesses in the last chapter. While it would be nice to eliminate all of your weaknesses and have only strengths, that is neither realistic nor all that necessary. More than likely, only one or two of these shortcomings stand between you and better race results. These key weaknesses are your "limiters."

Peak performance is a consequence of matching your individual strengths with the requirements of an event. This is similar to comparing your lottery ticket to the winning numbers and finding out that you had five of the six numbers right—close, but no million-dollar prize. Racing is like this. Having two of the three qualities necessary to race at the front isn't good enough. The one you're missing is the limiter. By correcting it, regardless of your other weaknesses, you're a contender. So it's really not weaknesses that should concern you, it's limiters.

A limiter is a race-specific weakness. For example, let's say you are training for a hilly, A-priority road race that is always won or lost on the last climb and one of your weaknesses is climbing. This weakness is obviously a limiter—it prevents you from performing at the level required for success. But if your other weakness is sprinting, this would not be a limiter for this race. So while you have two weaknesses—climbing and sprinting—only one is limiting your performance in this important event.

What you should closely watch for in this chapter are the necessary requirements to race well in the types of races you do, and which of those requirements you are missing. Later I'll show you how to strengthen your limiters.

Basic Racing Abilities

In Chapter 5, I mentioned the three basic abilities required in all sports: endurance, force, and speed skill. Different types of races, from hilly or flat to long or short, require different mixes of these abilities. The basic abilities are the ones with which an athlete should start his or her training year. They also should be the foundations of the novice cyclist's development in the sport for the first year or two.

It may help to understand where this discussion is going if you see the basic racing abilities as the corners of a triangle. While endurance, force, and speed skill sound simple enough, it may be helpful to explain how those terms are used here.

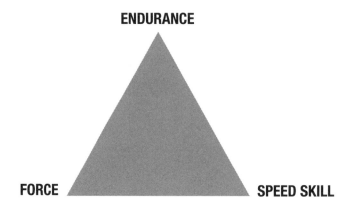

Figure 6.1
Basic abilities triangle

Endurance

Endurance is the ability to continue working by delaying the onset of fatigue. Within the context of this book, it implies an aerobic level of exertion. Endurance is specific to the event. For example, a one-hour race does not require the endurance to ride for five hours.

As with other aspects of fitness, endurance is typically developed by starting with general endurance training and progressing to more specific training. This means that an aerobic endurance base is built first in the winter months by developing the capabilities of the cardiorespiratory system (heart, lungs, blood, blood vessels), usually with crosstraining activities such as skiing or running. For those of you strongly committed to riding your bikes year-round, consider cyclo-cross training since it combines running with cycling and lets you hone your handling skills. Later in the winter, training will become more specific as the length of the longest rides are extended to a minimum of two hours or the duration of the longest race, whichever is longer.

For the novice cyclist, endurance is the key to progress. After all, the sport of road racing is primarily an endurance sport. If you don't have the endurance to finish the race, it doesn't matter how well developed any of your other abilities may be. This ability has to be nurtured before others are emphasized.

Force

Force, or strength, is the ability to overcome resistance. In cycling, force comes into play on hills and when riding into the wind. It also has a lot to do with how big a gear you can turn any time you want to go fast. You develop muscular force by progressing from general to specific training during the year. This starts with weight lifting early in the season and eventually becomes big-gear repeats and then hill work. This progression, by the way, is typical of the general to specific preparation so common in proper training. When lifting weights you are engaged in general training as no bike is involved, but when suffering through big-gear hill repeats the training is specific to the demands of the sport. I mention this now because it will continue to be an important point in the development of all of the race abilities described here.

Speed Skill

Speed skill is the ability to move quickly and efficiently. It is the ability to pedal smoothly at a high cadence and to negotiate turns quickly without wasted movement. It is not used here as a measure of your race times or velocity, although these are related issues. As speed skills improve, so do race performances. Some aspects of this ability, such as 200 rpm pedaling, are typically genetic. Athletes with world-class speed have been found to have a high percentage of fast-twitch muscles that are capable of rapid contraction, but they tend to fatigue quickly. It's possible, however, to improve speed skill by improving economy—quick movement with little wasted energy. Several scientific studies have demonstrated that leg turnover is trainable given the right types of workouts and consistency of purpose.

Just as with force, speed skill training progresses from the general to the specific. The goal for this ability is to be able to pedal comfortably (in other words, with a lower energy expenditure) at a higher cadence than you are capable of now. Such training will start with drills (general) and slowly move toward riding with a higher cadence than you currently employ (specific).

Advanced Racing Abilities

The triangle diagrammed in Figure 6.1 may be further defined. The basics of endurance, force and speed skill make up the corners, but each of the sides of the triangle represents a more advanced ability. These are the abilities the experienced athlete will emphasize in the later periods of training, once the basic abilities have been fully developed.

Muscular Endurance

Muscular endurance (ME) is the ability of muscles to sustain a high load for a prolonged time. It is the combination of the basic force and endurance abilities. In the world of cycling, muscular endurance is the ability to repeatedly turn a relatively high gear for a relatively long time. For the road cyclist, this is a critical ability. ME is what allows you to ride in a fast-moving group without suffering, to time trial faster than you have done before, and to hang with the leaders on a very long, steady grade.

Excellent muscular endurance is evidenced by a high level of fatigue resistance when turning a big gear. It is so critical to performance in road cycling that we will work on it almost as much as the more basic ability of pure endurance.

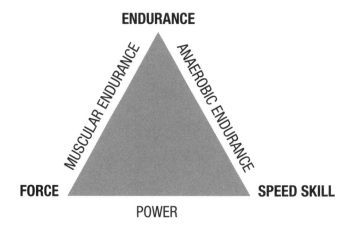

Figure 6.2

Higher abilites triangle

The "general" aspect of muscular-endurance training is the development of the accompanying corners—endurance and force. Once these abilities are deep-rooted, ME training begins with long repeats (endurance) in a higher-than-normal gear (force). The intensity is not high at first, being well below the lactate threshold, but eventually such training approaches and often surpasses threshold effort. As the early-season training progresses, the work intervals gradually get longer as the recovery intervals remain quite short—about one-fourth of the work interval duration.

Anaerobic Endurance

Anaerobic endurance (AE) is the ability to resist fatigue at high cadence while turning a big gear. In advanced athletes, it is the blending of speed skill and endurance. Anaerobic endurance is fundamental to races in which long sprints determine success. A rider with the ability to maintain sprint speed for several hundred meters can often dictate the outcome of a race either as a strong lead-out or as a solo effort. AE is also present in the rider who is capable of single-handedly bridging a gap. Another time when this ability is needed is when climbing steep hills that take only a couple of minutes to ascend. In short, fast events such as criteriums, AE is challenged by the many surges that take place. Such rapid changes of effort cause the creation of high levels of lactic acid. Without well-developed anaerobic endurance a rider would quickly fatigue as lactate accumulates.

From this discussion, it should be evident that any rider who wants to compete at the highest levels must fully hone his or her anaerobic endurance. But for the novice, AE training is to be avoided for at least the first year. This is a very stressful type of training that is most likely to lead to injury, overtraining, and burnout. The recovery requirements for this type of training are also the highest of any.

There are two types of anaerobic-endurance workouts. Both are interval-based. One is done at a power output roughly equivalent to what you would experience at the highest levels of your aerobic capacity (VO$_2$max). If you have a powermeter, this is your CP6 zone. If you train only with a heart rate monitor or ratings of perceived exertion, the heart rate zone is 5b and the RPE is 18 to 19 on the 6 to 20 scale. The work intervals are about three minutes long with equal recovery intervals. As the season progresses and fitness improves, the work intervals are shortened.

The second type of AE interval workout prepares you for the stresses common when repeated surges occur. Short repetitions (less than a minute long) at very high power outputs are completed with only short recoveries between them. This is exactly what you experience in a criterium. The idea of these workouts is to challenge the body's lactate-clearance and buffering system so that eventually you will be able to remove and cope with so much lactate so quickly that staying with such a demanding event becomes considerably easier—but never easy. It is not the sort of training you want to do frequently or for many weeks. This is the most demanding of all workouts.

Power

Power is the ability to apply maximum force in the shortest time possible. It results from having high levels of the basic abilities of force and speed skills. Well-developed power, or the lack of it, is obvious on short hills, in sprints, and in sudden pace changes.

Since it is based on the speed skills and force components of the triangle, power is in the realms of the nervous and muscular systems. It's dependent on the nervous system to send signals to the proper muscles, initiating their contraction at just the right times. The muscles then must produce a large contraction force.

Training for greater power involves short, all-out efforts in the power CP0.2 zone or at RPE 20 followed by long recoveries to allow the nervous system and muscles to fully recover. Inadequate recovery will diminish the value of this workout. These repetitions are quite short—in the neighborhood of eight to twelve seconds or less. Heart rate monitors are of no use in power training.

Attempting to improve power while fatigued is counterproductive. Such training is best done when you are rested and early in a training session when the nervous system and muscles are most responsive. This is not to say that you should never work on sprinting late in a workout. You should at some time in the season prepare to sprint when tired as that is what usually happens in a race. But when trying to improve power earlier in the season be sure to be well-recovered.

Limiters and Racing

Let's return to the discussion of limiters, which were previously defined as race-specific weaknesses. By now you should have a good idea of what your physical ability limiters are. The basic abilities of endurance, force, and speed skill are easily identified.

The advanced abilities are somewhat more difficult to recognize. But since the higher abilities are based on the combination of the basic abilities, a weakness in basic abilities produces a weakness in the higher abilities. For example, if your endurance is weak it will limit both muscular endurance and anaerobic endurance. If endurance is good but force is lacking, muscular endurance and power are negatively affected. Poor speed skill means low power and inferior anaerobic endurance.

As mentioned, the types of races you do determine what strengths are needed and how your weaknesses limit you. Matching your abilities to the demands of the event is critical for success. Let's examine how that works.

Race Prescription

There are several variables that define the demands of a road race. For example, races vary not only in course length, but also in terrain characteristics such as hills and corners. Other variables include wind, temperature, and humidity. Perhaps the most significant variable in road racing is the competition. Matching your physical fitness to the demands of the most important events for which you are training produces the best results.

The longer the race is, the more it favors the basic abilities. Conversely, the shorter the race, the more important the higher abilities are. In preparing for a longer race, endurance is paramount, but force is also necessary to deal with hills, and good fuel economy resulting from good speed skill conserves energy. Muscular endurance plays an important role, but training for anaerobic endurance and power is of less value.

In the same way, a short race such as a criterium favors the higher abilities, especially anaerobic endurance and power. That doesn't mean that endurance and force aren't needed, just not to the same extent as for the endurance events. Speed skill training is critical for short races, and muscular endurance also plays a role.

Training for an important event means first deciding what is important for success and then improving your weaknesses that don't match the demands of the event, while maintaining strengths that already fit its demands.

Other Limiters

Besides the event-specific ability limiters discussed here, there are other factors that may also hold you back from achieving race goals. One of the most critical is a lack of time to train. This is perhaps the most common limiter. If this is a limiter for you, when designing a program consider that the specificity of training discussed in Chapter 3 becomes increasingly important as the hours available to work out diminish. In other words, when time becomes scarce, your training must increasingly simulate racing. So as volume declines, workout intensity specific to the event increases. The next chapter will help you decide how many weekly training hours are reasonable and necessary.

Table 6.1
Summary of Abilities

ABILITY	WORKOUT FREQUENCY*	INTERVALS DURATION**	ZONES WORK	RECOVERY***	RPE	HEART RATE	POWER	BENEFIT	EXAMPLE
Endurance	1–4/week Continuous	20'–6 hrs.	N/A	N/A	2–6	1–3	CP180	a. Delay fatigue b. Build slow twitch c. Economy	3 hrs. on flat course
Force	1–2/week Intervals	20–90'	30"–2'	1:2	7–9	4–5b	CP12–60	a. Muscular strength b. Economy	Seated hill repeats
Speed Skills	1–4/week	20–90'	10–30"	1:2–5	9–10	N/A	CP1	a. High cadence b. Economy	30" spin-ups
Muscular Endurance	1–2/week	30'–2 hrs. Intervals/continuous	6–20'	3–4:1	7–8	4–5a	CP30–90	a. Strength endurance b. Race-pace comfort c. Boost LT velocity	4 x 6' (2' RI)
Anaerobic Endurance	1–2/week	30–90'	3–6' 30–40"	2:1–2 2–3:1	9	5b	CP6	a. Raise VO$_2$max b. VO$_2$max velocity c. Lactate clearance d. Lactate tolerance	5 x 5' (5' RI) 4 x (4 x 40" (20" RI)) Fartlek between sets
Power	1–3/week	20–90'	8–12"	1:10	10	N/A	CP0.2	a. Muscular power b. Fast starts c. Short hills d. Sprints	10 x 8" (80" RI)

* Varies with individual, time of season and time available to train.

** Total workout time including the portion of workout that develops the ability.

*** Work interval-to-recovery interval ratio. Example, 3:1 means rest ("off") 1 minute for every 3 minutes of work ("on") time.

Note: ' = minutes, " = seconds, hrs = hours, RI = recovery ("off") interval

Training of Abilities

As you can see from the brief discussion of abilities, there are training patterns that progress from the general to the very specific. Figure 6.3 illustrates this concept. At the start of the training year, much of the work is general in nature, meaning that it may not include a bicycle or may involve riding in an unusual fashion, as when doing drills. Force (strength) training serves as a good example of the progression from general to specific. Early in the training year, weight workouts take up a large portion of training time. Later in the winter, weight room training is cut back as the number of hilly rides increases—especially in a high gear with low cadence. Eventually, the athlete may progress to hill repeats or hill intervals, and, finally, to racing on hilly courses—the most specific of force-related work.

Each ability has a unique method of training associated with it throughout the season. Here is a brief and simplified summary of how to train abilities from the start of the season through the end. Chapter 8 will provide details of how to blend all of the abilities, and Chapter 9 will furnish workout menus and the criteria for selecting workouts for each of these abilities.

Figure 6.3
General to specific training emphasis throughout the training year

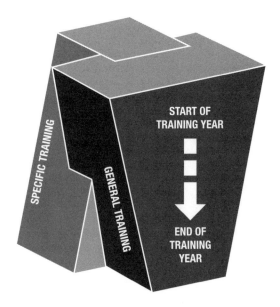

SPECIFIC TRAINING

GENERAL TRAINING

START OF TRAINING YEAR

END OF TRAINING YEAR

Endurance

Endurance training starts in early winter with aerobic crosstraining activities such as Nordic skiing or in-line skating. These modes of training will provide enough stress to the heart, lungs, blood, and blood vessels to improve their endurance qualities. By mid-winter, the program calls for a gradual phasing-in of on-bike training and the gradual elimination of crosstraining. Late-winter or early-spring rides should increase until they are at least as long as the longest race of the upcoming season. By this point, you have already established a good level of stamina and you begin to favor high-intensity workouts over endurance training. During the Transition period from the end of the race season to the beginning of the Base period, you can maintain a minimum level of endurance with crosstraining.

Force

Force development begins in early winter with training in the weight room. If you have followed the schedule, you should attain the maximum strength necessary by the end of Base 1 near mid-winter. You should then shift your emphasis toward improving your force when on the bike. Depending on the weather, late winter is the best time to begin riding in the hills. Later, hill work may evolve into hill intervals and repeats, depending on your weaknesses. A rider can work to maintain strength throughout the season with weight room training and hill work. This is especially helpful for women and masters.

Speed Skill

As with force, speed-skill development improves pedaling economy. Frequent drill work, especially in the winter months, teaches big and small muscles exactly when to contract and when to relax. As the muscles involved in pedaling are activated with precise harmony, precious fuel is conserved. Just as with endurance and force, speed skill training begins in the late fall or early winter, depending on the race schedule, and continues at a maintenance level throughout the rest of the season.

Muscular Endurance

Muscular-endurance work begins in mid-winter with sustained efforts of several minutes in the heart rate zone 3 or power zone CP90. By late winter, it gradually progresses to interval training in the heart rate zones 4 and 5a or CP30 to CP60. The work intervals gradually get longer as the recovery intervals shorten. By spring, the athlete is riding up to an hour in these zones. The effort is much like "controlled" time trialing and tremendously effective in boosting both aerobic and anaerobic fitness with little risk of overtraining. Throughout the Race period, muscular endurance is maintained.

Power

Power may be the most misunderstood aspect of training in cycling. Most athletes do sprints with brief recovery periods to try to improve their power. They are really working on anaerobic endurance. You can improve power with brief sprints at near maximum exertion followed by long recovery intervals. Natural sprinters love these workouts. Those with little power—riders possessing great endurance and little speed skill or force—find power workouts painful and dread doing them. For these cyclists the blending of speed skill and force training into power development will lead to an effective jump at the start of sprints.

Anaerobic Endurance

Anaerobic-endurance training includes aerobic capacity–developing intervals and lactate tolerance repetitions. At the start of the Build period of training, the experienced athlete should phase into interval training to bring his or her aerobic capacity to a peak. During the last weeks of the Build period, lactate-tolerance work trains the body to dissipate lactate from the blood and to buffer its usual effects. Anaerobic-endurance training is quite stressful and should not be a part of the novice cyclist's regimen. Both speed skill and endurance should be well established with at least two years of training before regularly attempting these workouts. The likely results of too much anaerobic-endurance work too soon are burnout and overtraining.

Ability Regions

In this section, it may sound as if I'm encouraging you to specialize in a particular category of races. I'm not. My purpose here is to show you how to blend the six abilities previously discussed to produce optimal performance for specific types of races. Your strengths will favor success in some of these, but it is likely that you will still need to improve limiters for complete mastery. It will also help you to begin seeing how strengths and limiters are blended into a comprehensive training program.

To understand the requirements of various types of races, it is helpful to further refine the triangle as in Figure 6.4.

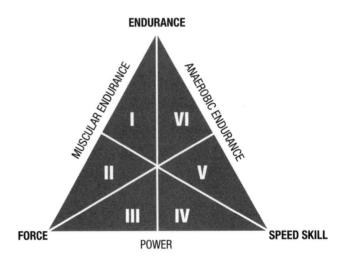

Figure 6.4
Racing abilities regions

Note that the triangle is divided into six regions, each representing a specific set of ability requirements. By now, you should be able to position yourself within one of the regions based on your known strengths. For example, if endurance is your number one ability and force is second, then you are a region I cyclist—high in muscular endurance with a tendency toward endurance. If two or all three of the natural abilities are equal for you, then your proficiencies may help define your region. Sprinters usually fit into the speed skill regions (IV–V), climbers into the force regions (II–III), and time trialists into the endurance regions (I–VI).

Races may also be divided into these same six regions based on their type, distance, and terrain. If you are a region I cyclist, then you will do best in region I races. The ability regions triangle also helps you decide what to work on in order to perform better in any of the other regions.

Following is a race description by ability regions and a prioritizing of the abilities you must train for each type. Obviously, your strengths will require less training time than your limiters. Chapter 8 will teach you how to blend the training of the various abilities, and Chapter 9 will provide detailed workouts to support each of these ability requirements.

The priorities of training that are listed here for each region do not imply an order of training, but rather an emphasis in training. Given that you have time and energy constraints placed on your training (career, family, home maintenance, etc.), it is necessary to decide what is most important in order to properly focus. If any of the first three abilities in a given list is a personal weakness, and this is the type of A-priority race you are training for, then you must elevate the identified ability to first priority when it comes to training. The last three abilities in each priority list have limited value for the type of race for which you're training. Do not avoid these areas, but do assign them less training time and energy. If a strength area falls into one of the last three abilities, you need place only minor emphasis on it. Realize that you can't be good at everything. And also realize that we are working within the concept of limiters. Determine what's holding you back and then correct that weakness.

Region I

Region I includes the long, flat to rolling races that are so common in the northwestern European countries of the Netherlands and Belgium. In the United States, races of more than 100 miles are becoming harder to find. Wind direction, team tactics, and mental tenacity go a long way toward determining the outcome of those races. Riders with excellent endurance and time trialing proficiency are likely to emerge victorious. These races are also likely to come down to a pack sprint.

Also included in this region are time trials that are 30 kilometers or longer. Indeed, time trialing proficiency is critical to performance in region I races. If your weakness is time trialing, you need to put a great deal of emphasis on muscular-endurance training in order to race well. Good time trialists have exceptional lactate thresholds relative to their aerobic capacities and maximum power outputs. They develop the ability to ride comfortably in an aerodynamic position and minimize wasted energy in pedaling. They also have superior ability to concentrate despite great suffering.

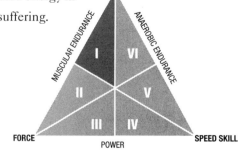

Priorities for region I training

Primary importance

    1. Endurance

    2. Muscular endurance

    3. Force

Secondary importance

    4. Anaerobic endurance

    5. Speed skill

    6. Power

Region II

Region II races include time trials of about 15 to 30 kilometers and road races of less than three hours. Hills are usually the element that determines outcomes. These are common road races in U.S. cycling.

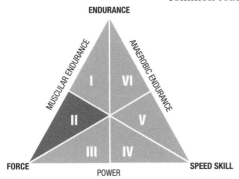

Climbing is a central proficiency skill for region II. What makes for champion climbers? Typically, they have less than two pounds of body weight for every inch of height. They are capable of generating high wattage per pound of body weight in sustained efforts. This requires a high lactate threshold–power output and a large aerobic capacity. Natural climbers have an economical climbing style and are especially nimble on the pedals when out of the saddle on a climb.

Priorities for region II training

Primary importance

    1. Force

    2. Muscular endurance

    3. Endurance

Secondary importance

    4. Power

    5. Speed skill

    6. Anaerobic endurance

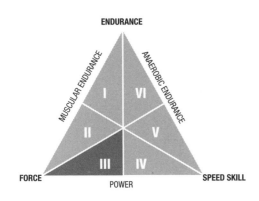

Region III

Region III in road racing is found only in short prologues of stage races. These are generally individual time trials on hilly courses taking only a few minutes to complete. As such, there is no need for the road racer to train for these events. The stage racer must simply grin and bear the agony.

Region IV

Region IV is in the domain of the track racer, especially the match sprinter. Training for this region is not within the scope of this book.

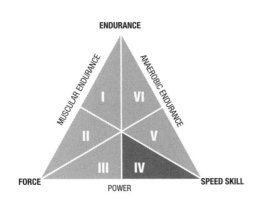

Region V

Region V includes short criteriums that are typical of many masters, women's, and juniors races. These are forty-five minutes or less and have a high requirement for speed skill and anaerobic endurance. You must also realize that while this is a short event with much sprinting, it is still an endurance race. Don't disregard the development of this primary ability.

Short criteriums attract riders who are good sprinters. They usually have great total body strength and a capacity to produce extremely high power outputs instantaneously. This power is often marked by the ability to produce vertical jumps in excess of 22 inches. Champion sprinters have the dynamic balance of a gymnast and can turn the cranks at extremely high cadences. In close-quarters sprints, they race aggressively with no thought given to "what would happen if . . . "—they are confident in their ability to win the close one.

Priorities for region V training

Primary importance

   1. Speed skill

   2. Anaerobic endurance

   3. Endurance

Secondary importance

   4. Power

   5. Force

   6. Muscular endurance

Region VI

Region VI races are long criteriums and circuit races. This is the most common type of race in the United States. Notice that the primary quality of criterium racing is still endurance. Criteriums, however, requires less endurance ability than do longer road races. The ability to maintain speed and repeatedly sprint out of corners is necessary for success, as are superb bike handling skills when cornering, bumping, and balancing.

If in a particular race, a hill or hills are the deciding factor, then force may replace speed skill as a success characteristic.

Priorities for region VI training

Primary importance

   1. Endurance

   2. Anaerobic endurance

   3. Speed skill

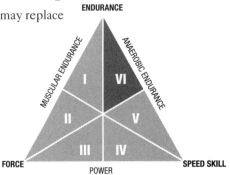

Secondary importance

    4. Muscular endurance

    5. Force

    6. Power

References

Bompa, T. *Theory and Methodology of Training.* Dubuque, IA: Kendall/Hunt Publishing, 1994.

Brunner, R., and B. Tabachnik. *Soviet Training and Recovery Methods.* Sport Focus Publishing, 1990.

Freeman, W. *Peak When It Counts.* Mountain View, CA: Tafnews Press, 1991.

Maglischo, E. *Swimming Faster.* Palo Alto, CA: Mayfield, 1982.

Martin, D.E., and P.N. Coe. *Training Distance Runners.* Champaign, IL: Leisure Press, 1991.

Sleamaker, R. *Serious Training for Serious Athletes.* Champaign, IL: Leisure Press, 1989.

PART FOUR

PLANNING

HISTORICAL PERSPECTIVES

Modern European Training Methods
by Jack Heid
As it appeared in *Cycling Almanac*, 1951

No one can tell you exactly how to train. It is something you have to work out according to the time at your disposal and the roads and companionship available. However, there are some basic things that you can make your training plans around, which you can copy from my present training methods that I assure you I copied from the European "masters" who have taught me to the point that I feel I have the ability to stay with many of them.

No matter how much training you do on the road with 70 gear or lower, you cannot go stale. You must get in the hours and the mileage. There is no substitute for it. Great riders like Harris and Coppi, who have entirely different actual racing styles, attest to this. Road riders here sit on their bikes all day and do 150 miles one day and the other they rest in the woods doing calisthenics and much deep breathing.

For my track training, I first get on the track and ride around slowly for 5 minutes to warm up. Then we get into a group and for about one-half hour change off pace every 500 yards (about one lap of the track) traveling at 20 mph. Then we all take a 15-minute rest and then go out taking turns leading out for sprints of 250 yards. We have three or four of these 15-minute turns, always resting off the track between. The same can be done on a piece of road measured off for 250 yards.

Developing a jump can be practiced afterwards by coming to an almost dead stop and jumping hard to get up top speed, then rolling slowly to a stop and duplicating this procedure. Don't do too much in one day if you don't feel like it—don't ever force yourself in training.

PLANNING TO RACE 7

> The method is the same for you as it is for the pros. What is different is the workload.
> —MICHELE FERRARI,
> Italian cycling coach

Why do you train? Is it to enjoy fresh air, the companionship of friends, travel to exotic places, and the feeling of fitness? Or is it to prepare for the peak experience of racing near your limits?

Certainly all of these play a part in getting you out the door and onto a saddle, but since you're reading this book, I suspect the latter choice is correct. All of us want to see how well we can perform, to get new glimpses of our potential, to push the limits of fitness, and to bask in the glow of success.

This chapter lays the groundwork for chapters 8 and 9, in which you will develop your own personalized training plan.

Training Systems

Cyclists typically gravitate to one of three training systems in order to prepare for racing. Each has produced champions. Most athletes don't consciously select a system—it just happens. They roll out of the driveway every day and then do what they feel like once on the road, or they meet with a group and let the top riders determine the day's workout. This is not the way to achieve your true potential as a bicycle racer. The road to racing success begins with understanding where you are headed and how you will get there. The starting point is a decision to train purposefully. Until haphazard workouts are replaced with systematic training, approaching your potential is highly unlikely.

Selecting a training system has a lot to do with this decision. Let's examine the three training systems most commonly used by cyclists: race into shape, always fit, and periodization.

Race into Shape

The most common training system used by cyclists is racing into shape. It traces its roots back to the days of wool jerseys and nail-on cleats. Even in the age of the power-meters, fingertip shifters, and titanium components, racing into shape is still the system used by most cyclists. It's easy to do—there are only two steps.

Step 1 involves building a large aerobic base by pedaling one thousand miles easily. Nearly every rider I talk with knows this number and speaks of it with quiet reverence. Interestingly, the thousand-mile goal does work well for some athletes. But it doesn't work for everyone. For some, it is way too much, and for others it is simply not enough.

Once you have established aerobic endurance, step 2 commences: race. The idea is that by going to a race every weekend, and club races at mid-week, a high level of fitness will result.

There are some good reasons to train this way, the most important being that the fitness developed is specific to the demands of racing. What could be more similar to racing than racing? There are, however, some problems. Training this way is very unpredictable. It's just as likely that great fitness will occur at the wrong time as at the right time relative to the most important races of the season. Another problem is that there is no planned rest. Racing into shape frequently leads to overtraining. It is also likely to lead to premature burnout. Every time you put your wheel on a starting line there is an emotional investment. After some number of these in a short period of time the rider loses enthusiasm. It's as if you have only so many matches to burn and once they are all used up the body and mind are unwilling to continue.

Always Fit

In warmer climates such as Florida, southern California, and Arizona, cyclists often try to stay in racing shape year-round. The cooler weather and availability of training races throughout the winter entice them to keep a constant level of fitness by doing the same training rides every week. Due to weather constraints, athletes in other parts of the country never even consider this system. That's a good reason why sloppy weather and frigid temperatures are probably an advantage for training.

The greatest issues facing the always-fit trainer are boredom and burnout. After 220 to 250 days of high-level training, an athlete becomes toast. Burnout is not a pretty sight. All interest in training, racing, and life in general vanishes. It sometimes takes months to regain enthusiasm for riding, if it's regained at all. (Chapter 17 will discuss burnout in detail.)

Another problem has to do with physiology. After about twelve weeks of training in the same way, improvement seems to plateau. And since fitness is never stagnant, if it's not improving, it must be getting worse. Trying to maintain fitness at a high level all the time really means trying to minimize losses. It just doesn't work.

Periodization

Periodization is the system used by most successful athletes today, and the one I propose you use. The rest of Part IV describes how to incorporate it into your training.

In Chapter 6, I mentioned periodization in relation to the works of Romanian scientist Dr. Tudor Bompa who contributed the foreword to this book. In the late 1940s, Soviet sports scientists discovered that athletic performance improved by varying the training stress throughout the year rather than maintaining a constant training focus. This led to the development of annual training plans that varied the stress of training over periods of time. The East Germans and Romanians further developed this concept by establishing goals for the various periods, and the system of periodization was born. Bompa so refined the concept that he is known as the "father of periodization." His seminal work, *Theory and Methodology of Training*, introduced Western athletes to this training system. The most recent edition of this work is called *Periodization, Theory and Methodology of Training*.

While athletes and coaches have "Westernized" periodization, they have done so largely without the help of science. Scientific literature offers little in the way of direction as to a long-term training approach for endurance athletes.

The basic premise of all periodization programs is that training should progress from the general to the specific. For example, early in the season, the serious cyclist uses much of the available training time to develop general strength with weights, while also crosstraining and doing some riding. Later in the season, more time is spent on the bike in conditions that simulate bicycle racing. While there is no scientific evidence to support such a pattern of training, logic seems to support it. In fact, most of the world's top athletes adhere to this principle.

Of course, periodization means more than simply training more specifically. It also involves arranging the workouts in such a way that the elements of fitness achieved in an earlier phase of training are maintained while new ones are addressed and improved. This modular method of training means making small changes in workouts during four- to eight-week periods. The body will gradually become more fit with such a pattern of change.

Flexibility of training, or lack of it, may be the biggest obstacle facing a cyclist using periodization. Once a rider has outlined a plan, there is often a reluctance to vary from it. Successful periodization requires flexibility. I've never coached an athlete who got through an entire season without a cold, work responsibilities, or a visit from Aunt Bessie getting in the way of the plan. That's just the way life is. An annual training plan should never be viewed as "final." You must assume from the outset that there will be changes due to unforeseen and unavoidable complications. Remember this in the next chapter when you sit down to write your training plan.

Another problem with periodization is all the scientific mumbo-jumbo that goes along with it. The language of periodization seems to confuse many, including coaches. Figure 7.1 illustrates the terms as used for blocks of time in periodization. For the purposes of this book, when referring to specific mesocycle periods, the bold terms in Figure 7.1 are used: Preparation, Base, Build, Peak, Race, and Transition.

MACROCYCLE	TRAINING YEAR					
MESOCYCLES	PREPARATION			COMPETITION		TRANSITION
	GENERAL PREPARATION	SPECIFIC PREPARATION	PRE-COMP	COMPETITION		TRANSITION
	PREP	BASE	BUILD	PEAK	RACE	TRANSITION
MICROCYCLES	1 2 3	4 5 6 7 8	WEEKS 9–42	43 44 45 46	47 48 49	50 51 52

Figure 7.1
The training year divided into mesocycles and microcycles

Training Periods

The reason for dividing the season into specific periods in a periodization plan is that this division allows for emphasis on specific aspects of fitness, while maintaining others developed in earlier periods. Trying to improve all aspects of training at the same time is impossible. No athlete is capable of handling that much simultaneous stress. Periodization also allows for two of the training principles discussed in Chapter 3—progressive overload and adaptation.

Figure 7.2 diagrams the process of periodization, describes the focus of each mesocycle period, and suggests a time frame for each period.

If you add up the suggested times for each period you'll find a range of 21 to 38 weeks—well short of a year. The reason for this is that I've found cyclists perform best when they peak two or three times during a year. Multi-peak seasons allow for rest and recovery more frequently, are less likely to cause burnout or overtraining, and keep training and racing fun. If you do things right—instead of losing fitness as a long race season progresses—each subsequent peak is higher than the previous one. In Chapter 8, I'll explain how to design such a multi-peak season.

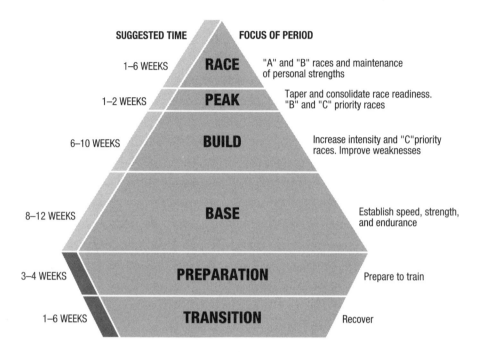

Figure 7.2

Using training periods to peak at pre-selected times

In the remainder of this chapter, I'll introduce you to each period in detail. Every aspect of periodization is described, along with suggestions for how to train the racing abilities discussed in the last two chapters. As you read about the period, use Figure 7.3 to see how volume and intensity blend in this hypothetical season. While will not look exactly the way yours will, it probably comes close. The elements common to most periodization plans are increased volume at the start of the training year followed by increased intensity as volume declines. Notice that there are reduced-volume recovery weeks scheduled periodically throughout the Base and Build periods. These are important—don't pass them up.

Figure 7.3

Hypothetical training year divided into periods showing the interplay of volume and intensity

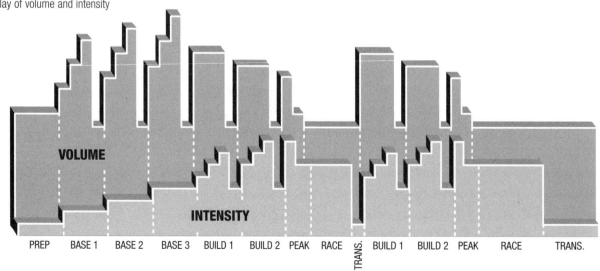

Accompanying each period description in the following section is a diagram that illustrates the mix of racing abilities for that period. It is especially important to note that the portion of the pie chart devoted to each ability is not exact. The amount of time spent working on each fitness ability will vary with the individual's strengths and limiters. Use the pie chart only as a rough guide of how to proportion training time.

Preparation Period

The preparation period generally marks the start of the training year and is included only if there has been a long transition following the end of the racing season. It is usually scheduled for the late fall or early winter, depending on when the last race was and the length of the transition.

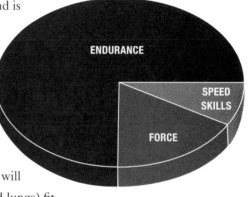

Figure 7.4A
Preparation

The purpose of this period is to prepare the athlete's body for the periods to follow. It's a time of training to train. Workouts are low intensity with an emphasis on aerobic endurance, especially in the form of crosstraining. Activities such as running, vigorous hiking, cross-country skiing, snowshoeing, swimming, and in-line skating will maintain or improve cardiorespiratory (heart, blood, blood vessels, and lungs) fitness. The total volume of training is low when compared with most other periods.

Strength training begins with the Anatomical Adaptation (AA) phase that prepares the muscles and tendons for the heavier stresses to follow later. (Strength training is discussed in detail in Chapter 12.)

Speed skills can be developed through drills, usually done on an indoor trainer or rollers. This will reawaken the legs to spinning fluidly in smooth circles.

Base Period

The Base period is the time to fully establish the basic fitness abilities of endurance, force, and speed skills. Base is generally the longest period of the season, lasting eight to twelve weeks. Some athletes are careless with Base training, ending it too soon. It is essential that the basic abilities have a strong foothold before launching high-intensity training.

In the warm-winter states, there may be races available during this period. I usually recommend that these be avoided. They are often demoralizing since some riders are in good shape (the always-fit ones), and you won't be, if you're following this plan. If you must do one of these races, treat it as a workout and do not take the results seriously. Remember that it is okay to abandon the race. These races are of no consequence for your season ahead.

Since this is such a long period and there will be many changes taking place in your fitness throughout, the Base period is divided into three segments: Base 1, Base 2, and Base 3. The volume of training grows in each base period as crosstraining phases into on-bike training. Intensity rises slightly (see Figure 7.3).

Base 1 marks the start of steady increases in volume to boost aerobic endurance and increase the body's resiliency to large workloads. In the more northern latitudes, you accomplish most of this through crosstraining. Cyclists in the warm-winter states should still consider crosstraining instead of spending all of their time on a bike. It's a long season, and many of the elements of fitness developed now can be accomplished off the bike.

Strength training in Base 1 places an emphasis on establishing Maximum Strength (MS) with the use of high-resistance loads and low repetitions. The shift to these greater loads should be gradual so as not to cause injury.

Speed-skills work continues just as in the Preparation period with drills that emphasize high cadence and smooth technique on a trainer or rollers.

In Base 2, on-bike endurance work begins to replace crosstraining as the volume rises. As the road rides become longer, the companionship of a group helps the time to pass faster. Be careful, however, not to ride with groups that turn these endurance rides into races. This time of year you will find many "Christmas stars"—riders who are in great race shape in the winter, but aren't around when the serious racing starts in the summer.

You should plan the majority of your road workouts each week on continuously rolling to hilly courses that place controlled stress on the muscular system. The best courses at this time of the season keep effort below the lactate threshold and allow cadences of 80 rpm and higher while seated on a hill. Staying in the saddle is important for these workouts to develop greater hip extension strength for the next period.

Weight room training shifts toward maintenance of strength gains made in the previous period. Also, speed-skills work moves outside, weather permitting. Otherwise, indoor workouts continue. Whenever possible, use the road to refine your sprinting form.

Muscular-endurance training is also introduced in Base 2, with tempo workouts based on heart rate or power output (see Chapter 4 for details).

Base 3 marks a phasing-in of higher-intensity training with the introduction of hill work done at or slightly above lactate threshold. In Base 2, somewhat hilly courses ridden in the saddle complemented the weight room workouts by creating greater hip extension force. Now you should seek out serious hills with long climbs, still riding them mostly in the saddle.

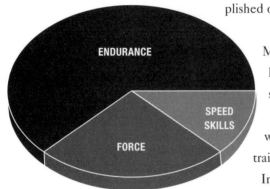

Figure 7.4B
Base 1

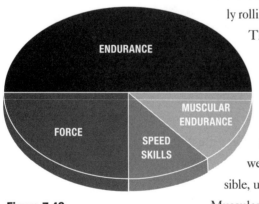

Figure 7.4C
Base 2

The total weekly volume of training progresses to the highest point of the season in Base 3, with aerobic-endurance rides on the road accounting for about half of all training time. The longest workouts now should be at least as long as your longest race of the season or two hours, whichever is longer. Group rides are still the best way to get in these long efforts. Some in the group may be ready for higher-intensity training and so these rides will typically become faster. While it's okay to occasionally put the hammer down in a sprint for the city limits sign, don't turn these into races. This is not easy to do as the pressure to "race" will be high. Be patient and sit in. Your purpose is to get as fast as you can with low-effort rides before turning up the heat in the next period. Later in the season, you'll be glad you held back.

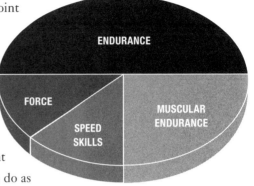

Figure 7.4D
Base 3

Muscular-endurance training is increased and weight workouts continue as maintenance. Several weekly workouts should now take you to the lactate threshold intensity training zones.

Speed-skills work, done mostly as form sprints, must now be on the road.

Build Period

A multi-peak season includes two or more full Build periods. This is shown in Figure 7.3. As you can see, Build 1 maintains the volume of training at a relatively high level, although less than that achieved in three of the previous eight weeks. That means when it is time to return to Build 1, following the first Race period, you may need to re-establish your endurance, force, and speed skills.

The Build period is marked by the introduction of anaerobic-endurance training. Just as with force, hill work, and muscular-endurance training, this should be done cautiously to avoid injury.

There will probably be criteriums and road races throughout this period. These should mostly be low-priority, and you can regard them as a substitute for anaerobic-endurance training. Anaerobic-endurance workouts may also include intervals and fast group rides.

During Build 1, endurance work is reduced, but is still a prominent focus of training. At this time in the season such rides may occur less frequently than in the Base period. You will be much better served by doing your long, easy endurance rides during this period with one or two teammates rather than with a large group. Use the group rides for the development of muscular endurance and anaerobic endurance. It is important to avoid overtraining during this phase of training. Now is the time it can easily happen. Pay close attention to your fatigue level during group rides. If you feel dead in the saddle, don't work hard with the group. Either sit in, getting as much of

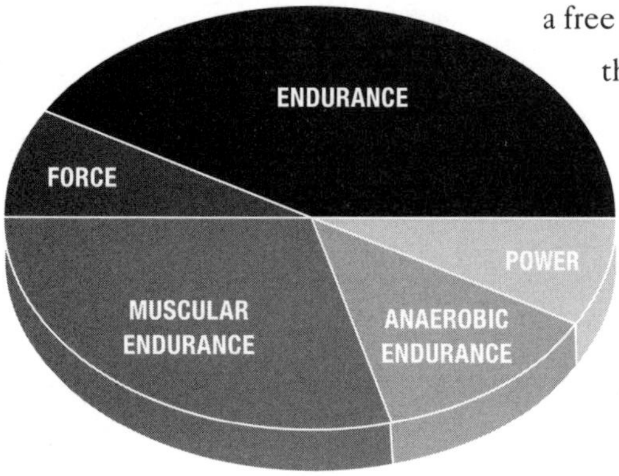

Figure 7.4E
Build 1

Figure 7.4F
Build 2

a free ride as you can, or turn off and ride alone. Be smart. You're not doing this to impress your friends. Save that for the races.

Force training in the weight room is either eliminated or cut back to one day a week now as the duration of such sessions gets shorter. Strength maintenance is the only purpose. For the athlete limited by force, hill work continues to be a primary focus. This may be in the form of muscular-endurance or anaerobic-endurance intervals done on a hill. Appendix C is a workout menu that will offer further suggestions. Anaerobic-endurance workouts can be done with one or two other riders close to your ability. Muscular-endurance training is best done alone to prepare you for the focus needed in time trialing and to keep you in the narrow threshold training zones.

Power may now replace speed skills work. Power training can be combined with other workouts, such as anaerobic-endurance sessions. If so, initially incorporate the power-training portion of your routine early in the workout when the legs are still fresh. At first, don't make the common mistake of doing power training at the end of workouts. Reserve that for anaerobic endurance and muscular endurance. In Build 2 power may be shifted to the end of workouts to simulate the demands of sprinting late in a race.

Build 2 slightly decreases the volume of training while increasing the intensity. Notice that intensity in Figure 7.3 is increased each of the three weeks just as volume increased in the Base period. By now you should be experiencing increasing levels of fatigue and you will need to continue being cautious with anaerobic intensity. If you are unsure about whether you should do a certain workout, be wise and either leave it out or shorten it. The mere fact that you're questioning it is enough reason to do so. When in doubt—leave it out.

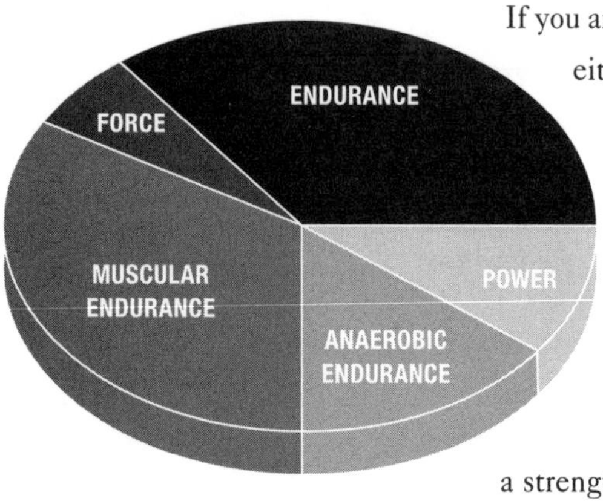

Training in Build 2 emphasizes intensity to a greater extent than in the previous four weeks. Anaerobic-endurance and muscular-endurance sessions become longer with decreasing recovery intervals. At this point, muscular endurance should be long, continuous exertions just as in time trialing.

Weight room training remains at once a week, if at all, and follows a strength maintenance plan. Riders for whom force is not a limiter may stop weight training in this period. I recommend, however, that masters and women continue, but the choice is up to you. Power training may continue as in Build 1.

Peak Period

The Peak period is when you consolidate racing fitness. It is time to reduce volume and keep intensity levels high relative to the expected demands of the targeted races while emphasizing recovery between workouts. It is now best to train at race-like intensities every 72 to 96 hours. The idea is to be rested and ready to push the limits of the fitness envelope when it's time for a quality workout. These workouts may also be B- or C-priority races that serve as tune-ups for the A-priority races to follow.

Tapering brings added rest that sometimes causes athletes to question whether they are doing enough. If you've designed your season correctly and followed the plan, you will be ready. And, even if you aren't ready, there's nothing you can do about it now.

The purpose of periodization is to reach peak form just as the most important races occur. Since these races are seldom on back-to-back weekends and may be separated by several weeks, it's usually necessary to peak more than once. I've found that the athletes I train race best when they peak two times each season. I believe you'll find that this works for you, also. Chapter 8 will help you design a twin-peaks season using the same procedure I use when training riders.

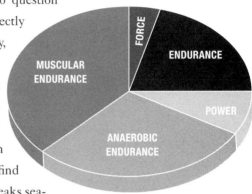

Figure 7.4G
Peak

Race Period

This is what you've been waiting for. The fun time of the year is starting. Now all that's needed is to race, work on strength areas, and recover. The races will provide adequate stress to keep your systems working at a maximum level. Your anaerobic fitness should stay high. In weeks when there are no races, a race-effort group ride is the best option.

Up until now, you've been working on your limiters. Now is the time to take your strength areas to a new level by emphasizing them. If muscular endurance is a strength, time trial at mid-week. If you're a strong sprinter, work on that. If climbing is your forte, then climb. Make your strength as strong as possible.

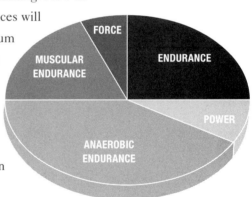

Figure 7.4H
Race

Transition Period

The Transition period is a time of rest and recovery following a Race period. This should always be included after the last race of the year, but may also be inserted early in the season following the first Peak period to prevent burnout later in the year. Early season Transition periods may be brief, perhaps only five to seven days, whereas at the end of the season such a break may be four weeks or so.

The Transition period should have little regimentation. My only admonition is to do what you feel like doing during this period, as long as it is low intensity and low volume. Crosstraining is a good idea. Use this time to "recharge your batteries." The time away from your bike will pay off with higher motivation for training and

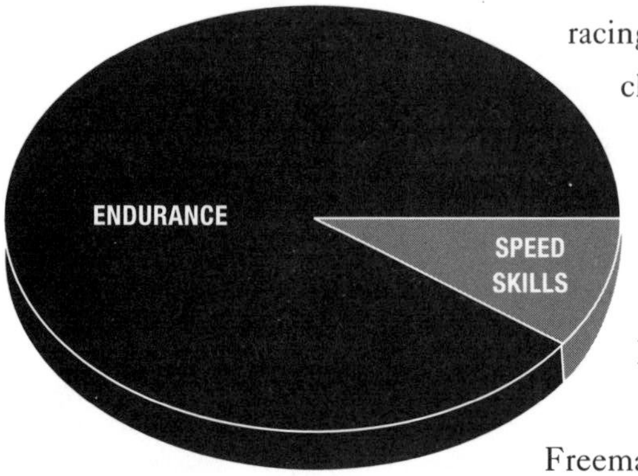

Figure 7.4I
Transition

racing, the healing of minor muscle damage, and the reduction of psychological stress.

References

Bompa, T. *Periodization of Strength*. Sedona, AZ: Veritas Publishing, Inc., 1993.

Bompa, T. *Periodization, Theory and Methodology of Training*. Champaign, IL: Human Kinetics, 1999.

Freeman, W. "Peak When It Counts." Tafnews, 1989.

Rogers, J. "Periodization of Training," *Endurance Training Journal* 2 (1992): 4–7.

Sleamaker, R. *Serious Training for Serious Athletes*. Champaign, IL: Leisure Press, 1989.

VanHandel, P.J. "Periodization of Training." *Bike Tech* 6, no. 2 (1987): 6–10.

VanHandel, P.J. "Training for Cycling I." *Conditioning for Cycling* 1, no. 1 (1991): 8–11.

VanHandel, P.J. "Training for Cycling II." *Conditioning for Cycling* 1, no. 2 (1991): 18–23.

THE TRAINING YEAR

I used to train too much, too many hours. In my first year as a pro I trained thirty-five hours a week, which is too hard.
—TONY ROMINGER

Now it's time to begin designing an annual training plan. The best time of year to do this is shortly following the end of your last Race period, when you're ready to start the Preparation period. If you've purchased this book after your season has already begun, it's still a good idea to plan the rest of your year. Better late than never.

I'm about to take you through a simple six-step process of annual planning that will have you on the way to a better season before you even turn a crank. This will require some writing, but use a pencil as you'll need to make changes later. The Annual Training Plan worksheet is in Appendix B. You should make a copy before starting to work. If you prefer to work on your plan electronically, you will find an electronic version of the Annual Training Plan along with other tools for self-coaching at www.TrainingBible.com.

The danger in following a methodical process to arrive at a training plan is that you'll be so engrossed in procedures and numbers that you might forget to think in a realistic way. The purpose is not simply to write a plan; the purpose is to race better than ever before. At the end of a successful season, you'll realize how important it was to have a written plan.

Writing and following an annual training plan is somewhat like climbing a mountain. Before you take the first step, it's a good idea to know where the peak of the mountain is and how you plan to get there. It also helps if you know what problems you're likely to encounter along the route so you can be prepared to deal with them. While ascending the mountain, you'll stop occasionally to look at the peak and check your progress. You may decide to change the route based on new conditions such as bad weather or unexpected obstacles. Arriving at the peak you'll be elated, but looking back down you will remember all of the challenges you overcame along the way and how the plan gave you direction.

Remind yourself throughout this chapter that you're not writing an annual plan to impress anyone or simply to feel organized. The purpose is to create a useful and dynamic guide for your training. You will refer to the plan regularly to make decisions as your training progresses. The plan will help you to keep an eye on the goal and not get lost in "just going to races." A training plan is dynamic in that you will frequently modify it as new circumstances arise.

The Annual Training Plan

It's time to get started planning. The six steps you'll complete in this chapter are:

1. Determine season goals
2. Establish supporting objectives
3. Set annual hours
4. Prioritize races
5. Divide year into periods
6. Assign weekly hours

In Chapter 9, you will complete the annual plan by assigning weekly workouts based on abilities. This probably sounds like a lot to accomplish. It is, but the system I've set out here will make it easy to do.

A working version of the Annual Training Plan appears in Figure 8.1. Notice that there are several parts to the Plan. At the top left of the page are spaces for annual hours, season goals, and training objectives. The left column assigns a number to each week of the year. You should write in the date of the Monday of each week of the season. For example, if your first week of training at the start of the next season will be the week of November 3–9, write "Nov. 3" in week 1 and do the same for the remaining weeks of the coming season. There is a column to list the races, their priorities (pri), the period, and weekly hours for each week. The small boxes down the right side will be used to indicate categories of workouts by abilities as listed at the top of the page. Chapter 9 will explain this last part.

Step 1: Determine Season Goals

Start with the destination: What racing goals do you want to accomplish this season? It could be to upgrade, to place in the top five at the district road race, or to finish a

ANNUAL TRAINING PLAN

Annual Hours:
Seasonal Goals:
1.
2.
3.
Training Objectives:
1.
2.
3.
4.
5.

WORKOUTS

WK#	MON	RACE	PRI	PERIOD	HOURS	DETAILS	WEIGHTS	ENDURANCE	FORCE	SPEED SKILL	MUSCULAR ENDUR.	ANAEROBIC ENDUR.	POWER	TESTING	
01	/														
02	/														
03	/														
04	/														
05	/														
06	/														
07	/														
08	/														
09	/														
10	/														
11	/														
12	/														
13	/														
14	/														
15	/														
16	/														
17	/														
18	/														
19	/														
20	/														
21	/														
22	/														
23	/														
24	/														
25	/														
26	/														
27	/														
28	/														
29	/														
30	/														
31	/														
32	/														
33	/														
34	/														
35	/														
36	/														
37	/														
38	/														
39	/														
40	/														
41	/														
42	/														
43	/														
44	/														
45	/														
46	/														
47	/														
48	/														
49	/														
50	/														
51	/														
52	/														

Figure 8.1
Annual training plan

stage race. Studies have shown that clearly defined goals improve one's ability to achieve them. A successful mountain climber always has the peak in the back of his or her mind. If you don't know where you want to go, by the end of the season you will have gone nowhere.

Don't get goals confused with wishes and dreams. The athletes I train sometimes dream about what they wish to accomplish, and I encourage them to do so. Dreaming is healthy. Without dreams there is no vision for the future, no incentive. Dreams can become realities. But wishes and dreams take longer than one season to accomplish. If you can achieve it this season, no matter how big it is, it's no longer a dream—it's a goal. Also, dreams become goals when there is a plan for accomplishing them. So we are dealing strictly with goals for the purpose of planning a season.

Let's be realistically optimistic. If you had trouble finishing club rides in the past season, winning a stage race this season is a wish, not a goal. "But," you say, "if you don't set high goals you never achieve anything." That's true, but the problem with wishes is that you know down deep you really aren't capable of achieving them this season, so there's no commitment to the training required. A challenging goal will stretch you to the limits, and may require you to take some risks, but you can imagine yourself accomplishing it in the next few months. Ask yourself: "If I do everything right, can I imagine success with this goal?" If you can't even conceive of achieving it now, you're wasting your time. If you can, it's a good goal. Otherwise, it's just another dream. There are four principles your goals must adhere to:

1. **Your goal must be measurable.** How will you know if you're getting closer to it? How do business people know if they're achieving their financial goals? By counting their money, of course. Rather than saying "get better" in your goal statement, you might say, "complete a 40k time trial in less than 58 minutes."

2. **Your goal must be under your control.** A successful person does not set goals based on other people. "If Jones misses the break, win XYZ race," is not a goal that demands your commitment. "Make the winning break at the Boulder Road Race," however, gets your juices flowing.

3. **Your goal must stretch you.** A goal that is too easy or too hard is the same as having no goal. For a Category 3 racer, winning the National Pro Championship this year is more than a stretch, even though it's a great dream. On the other hand, "finish the club's eight-mile time trial" isn't much of a challenge. But upgrading to Category 2 would, perhaps, be an excellent stretch.

4. **Whatever your goals, state them in the positively.** Whatever you do while reading this paragraph, don't think about pink elephants. See what I mean? Your goal must keep you focused on what you want to happen, not what you want to avoid.

Guess what happens to people who set a goal such as "Don't lose the Podunkville Criterium." You got it, they lose because they didn't know what they were supposed to do. Knowing what *not* to do is of little benefit.

The goal should also be racing-outcome oriented. For example, don't set a goal of climbing better. That's an objective, as we'll see shortly. Instead, commit to a faster time for the Mount Evans Road Race, for example. Table 8.1 offers some examples of racing-oriented goals to help you.

GOALS
Top 10 finish in district Category III road race
Break one hour in 40-km time trial in August
Finish in top five in two out of three A-priority criteriums
Upgrade to Category II.
Rank in top five in district Category III B.A.R.
Finish in top three in masters nationals road race
Place in top 25 in Category III G.C. at Mike Nields Stage Race

Table 8.1
Goal Setting Examples

After establishing a racing-oriented goal, you may have one or two others that are important to you. Give them the same consideration you did the first goal. Stop at three goals so things don't get too complicated in the coming months. All of your goals should be listed at the top of the Annual Training Plan.

Step 2: Establish Training Objectives

In Chapter 5, you determined your strengths and weaknesses. After doing this you completed the Cyclist Assessment form. Look back at that form now to refresh your memory: What are your strengths and weaknesses? Which of your weaknesses is a limiter?

You may remember that in Chapter 6, I described the concept of limiters. These are the key race-specific weaknesses that hold you back from being successful in certain races. In Chapter 6, I explained abilities required for different types of races. By comparing your weaknesses with the race's requirements, you will know your limiters. For example, a hilly race requires good force and climbing proficiency. A weakness in either of these areas means you have a limiter for A-priority, hilly races. You must improve in that area if you're to be successful in hilly races.

Read your first season goal. Do any of your weaknesses (score of 3 or lower on the Cyclist Assessment) present a limiter for this goal? If so, you'll need to train to improve that specific weakness. Under training objectives list the limiter. In the coming weeks of the Annual Training Plan, you'll work on improving this race-specific weakness. Chapter 9 will show you how to do that. For now the challenge is knowing when you have improved a limiter—in other words, being able to measure progress.

There are several ways to measure progress. Chapter 5 presented several tests you could conduct, but races and workouts also serve as good progress indicators. Table 8.2 provides examples of training objectives for hypothetical limiters associated with specific goals. You should write your training objectives for each goal in a similar manner so you know how to determine when progress is being made. Notice that time limits are set for each objective. To accomplish the goal, you must meet the training objective by a certain time of the season. Too late is as good as never.

By the time you are done with this part of the Annual Training Plan, you will probably have three to five training objectives listed. These are short-term standards against which you will measure progress.

Step 3: Set Annual Training Hours

The number of hours you train in the coming season—including on the bike, in the weight room, and crosstraining—partly determines the stress load you carry. It is a balancing act: an annual volume that is too high will probably result in overtraining; too low and you begin to lose endurance. Setting annual training hours is one of the most critical decisions you will make about training. If you make an error here, make it on the side of too few hours.

Before discussing how to arrive at this number, I'd like to make a case for training based on time rather than on distance. Training by miles encourages you to repeat the same courses week after week. It also causes you to compare your time on a given course today with what it was last week. Such thinking is counterproductive. Using time as a basis for training volume allows you to go wherever you want, so long as you finish within a given time. Your rides are more enjoyable due to the variety and less concern for today's average speed.

How do you determine annual hours if you haven't kept track of time in the past? Most cyclists keep a record of the miles they've ridden. If you have such a record divide the total by what you guess the average speed to have been—18 miles per hour would be a reasonable guess. If you've also crosstrained and lifted weights, estimate how many hours you put into those activities in the past year. By adding all of the estimates together, you have a ballpark figure for your annual training hours.

Looking back over the last three years you can easily see trends in training volume. If so, did you race better in the high-volume years or worse? There were undoubtedly other factors in your performance at those times, but this may help you to decide what the training volume should be for the coming season.

GOAL	TRAINING OBJECTIVES
TOP 10 FINISH IN DISTRICT CATEGORY 3 ROAD RACE	1. **IMPROVE MUSCULAR-ENDURANCE:** Complete a sub-57 minute 40-km TT in June 2. **IMPROVE CLIMBING:** Squat 320 pounds by end of Base 1.
BREAK ONE HOUR IN 40-KM TIME TRIAL IN AUGUST	1. **IMPROVE FOCUS:** Feel more focused in tempo work outs and races by July 31 (subjective measurement). 2. **IMPROVE MUSCULAR ENDURANCE:** Increase lactate threshold power to 330 watts by end of Base 3.
FINISH IN TOP FIVE IN TWO OUT OF THREE A-PRIORITY CRITERIUMS	1. **IMPROVE SPEED-ENDURANCE:** Increase speed score on Natural Abilities Profile by end of Base 3. 2. **IMPROVE SPRINTING:** Increase average watts to 700 on power test by end of Base 3.
UPGRADE TO CATEGORY II	1. **IMPROVE CLIMBING:** Increase power-to-weight index by 10% by end of Base 3. 2. **IMPROVE TRAINING CONSISTENCY:** Complete all BT workouts in Build period.
RANK IN TOP FIVE IN DISTRICT IN CATEGORY III B.A.R.	1. **IMPROVE SPEED:** Spin at 140 rpm and remain in contact with the saddle (no bouncing) by February 12. 2. **IMPROVE SPEED ENDURANCE:** Continue for four minutes beyond 165 heart rate on lactate threshold test by end of first Build 2 period.
FINISH IN TOP THREE IN MASTERS NATIONALS ROAD RACE	1. **IMPROVE SPRINT:** Produce 950 watts on max power test by end of Base 3. 2. **IMPROVE CLIMBING:** Climb Rist Canyon in 28 minutes by May 31.
PLACE IN TOP 25 IN CATEGORY III G.C. AT MIKE NIELDS STAGE RACE	1. **IMPROVE MUSCULAR ENDURANCE:** Climb Poudre Canyon six times in 10 weeks prior to race. 2. **IMPROVE TIME TRIALING:** Lower 8-mile TT self-test to 19:12 by April 15.

Table 8.2

Limiters and Training Objectives by Goal

Even without records of annual miles or hours trained, you may be able to produce an estimate. That will give you a starting point. To do this, jot down on a piece of paper what a typical training week looks like for you—neither your highest or lowest volume. Add these daily times and multiply by 50 for a very rough gauge of how many hours you train annually.

Table 8.3 offers a rough guideline of the annual hours typical of cyclists by racer category. This should not be considered a "required" volume. I know of many riders with ten or more years of racing who put in fewer miles than those suggested here for their category and yet race quite well. The volume of training has a lot to do with developing endurance. With endurance already established by years of riding, you can shift your emphasis toward intensity.

Limiting the number of hours an athlete trains produces better results than struggling through an overly ambitious volume. If you have a full-time job, a family, a home to maintain, and other responsibilities, be realistic—don't expect to train with the same volume as the pros. Training is their job.

If, however, you have not been competitive in the past, and fall well below the suggested annual hours for your category, it may be wise to consider increasing your volume to the lower figure in your category range so long as this is not more than a 15-percent increase. Otherwise, increases in your annual hours from year to year should be in the range of 5 to 10 percent.

Many professional business people have limitations imposed on their training time by travel and work responsibilities. Determining annual hours in this case is based strictly on what is available. Write your annual training hours at the top of the Annual Training Plan. Later you'll use that figure to assign weekly training hours.

Table 8.3
Annual Training Hours
by Racer Category

CATEGORY	HOURS/YEAR
PRO	800–1,200
1–2	700–1,000
3	500–700
4	350–500
5/junior	200–350

Step 4: Prioritize Races

For this step you need a list of the races you will be doing. If the race schedule has not been published yet, go back to last year's race calendar and guess which days they'll be on. Races nearly always stay on the same weekends from year to year.

On the Annual Training Plan, list all of the races you intend to do by writing them into the "Races" column in the appropriate date rows. Remember that the date indicated is the Monday of that week. This should be an inclusive list of tentative races. You may decide later not to do some of these races, but for now you should assume you'll do them all.

The next step is to prioritize the races into three categories—A, B, and C—using the criteria that follows. If your team is well organized, the team manager may have some input on the priorities of the season. Better check with him or her before going beyond this point.

A Races

Pick out the three or four races—no more than this—that are most important to you this year. A stage race counts as one race and two A-priority races on the same weekend count as one race. An A-priority race isn't necessarily the one that gets the most press or has the biggest prize purse. It could be the Nowhereville Road Race, but if you live in Nowhereville, that could be the big race of the year *for you.*

The A-priority races are the most important on the schedule and all training will be designed around them. The purpose of training is to build and peak for these A races.

It's best that these races be clumped together in two or three weeks or widely separated by eight or more weeks. For example, two of the races may fall into a three-week period in May and the other two could be close together in August. Then again, two may occur in May, one in July, and the other in September. The idea is that in order to come to a peak for each of these most important races, a period of several weeks will be needed. During this time between A races you will still race, but won't be in top form. Realize that every time you go through the tapering and peaking process you lose some base fitness. So if your A-priority races occur frequently with little time to re-establish the most basic abilities of fitness between them, performance will decline. This is why the number of A races is limited to three or four, and it is best if they are widely separated on the calendar. It's generally best for the single most important race of the year to come near the end of the season when your fitness is likely to be at the highest level possible.

If your A races aren't neatly spaced or grouped as I've described here, don't worry. Season priorities are not determined by the calendar, but rather by goals. A schedule, however, that doesn't conveniently space the races makes planning and coming to a peak much more difficult, as you will see.

In the "Pri" column write in "A" for all of your A-priority races. Again, there should be no more than three or four of these.

B Races

These are important races at which you want to do well, but they're not as critical as the A races. You'll rest for a few days before each of them, but not build to a peak. There may be as many as twelve of these, and as with the A-priority events, stage races count as one as do two B races on the same weekend.

In the Pri column write in "B" for all of these races.

C Races

You now have up to sixteen weeks dedicated to either A or B races. That's most of the racing season. All the other races on the list are C-priority. C races are done for experience, as hard workouts, as tests of progress, for fun, or as tune-ups for A races. You will "train through" these races with no peaking and minimal rest before each one. They are essentially hard workouts. It's not unusual to decide at the last moment not to do one of these low-priority events. If your heart isn't in it, you'd be better off training that day—or resting.

Be careful with C races. They are the ones in which you're most likely to crash or go over the edge into a state of overtraining, since you may be tired and have low motivation to perform well. They are also usually associated with haphazard racing and confused incentives. Every race should have a meaning in your schedule, so decide before a C race what you want to get out of it. The more experienced you are as a racer, the fewer C races you should do. Conversely, juniors and Category IV and V riders should do several to gain experience.

Just because you classified a race as a C-priority doesn't mean that you won't give it your best shot. It merely means that this is a workout and you're probably coming into it carrying a bit of fatigue. You may still give it everything you've got, if that fits with your purpose in doing a given race, but realize that if the outcome isn't what you'd like that there are reasons for this—and it was just a C race anyway.

Step 5: Divide Year into Periods

Now that the times in the year when you want to be in top form are known (where the A-priority races are listed), periods can be assigned. Chapter 7 described the six training periods of the year. To refresh your memory, Table 8.4 summarizes each.

Table 8.4
Periodization Summary

PERIOD	DURATION	TRAINING FOCUS
PREPARATION	3–4 weeks	General adaptation with weights, crosstraining and on-bike drills.
BASE	8–12 weeks	Establish strength, speed and endurance. Introduce muscular endurance and hill work.
BUILD	6–10 weeks	Develop muscular endurance, speed endurance, and power.
PEAK	1–2 weeks	Consolidate race readiness with reduced volume and race tune-ups.
RACE	1–3 weeks	Race, refine strengths, and recover.
TRANSITION	1–6 weeks	Rest and recover.

Find the week of your first A race on the schedule and in the "Period" column write in "Race." This first Race period extends throughout your clumping of A races and could be as long as three weeks. Count (up the page) two weeks from "Race" and write in "Peak." Now work backward three (those over 40 years of age or so) or four weeks from Peak and indicate "Build 2." Using duration as indicated in Table 8.4, do the same for Build 1 (3–4 weeks), Base 3 (3–4 weeks), Base 2 (3–4 weeks), Base 1 (3–4 weeks), and Prep (3–4 weeks). The first part of the year is now scheduled.

Go to your second A race and write in "Race" as you did above. Count backward two weeks and write in "Peak" again. Then count back three or four weeks for Build 2 and another three or four for Build 1. It's not necessary to repeat the Base period unless your first peak has a two- or three-week Race period, or you feel that your base abilities, especially endurance and force, are being lost, or you included a Transition period following your first Race period of the season (which, by the way, is a very good idea).

It's unlikely that the Build-Peak period between your two Race periods will work out exactly with this number of weeks assigned to each period. Once you have the second Race period scheduled, it may be necessary to change the lengths of the various periods to make it work out so that you both improve your fitness and allow for scheduled rest weeks. Remember that our purpose in assigning periods at this point is to make sure you are ready for the A-priority races. Only you can determine what this means in terms of training since you are the only one who knows what your fitness is like at a given point in the season. It may well be necessary to change your plan for the second peak of the season once you reach that point. Again, the Annual Training Plan as we develop it early in the year is merely a guide to get you started. Be prepared to change it as you progress through the year.

It's a good idea to schedule a five- to seven-day Transition after your first Race period to allow for recovery and to prevent burnout later in the season. This always pays off with higher enthusiasm for training and greater fitness for late-season races. Following the last Race period of the season, schedule a longer Transition period.

If this step in the planning process seems confusing, you may want to look ahead to Chapter 11 where case studies describe the annual plan further.

Step 6: Assign Weekly Hours

Throughout the season there is a wave-like pattern of increasing and decreasing volume. Figure 7.3 also illustrates this. The purpose of this pattern is to make sure your endurance is maintained, but also to permit increases in intensity without overly stressing your body's systems. In this step, you'll write in the weekly training hours using Table 8.5 as a guide.

Table 8.5
Weekly Training Hours

PERIOD	WEEK	200	250	300	350	400	450	500	550	600	650
PREP	ALL	3.5	4.0	5.0	6.0	7.0	7.5	8.5	9.0	10.0	11.0
BASE 1	1	4.0	5.0	6.0	7.0	8.0	9.0	10.0	11.0	12.0	12.5
	2	5.0	6.0	7.0	8.5	9.5	10.5	12.0	13.0	14.5	15.5
	3	5.5	6.5	8.0	9.5	10.5	12.0	13.5	14.5	16.0	17.5
	4	3.0	3.5	4.0	5.0	5.5	6.5	7.0	8.0	8.5	9.0
BASE 2	1	4.0	5.5	6.5	7.5	8.5	9.5	10.5	12.5	12.5	13.0
	2	5.0	6.5	7.5	9.0	10.0	11.5	12.5	14.0	15.0	16.5
	3	5.5	7.0	8.5	10.0	11.0	12.5	14.0	15.5	17.0	18.0
	4	3.0	3.5	4.5	5.0	5.5	6.5	7.0	8.0	8.5	9.0
BASE 3	1	4.5	5.5	7.0	8.0	9.0	10.0	11.0	12.5	13.5	14.5
	2	5.0	6.5	8.0	9.5	10.5	12.0	13.5	14.5	16.0	17.0
	3	6.0	7.5	9.0	10.5	11.5	13.0	15.0	16.5	18.0	19.0
	4	3.0	3.5	4.5	5.0	5.5	6.5	7.0	8.0	8.5	9.0
BUILD 1	1	5.0	6.5	8.0	9.0	10.0	11.5	12.5	14.0	15.5	16.0
	2	5.0	6.5	8.0	9.0	10.0	11.5	12.5	14.0	15.5	16.0
	3	5.0	6.5	8.0	9.0	10.0	11.5	12.5	14.0	15.5	16.0
	4	3.0	3.5	4.5	5.0	5.5	6.5	7.0	8.0	8.5	9.0
BUILD 2	1	5.0	6.0	7.0	8.5	9.5	10.5	12.0	13.0	14.5	15.5
	2	5.0	6.0	7.0	8.5	9.5	10.5	12.0	13.0	14.5	15.5
	3	5.0	6.0	7.0	8.5	9.5	10.5	12.0	13.0	14.5	15.5
	4	3.0	3.5	4.5	5.0	5.5	6.5	7.0	8.0	8.5	9.0
PEAK	1	4.0	5.5	6.5	7.5	8.5	9.5	10.5	11.5	13.0	13.5
	2	3.5	4.0	5.0	6.0	6.5	7.5	8.5	9.5	10.0	11.0
RACE	ALL	3.0	3.5	4.5	5.0	5.5	6.5	7.0	8.0	8.5	9.0
TRANS.	ALL	3.0	3.5	4.5	5.0	5.5	6.5	7.0	8.0	8.5	9.0

700	750	800	850	900	950	1000	1050	1100	1150	1200
12.0	12.5	13.5	14.5	15.0	16.0	17.0	17.5	18.5	19.5	20.0
14.0	14.5	15.5	16.5	17.5	18.5	19.5	20.5	21.5	22.5	23.5
16.5	18.0	19.0	20.0	21.5	22.5	24.0	25.0	26.0	27.5	28.5
18.5	20.0	21.5	22.5	24.0	25.5	26.5	28.0	29.5	30.5	32.0
10.0	10.5	11.5	12.0	12.5	13.5	14.0	14.5	15.5	16.0	17.0
14.5	16.0	17.0	18.0	19.0	20.0	21.0	22.0	23.0	24.0	25.0
17.5	19.0	20.0	21.5	22.5	24.0	25.0	26.6	27.5	29.0	30.0
19.5	21.0	22.5	24.0	25.0	26.5	28.0	29.5	31.0	32.0	33.5
10.0	10.5	11.5	12.0	12.5	13.5	14.0	15.0	15.5	16.0	17.0
15.5	17.0	18.0	19.0	20.0	21.0	22.5	23.5	25.0	25.5	27.0
18.5	20.0	21.5	23.0	24.0	25.0	26.5	28.0	29.5	30.5	32.0
20.5	22.0	23.5	25.0	26.5	28.0	29.5	31.0	32.5	33.5	35.0
10.0	10.5	11.5	12.0	12.5	13.5	14.0	15.0	15.5	16.0	17.0
17.5	19.0	20.5	21.5	22.5	24.0	25.0	26.5	28.0	29.0	30.0
17.5	19.0	20.5	21.5	22.5	24.0	25.0	26.5	28.0	29.0	30.0
17.5	19.0	20.5	21.5	22.5	24.0	25.0	26.5	28.0	29.0	30.0
10.0	10.5	11.5	12.0	12.5	13.5	14.0	15.0	15.5	16.0	17.0
16.5	18.0	19.0	20.5	21.5	22.5	24.0	25.0	26.5	27.0	28.5
16.5	18.0	19.0	20.5	21.5	22.5	24.0	25.0	26.5	27.0	28.5
16.5	18.0	19.0	20.5	21.5	22.5	24.0	25.0	26.5	27.0	28.5
10.0	10.5	11.5	12.0	12.5	13.5	14.0	15.0	15.5	16.0	17.0
14.5	16.0	17.0	18.0	19.0	20.0	21.0	22.0	23.5	24.0	25.0
11.5	12.5	13.5	14.5	15.0	16.0	17.0	17.5	18.5	19.0	20.0
10.0	10.5	11.5	12.0	12.5	13.5	14.0	15.0	15.5	16.0	17.0
10.0	10.5	11.5	12.0	12.5	13.5	14.0	15.0	15.5	16.0	17.0

Now that you know annual hours and have divided the year into periods, you're ready to assign weekly training hours. Find the annual hours column in Table 8.5. In that column weekly hours are in half-hour increments. On the left side of the table are all of the periods and weeks. By reading across and down, determine the number of hours for each week and write those in under "Hours" on the Annual Training Plan. If you are over forty years of age or have scheduled some three-week periods during the season, leave out week 3 for each of these periods. There is a more complete discussion of training for older riders in Chapter 14.

You've now completed the Annual Training Plan with the exception of the workouts portion, which we will tackle in Chapter 9.

References

Bompa, T. "Physiological Intensity Values Employed to Plan Endurance Training." *New Studies in Athletics* 3, no. 4 (1988): 37–52.

Bompa, T. *Theory and Methodology of Training.* Dubuque, IA: Kendall Hunt Publishing, 1994.

Costill, D., et al. "Adaptations to Swimming Training: Influence of Training Volume." *Medicine and Science in Sports and Exercise* 23 (1991): 371–377.

Maglischo, E. *Swimming Faster.* Palo Alto, CA: Mayfield, 1982.

Martin, D., and P. Coe. *Training Distance Runners.* Champaign, IL: Leisure Press, 1991.

Matveyev, L. *Fundamentals of Sports Training.* Moscow: Progress Publishing, 1981.

Stucker, M. "Training for Cycling," unpublished manuscript, 1990.

USA Cycling. *Expert Level Coaching Manual.* USA Cycling Inc., 1995.

VanHandel, P.J. "Planning a Comprehensive Training Program" *Conditioning for Cycling* 1, no. 3 (1991): 4–12.

VanHandel, P.J. "The Science of Sport Training for Cycling I," *Conditioning for Cycling* 1, no. 1 (1991): 8–11.

VanHandel, P.J. "The Science of Sport Training for Cycling II," *Conditioning for Cycling* 1, no. 2 (1991): 18–23.

PLANNING
WORKOUTS

The novelty of riding thirty-hour weeks
wore off a long time ago.
—STEVE LARSEN

If there's one thing you're getting out of this book so far, I hope it's that training should be purposeful and precise to meet your unique needs. Training haphazardly brings results initially, but to reach the highest level of racing fitness, carefully planned workouts are necessary. Before starting any training session, from the easiest to the hardest, you must be able to answer one simple question: What is the purpose of this workout?

When training for high performance, that purpose is one of three possibilities: improvement of ability, maintenance of ability, or active recovery. How these three are mixed into every week of training ultimately determines how well you race. This chapter provides a method for designing your training week.

ATP Workout Categories

In the last four chapters, I've described a system of planning based on strengths and limiters. In this chapter, you will complete the training plan by scheduling daily workouts determined by your limiters. To intelligently select workouts, it's important that you know what your limiters are. If you haven't read Chapters 5 and 6, do so before planning workouts. Knowing what you need to work on will make your plan purposeful and precise.

You are not going to schedule every workout for all fifty-two weeks on your Annual Training Plan now. With the exception of endurance-maintenance workouts, you will only be determining the "breakthrough" (BT) workouts. These are the ones that provide the stress to start the adaptive process described earlier. Active recovery workouts, the ones you do between the BTs, will not be scheduled now, but will be a part of your weekly plan as you will soon see.

You should base these workouts on the abilities listed at the top of the Annual Training Plan (see Figure 8.1). Notice that there are two categories of workouts added to the abilities we've discussed before: "Strength Phase" and "Testing." It may be helpful before you start this planning step to review all of the workout columns listed.

Strength Phase

In this column you will schedule weight room workouts. This is an aspect of cycling training that is often neglected, especially by riders whose limiter is force. It has been my experience that measurable results on the bike are more evident from this type of training than any other in athletes who lack the ability to apply force to the pedals. They are always amazed at how strong they feel riding in the spring after a winter of weights.

The details of the strength phases listed below are discussed in Chapter 12, but with a little information you can complete the Strength Phase column now by penciling in the abbreviations for the various phases. Here's how to determine the duration of each weight room phase. If you're a bit confused, flip ahead to Chapter 11 for examples of completed Annual Training Plans.

Preparation Period: Anatomical Adaptation (AA) and Maximum Transition (MT)

On your Annual Training Plan, for the first two or three weeks of the Preparation period, write in "AA" under the Strength column. This weight room phase prepares the body for the stresses that are to follow. For the last week of the Preparation period include one or two weeks of MT (Maximum Transition). As the name implies, MT is a transitional phase that better prepares you for the heavier lifting of the MS phase.

Base 1 Period: Maximum Strength (MS)

Write in "MS" for each week of Base 1. If you are a master who is training in three-week periods, extend MS by one week into the Base 2 period so that you schedule four total MS weeks.

All Other Periods: Strength Maintenance (SM)

For the remainder of the season, basic strength is maintained with brief workouts and heavy loads. Riders in their twenties with good force may omit weight room strength training from their schedules starting with Build 1. All women and men over about forty years of age are advised to continue the SM phase of weights throughout the season. During the week of A-priority races schedule no weight training.

Endurance

Racing on the roads is primarily an endurance sport. The ability to delay the onset of fatigue during long rides is what sets road racers apart from track racers. For this reason, the Endurance column will be frequently selected on the Annual Training Plan form. You will work on endurance in some form nearly every week of the year, for once you have lost endurance, the time required to fully restore it is exorbitant. That's not to say that there won't be fluctuations in your endurance throughout the season. Following an extended Race period, your endurance is likely to wane, and you must work to rebuild it by returning to the Base period before you are able to attain another high peak.

Force

This Force column refers to on-bike workouts intended to improve muscle dynamics, while the Strength Phase column consists of off-bike workouts usually done in the weight room. If you don't live in a vertically challenged region, use hills for on-bike force training. Later on in the workout menu section of this chapter, I'll refer to hills by percentage grades. Here's a guide to help you select the proper types of hills for specific workouts.

2–4 percent grade: Slight hill. In a car on a 2 percent grade you may not even know there's a grade. You could easily ride these hills in the big chainring. These are often described as "gently rolling hills."

4–6 percent grade: Moderate hill. These hills get your attention in races, but are seldom determining factors. You could ride them in the big chainring, but may drop down to the small chainring.

6–8 percent grade: Steep hill. These are the steepest hills you generally find on state and federal highways. Such hills, especially if they're long, often determine the winning move. These are usually climbed in the small chainring.

8–10 percent grade: Very steep hill. These hills are always a determiner in a race. They are climbed only in the small chainring. A workout on such a hill is challenging for riders of all abilities.

10+ percent grade: Extremely steep hill. These hills are most often found in remote areas or in the mountains. In more populated areas, they are usually quite short. Everyone climbs in the small chainring. Some riders have difficulty just getting over them. They make you cry for your mother.

If you do live in a vertically challenged environment—the plains of Kansas or Florida's flat coastal terrain—don't despair. The real benefit of hills is that they offer greater resistance. You can achieve a similar result with big gears and head winds while sitting up, or on a good indoor trainer. Highway overpasses offer short hills of about 4 percent grade. Multilevel parking garages are great simulated mountains—just remember to ask the attendant's permission first.

Speed Skills

Do not get speed skills confused with anaerobic endurance. While working on speed skills you are not doing intervals or hammering on group rides. The purpose of workouts in this column is always to improve mobility—the ability to handle the bike efficiently and effectively while turning the cranks quickly and smoothly. In the Base period, many of these workouts will be drills on a trainer or rollers that exaggerate the mechanics of pedaling, typically in a low gear at a high cadence, in order to become more fluid and supple. On the road, speed-skill training involves form sprints, high-cadence pedaling, and the handling skills necessary for sprinting.

Muscular Endurance

Muscular endurance is the ability to turn a relatively high gear for a long time, as in time trialing. In many ways, this ability is at the heart of road racing. As one of the primary ingredients of road racing fitness, you need to emphasize this approach throughout the training year regardless of your limiters. All of the legendary champion road cyclists—Merckx, Hinault, LeMond, Carpenter, Indurain, and Longo—had great muscular endurance. This ability will be developed starting in the Base period and continue in various forms right through the Race periods.

Anaerobic Endurance

Anaerobic endurance involves training to continue working hard even though the body is crying out for relief. Long sprints and short climbs are the usual times for this to occur. If it is known to be a limiter (which is the case for nearly every athlete), schedule workouts for this ability at the start of the first Build period. Anaerobic-endurance training is excellent for improving aerobic capacity (VO_2max).

Power

For the rider whose ability limiter is power, these workouts mean the difference between success and failure in criteriums that require the ability to accelerate quickly out of corners and to contest field sprints. Workouts for power depend on speed and force, so these more basic abilities must be improved first. Power training may be included primarily in the Build and Peak periods.

Testing

Throughout the Base and Build periods, make regular progress checks about every four to six weeks. It's important to regularly know how your abilities are developing in order to make adjustments to training.

Ability Workouts by Period

The following will help you complete the workouts section of the Annual Training Plan. I'll start with the recovery and rest weeks since those are usually neglected, but are in some ways the most important.

If there is any confusion on how to mark the Annual Training Plan, see the examples in Chapter 11.

R & R Weeks

Reserve every fourth week (third week for over-forty riders) during the Base and Build periods for recovery and rest from the accumulated fatigue of the previous three weeks. Without such regular unloading of fatigue, fitness won't progress for long. You've already partially incorporated R & R by assigning reduced weekly hours during these weeks in the Base and Build periods. Now we'll assign the workouts to those low-volume weeks. (For more detail on recovery weeks, see Chapter 18.)

For each of the R & R weeks, place an "X" under the Endurance, Speed Skills, and Testing columns. Other than one weight room session, that's all for those weeks. The idea is to recover from the collected stress; feel rested by week's end; maintain endurance (with a late-week long ride), speed skills, and force; and test progress once rested. It may take you only three to five days to feel fully recovered so that's when the testing should be done. In the Build period, there may be a B or C race at week's end in place of a test.

In the workout menu in Appendix C (under Testing), I'll describe the tests you will do during R & R weeks.

Now you're ready to complete workouts for the other weeks of the year. The Workout Menu in Appendix C will be used at a later time to fill in the details of what you schedule here.

Preparation Period

Place an X in the Endurance and Speed Skills columns for each week of the Preparation period. Endurance training during this period concentrates on improving the endurance characteristics of the heart, blood, and lungs. Crosstraining by running, swimming, hiking, or cross-country skiing accomplishes the desired results while limiting the number of times each week that you're on an indoor trainer in the early winter months. Be cautious with your volume of indoor riding as it can be mentally and emotionally draining.

Base 1

Again, mark the Endurance and Speed Skills columns for each week of the Base 1 period. During this period, endurance training shifts slightly toward more time on the bike and less in crosstraining modes. Weather, however, is often the determining factor for the type of endurance training done now. A mountain bike is an excellent alternative during this period when the roads and weather don't cooperate. A good indoor trainer, especially CompuTrainer, is also an excellent way to train throughout the Base period when you can't get on the roads.

Base 2

Place an X in the Endurance, Force, Speed Skills, and Muscular Endurance columns for each week of the Base 2 period. As you will see in the Workout Menu (Appendix C), you should conduct force and muscular-endurance workouts at moderate heart rates and power outputs during this period. Endurance training should be mostly on the road by now with very little crosstraining. You will be doing some Force work in the form of endurance rides on rolling courses, staying in the saddle on the uphill portions. This can be an integral part of endurance training.

Base 3

Mark the Endurance, Force, Speed Skills, and Muscular Endurance columns for each week of the Base 3 period. Training volume tops out during this period. Intensity has also risen slightly with the addition of more hill work and higher effort muscular-endurance work.

Build 1

Schedule workouts for Endurance and Muscular Endurance for each week of the Build 1 period. Also select your greatest limiter and mark that column. If unsure of which limiter to schedule, choose Force. If you don't select Power or Anaerobic Endurance, also mark Speed Skills. A criterium may take the place of an Anaerobic Endurance or Power workout. Road races and time trials are substituted for Force and Muscular Endurance. Early-season races in this period are best as C-priority. Schedule each Build 1 period on your Annual Training Plan in this same way.

Build 2

Check off Endurance and Muscular Endurance for each week of the Build 2 period. Then mark two of your limiters. If unsure, or if you have only one limiter, mark Force and Anaerobic Endurance. Speed skills will be maintained either with Anaerobic Endurance or Power training. If there are B or C races scheduled during this period, substitute them for workouts. A criterium takes the place of either a Power or Anaerobic Endurance workout. Depending on the terrain, you may substitute a road race or time trial for a Force or Muscular-Endurance workout. The week of B-priority races, schedule only one limiter. Remember that you're training through C-priority races. Mark all Build 2 periods on your plan in the same manner.

Peak

Place an X in the Muscular Endurance column and that of your next greatest limiter for each week of the Peak period. If unsure of your next limiter, select Anaerobic Endurance. You may substitute races for workouts using the same criteria as in the Build periods. C races in the Peak period are excellent tune-ups for the approaching A-priority races as they get you back into a racing mode again. If there are no races, but you have a hard club ride available, that may be one of your Anaerobic Endurance sessions. There should be a race-specific intensity workout every 72 to 96 hours in a Peak week. Mark all Peak periods in this same way.

Race

During each week of this period either race or complete a race-effort group ride. If there is no group ride or race available, substitute an Anaerobic Endurance workout. Also mark Speed Skills and your strongest ability other than Endurance. If unsure about your strength, mark Muscular Endurance. All Race periods should be marked just as the first one was.

Transition

Mark Endurance, but keep in mind that this is a mostly unstructured period. By "mostly," I mean that your only purpose is to stay active, especially in sports that you enjoy other than cycling. These are often team games such as soccer, basketball, volleyball, or hockey. Such sports require some endurance and also encourage quick movement. Don't become a couch potato, but also don't train seriously.

Weekly Routines

Now that your Annual Training Plan is complete, the only issue left to decide is the weekly routine—on what day to do which workout and for how long. That's no small thing. You could have the best possible plan, but if you do not blend workouts in such a way as to allow for recovery and adaptation, then it's all for nothing. The problem is that you must blend both long and short duration workouts with workouts that are of high and low intensity.

Chapter 15 will provide you with a weekly training journal on which to record the days' scheduled workouts and their results. For now, let's examine ways to determine each day's routine.

Keep in mind that the workout options listed in Figure 9.1 are just that—options. These are not intended to be the only ways to organize a week. There are many possibilities. When it comes to selecting a workout for a given day choose one option—do not do all of the options. The option you select is determined by your limiters as discussed in Chapter 6.

Patterns

Figure 9.1 illustrates a suggested pattern for blending duration (or volume) and intensity for each week of the training periods plus the R & R and race weeks. Duration and intensity are indicated as high, medium, and low or recovery. Obviously, what is high for one cyclist may be low for another, so these levels are meaningful only to you. Also, what is high duration or high intensity in the Base 1 period may be moderate by Build 1 as your fitness improves. Recovery days may be active recovery (on the bike) or passive (complete rest), depending on your experience level.

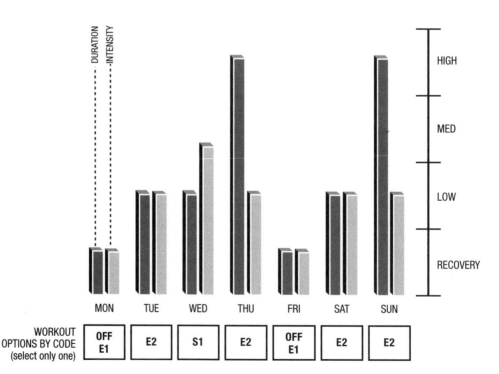

Figure 9.1
Weekly training patterns

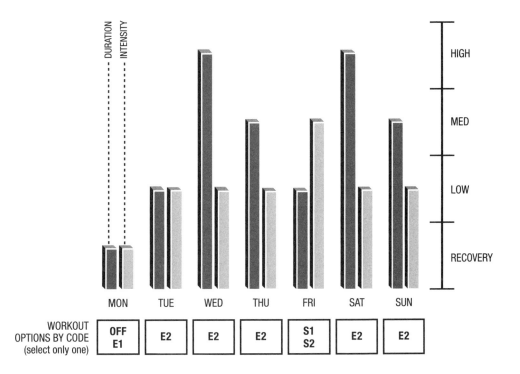

Figure 9.1
continued

BASE 1

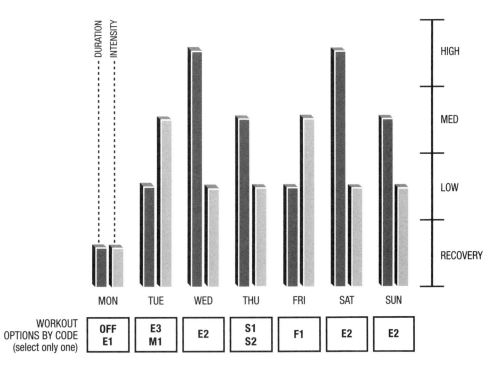

BASE 2

Figure 9.1
continued

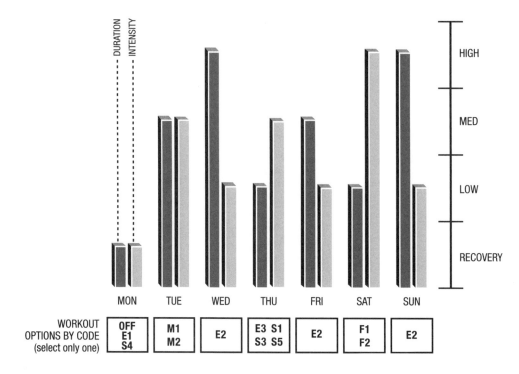

BASE 3

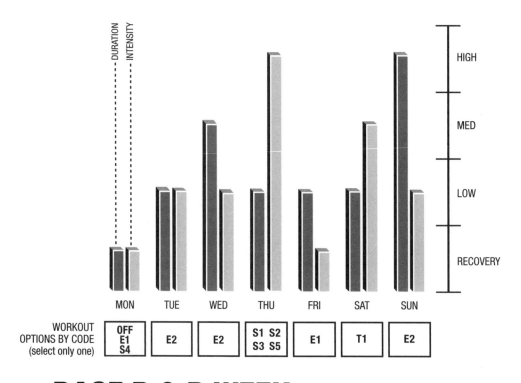

BASE R & R WEEK

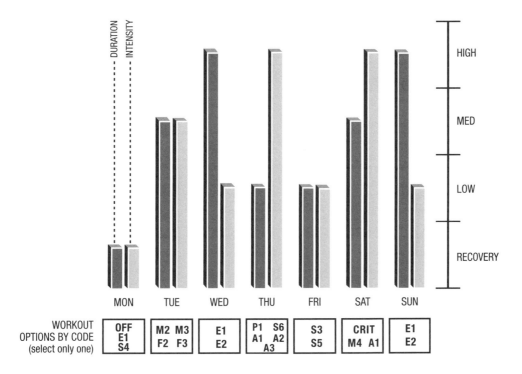

Figure 9.1
continued

BUILD 1

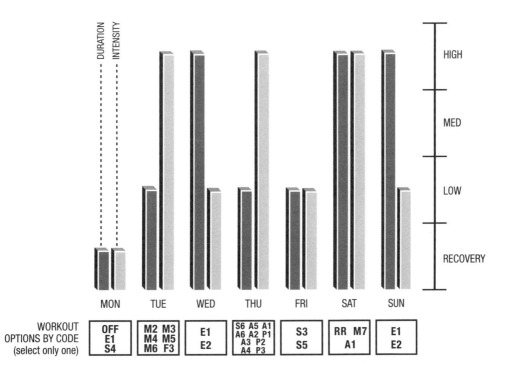

BUILD 2

Figure 9.1
continued

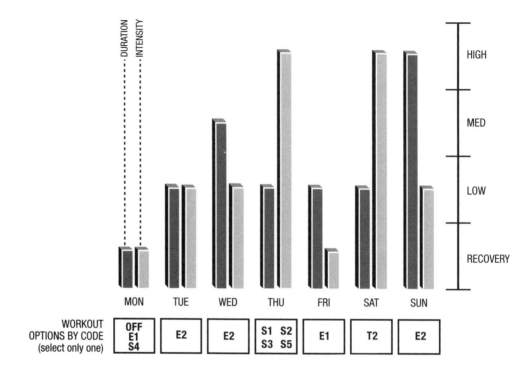

BUILD R & R WEEK

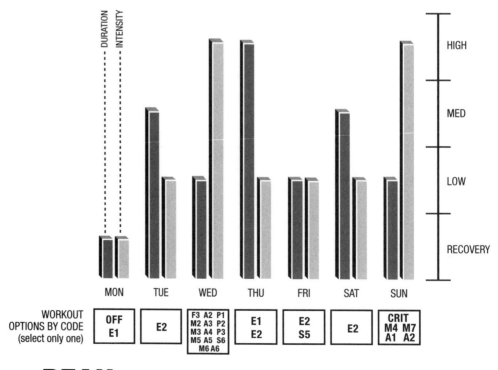

PEAK

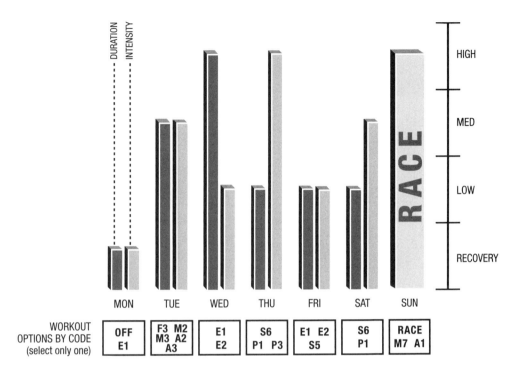

Figure 9.1
continued

RACE (A OR B) ON SUNDAY

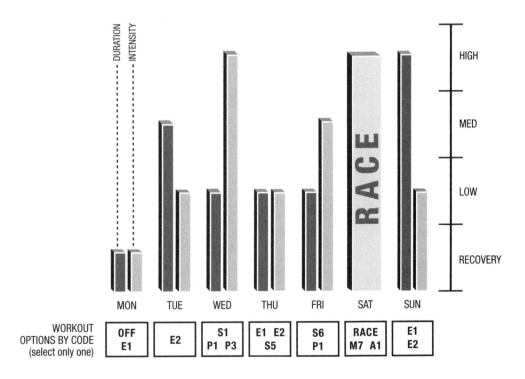

RACE (A OR B) ON SATURDAY

Figure 9.1
continued

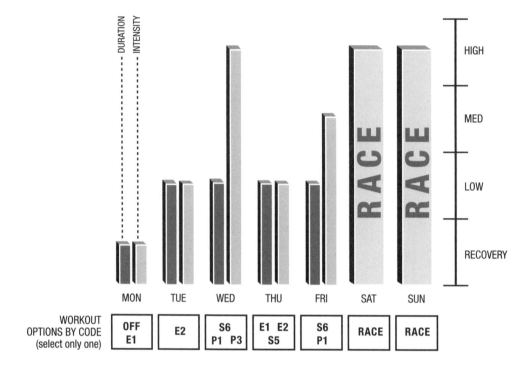

DURATION
INTENSITY

HIGH

MED

LOW

RECOVERY

MON TUE WED THU FRI SAT SUN

WORKOUT
OPTIONS BY CODE
(select only one)

OFF E1	E2	S6 P1 P3	E1 E2 S5	S6 P1	RACE	RACE

RACE (A OR B) ON SAT. & SUN.

Notice in the Base period that duration is high or medium, four times each week, while intensity is either medium or low, except for Base 3 when one high-intensity day is included. Also note in the Build period that intensity increases and duration decreases. In Build 2 there are no moderate workouts—everything is either high or low. The reason for this is to allow for adequate recovery since there is so much high intensity during this period. In Build 2, both high duration and high intensity are combined once each week for the first time. Training in this period takes on many of the characteristics of racing. Note that "high duration" and "high intensity" are relative to the A-priority event you are training for. The average intensity of a criterium is typically higher than that of a road race whereas road races generally are higher-duration events. The minimum high-duration workout is two hours.

Figure 9.1 also suggests a blending of duration and intensity for A- and B-race weeks. Of course, A-race weeks immediately follow a Peak period or a previous Race period week, so rest would be greater. B-race weeks would not necessarily have that advantage.

Workouts are suggested for each day by the alpha-numeric codes used in the "Workout Menu" in Appendix C. Weight room training has not been included in the suggested weekly patterns since some cyclists lift three times per week and

WEEKLY HOURS	LONG RIDE	MAY BE TWO-A-DAY WORKOUTS					
3:00	1:30	0:45	0:45	Off	Off	Off	Off
3:30	1:30	1:00	1:00	Off	Off	Off	Off
4:00	1:30	1:00	1:00	0:30	Off	Off	Off
4:30	1:45	1:00	1:00	0:45	Off	Off	Off
5:00	2:00	1:00	1:00	1:00	Off	Off	Off
5:30	2:00	1:30	1:00	1:00	Off	Off	Off
6:00	2:00	1:00	1:00	1:00	1:00	Off	Off
6:30	2:00	1:30	1:00	1:00	1:00	Off	Off
7:00	2:00	1:30	1:30	1:00	1:00	Off	Off
7:30	2:30	1:30	1:30	1:00	1:00	Off	Off
8:00	2:30	1:30	1:30	1:30	1:00	Off	Off
8:30	2:30	2:00	1:30	1:30	1:00	Off	Off
9:00	3:00	2:00	1:30	1:30	1:00	Off	Off
9:30	3:00	2:00	1:30	1:30	1:00	0:30	Off
10:00	3:00	2:00	1:30	1:30	1:00	1:00	Off
10:30	3:00	2:00	2:00	1:30	1:00	1:00	Off
11:00	3:00	2:00	2:00	1:30	1:30	1:00	Off
11:30	3:00	2:30	2:00	1:30	1:30	1:00	Off
12:00	3:00	2:30	2:00	2:00	1:30	1:00	Off
12:30	3:30	2:30	2:00	2:00	1:30	1:00	Off
13:00	3:30	3:00	2:00	2:00	1:30	1:00	Off
13:30	3:30	3:00	2:30	2:00	1:30	1:00	Off
14:00	4:00	3:00	2:30	2:00	1:30	1:00	Off
14:30	4:00	3:00	2:30	2:30	1:30	1:00	Off
15:00	4:00	3:00	3:00	2:30	1:30	1:00	Off
15:30	4:00	3:00	3:00	2:30	2:00	1:00	Off
16:00	4:00	3:30	3:00	2:30	2:00	1:00	Off
16:30	4:00	3:30	3:00	3:00	2:00	1:00	Off
17:00	4:00	3:30	3:00	3:00	2:00	1:30	Off
17:30	4:00	4:00	3:00	3:00	2:00	1:30	Off
18:00	4:00	4:00	3:00	3:00	2:30	1:30	Off
18:30	4:30	4:00	3:00	3:00	2:30	1:30	Off
19:00	4:30	4:30	3:00	3:00	2:30	1:30	Off
19:30	4:30	4:30	3:30	3:00	2:30	1:30	Off
20:00	4:30	4:30	3:30	3:00	2:30	2:00	Off
20:30	4:30	4:30	3:30	3:30	2:30	2:00	Off
21:00	5:00	4:30	3:30	3:30	3:30	2:00	Off
21:30	5:00	4:30	4:00	3:30	2:30	2:00	Off
22:00	5:00	4:30	4:00	3:30	3:00	2:00	Off
22:30	5:00	4:30	4:00	3:30	3:00	2:30	Off
23:00	5:00	5:00	4:00	3:30	3:00	2:30	Off
23:30	5:30	5:00	4:00	3:30	3:00	2:30	Off
24:00	5:30	5:00	4:30	3:30	3:00	2:30	Off
24:30	5:30	5:00	4:30	4:00	3:00	2:30	Off
25:00	5:30	5:00	4:30	4:00	3:00	3:00	Off
25:30	5:30	5:30	4:30	4:00	3:00	3:00	Off
26:00	6:00	5:30	4:30	4:00	3:00	3:00	Off

Table 9.1
Daily Training Hours

Table 9.1
continued

WEEKLY HOURS	LONG RIDE	MAY BE TWO-A-DAY WORKOUTS					
26:30	6:00	5:30	5:00	4:00	3:00	3:00	Off
27:00	6:00	6:00	5:00	4:00	3:00	3:00	Off
27:30	6:00	6:00	5:00	4:00	3:30	3:00	Off
28:00	6:00	6:00	5:00	4:00	3:30	3:30	Off
28:30	6:00	6:00	5:00	4:30	3:30	3:30	Off
29:00	6:00	6:00	5:30	4:30	3:30	3:30	Off
29:30	6:00	6:00	6:00	4:30	3:30	3:30	Off
30:00	6:00	6:00	6:00	4:30	4:00	3:30	Off
30:30	6:00	6:00	6:00	5:00	4:00	3:30	Off
31:00	6:00	6:00	6:00	5:00	4:00	4:00	Off
31:30	6:00	6:00	6:00	5:00	4:30	4:00	Off
32:00	6:00	6:00	6:00	5:30	4:30	4:00	Off
32:30	6:00	6:00	6:00	5:30	4:30	4:30	Off
33:00	6:00	6:00	6:00	5:30	5:00	4:30	Off
33:30	6:00	6:00	6:00	6:00	5:00	4:30	Off
34:00	6:00	6:00	6:00	6:00	5:30	4:30	Off
34:30	6:00	6:00	6:00	6:00	5:30	5:00	Off
35:00	6:00	6:00	6:00	6:00	6:00	5:00	Off

others only once or twice. Also, some riders, such as masters, may lift year-round, while others will stop once racing begins. It is best to substitute a weight room workout for "E" category workouts. Weight training is best done the day after a long or "BT" workout. Try to avoid doing weights the day before a BT. If weight training must be done the same day as a BT workout, lift after riding.

Daily Hours

In the Hours column of your Annual Training Plan, you've indicated the volume for each week of the season. All that remains is to decide how those hours should be spread during the week. Table 9.1 offers a suggested breakdown. In the left-hand column, find the hours you scheduled for the first week of the season. By reading across to the right, the weekly hours are broken into daily amounts. For example, find 12:00 in the Weekly Hours column. To the right are seven daily hours—one for each day of the week. In this case, 3:00, 2:30, 2:00, 2:00, 1:30, 1:00, and Off. So, the long workout that week is three hours. Do this as a continuous ride—not as two workouts of 1:30 each. The other daily hours may be divided between two workouts in the same day, especially in the Base period when volume is high. In fact, there are some advantages to working out two times a day, such as an increase in quality for each workout.

When it comes time to schedule hours for a given week, use Table 9.1 along with Figure 9.1 to assign high, medium, and low durations for each day of the week.

References

Birkholz, D., ed. *Training Skills*. United States Cycling Federation: 1991.

Bompa, T. "Physiological Intensity Values Employed to Plan Endurance Training." *New Studies in Athletics* 3, no. 4 (1988): 37–52.

Borysewicz, E. "Bicycle Road Racing." *VeloNews*: 1995.

Burke, E. *Serious Cycling*. Champaign, IL: Human Kinetics, 1995.

Daniels, J., et al. "Interval Training and Performance." *Sports Medicine* 1 (1984): 327–324.

Faria, I.E. "Applied Physiology of Cycling." *Sports Medicine* 1 (1984): 187–204.

Knuttgen, H.G., et al. "Physical Conditioning Through Interval Training with Young Male Adults." *Medicine and Science in Sports* 5 (1973): 220–226.

Okkels, T. "The Effect of Interval and Tempo Training on Performance and Skeletal Muscle in Well-trained Runners." Acoteias, Portugal: Twelfth European Track Coaches Congress (1983): 1–9.

Maglischo, E.W. *Swimming Faster*. Palo Alto, CA: Mayfield Publishing Co., 1982.

Phinney, D. and C. Carpenter. *Training for Cycling*. New York: Putnam, 1992.

USA Cycling Inc. *Expert Level Coaching Manual*, 1995.

VanHandel, P.J. "Specificity of Training: Establishing Pace, Frequency, and Duration of Training Sessions." *Bike Tech* 6, no. 3 (1987): 6–12.

Zappe, D.H., and T. Bauer. "Planning Competitive Season Training for Road Cycling." *Conditioning for Cycling* 1, no. 2 (1991): 4–8.

STAGE RACE TRAINING

10

There's a lot of feelings about racing you can
never communicate. They're your own, and
only you can identify with them.
—ALEXI GREWAL,
1984 Gold Medalist, road cycling

For the serious cyclist, a stage race is often the most important event of the year. With a season made up mostly of one-hour crits and 60-or-so-mile circuit races, few riders are ready to take on five or more days of back-to-back races including time trials, 90-minute criteriums, 75-mile circuits, and 100-mile road races in the mountains. Throw in the toughest competitors in the region, prize money, and crowds, and it's easy to see why stage races are often the high point of the season and the ultimate measure of a road racer.

Separate stage races into two broad categories for training purposes—short events with four or fewer stages and long events with five or more stages. Short stage races require no specific preparation for the cyclist who frequently competes in two races on the same weekend. Long stage races, however, are a whole different game demanding exceptional raw endurance, muscular endurance, and usually force for climbing. Combine that with the need to recover quickly in order to be ready for the next stage and it's apparent why long stage races have such a high attrition rate. It's survival of the fittest.

Training to race well in a long stage race requires a focused six- to eight-week training program to prepare for the unique stresses. Stage races not only require a rider's fitness to be at peak, but recovery methods must also be perfected. All of this, of course, happens within the context of an ongoing weekly race schedule.

It is important not to take stage race preparation lightly. The stress resulting from high volume, intensity, and short recoveries threatens health, fitness, work performance, and family relations. Overtraining is a definite possibility. Approach this training with great caution.

Crash Cycles

Training for a long stage race is much like doing a short-stage race several times in the weeks building to the event. High-quality workouts are gradually brought closer together with the purpose of overloading the body's systems. That results in a delay in recovery, further increasing the stress load. This process is sometimes called "crashing"—a descriptive, if somewhat threatening title.

With the inclusion of a recovery period following the crash, there is a greater-than-normal training adaptation known as "supercompensation."

Two studies looked at supercompensation resulting from crash cycles. In 1992, a group of seven Dutch cyclists crashed for two weeks by increasing their training volume from a normal 12.5 hours per week to 17.5. At the same time, their high intensity training went from 24 to 63 percent of total training time. The immediate effect was a drop in all measurable aspects of their fitness. But after two weeks of recovering with light training, they realized a 6-percent improvement in power, their time trial improved by an average of 4 percent, and they had less blood lactate at top speed compared with pre-crash levels. Not bad for two weeks of hard training.

A similar study in Dallas put runners through a two-week crash cycle with positive results similar to the Dutch study, plus an increase in aerobic capacities. Again, it took two weeks following the crash cycle to realize the gains. Other studies suggest an increase in blood volume, greater levels of hormones that cause muscle growth, and an improved ability to metabolize fat result from a high-stress crash and recovery period and the subsequent supercompensation.

Be careful with crashing. The risk of overtraining rises dramatically during such a build-up. If the typical signs of overtraining appear, such as a greatly changed resting heart rate or feelings of depression, cut back on the intensity of training immediately. High-intensity training is more likely to magnify or cause overtraining than is low-intensity work.

Planning

Designing a stage race training plan is a complex task—almost as complex as designing an entire season. The key is to decide, just as you did when putting your Annual Training Plan together, what it takes to achieve your goals in the targeted stage race and how those demands match with your own strengths and limiters. The key limiters for long stage races typically are endurance, muscular endurance, and force for climbing.

Speed skill, power and anaerobic endurance play a lesser part, depending on the number and relative importance of criteriums, which seldom play a significant role in the outcome on the general classification. The objective of winning a criterium stage, however, would increase the importance of anaerobic endurance in stage race planning and preparation. Otherwise, the amount of endurance, muscular-endurance, and force training you do will primarily determine your success.

For an A-priority stage race, start by finding out exactly what the stages will be, their order, how much time separates them, the terrain, and what the weather is expected to be—especially heat, humidity, and wind. Then try to simulate these conditions as closely as possible during the build-up weeks.

Table 10.1 provides an eight-week stage race build-up emphasizing the above limiters. This suggested plan assumes that base fitness is well established. That means you have been putting in adequate miles, hills, pedaling drills, and weight room training, if appropriate, for at least six weeks before starting.

Notice that quality workouts are clumped together in two Build weeks of high volume and intensity and then followed by a week of recovery. The workload (combined volume and intensity) in Build 1 period is not as great as in Build 2, so the first recovery period is only one week. A recovery week and a reduced-volume Peak week follow Build 2, allowing fitness to soar.

Three-week cycles are used instead of the more typical four-week cycles due to the greater accumulated stress and more frequent need for recovery. If there's any question about your readiness for a breakthrough workout, don't do it. Better to be mentally and physically sharp, but somewhat undertrained, rather than the opposite. As always, when in doubt, do less intensity.

Week 1	Build 1
Week 2	Build 1
Week 3	Recovery
Week 4	Build 2
Week 5	Build 2
Week 6	Recovery
Week 7	Peak
Week 8	Race

Table 10.1
Eight-Week Stage Race Preparation

Also, note in Figure 10.1 that the most intense workouts are clumped closer together in Build 2 than in Build 1. This is the basis of crash training—providing increasing dosages of high intensity within short spans of time and then allowing for complete recovery.

During the Build weeks, be sure to practice recovery techniques following each of the intense workouts. This includes massage, stretching, fuel replacement, elevating legs, high fluid intake, staying off your feet, and extra rest (see Chapter 18 for a complete discussion of recovery methods). Find out what works best for you, and be ready to use the best options between stages when it comes time to race. Once you have built your fitness, quick recovery is the key to stage racing success.

Figure 10.1
Weekly training patterns to
prepare for a stage race

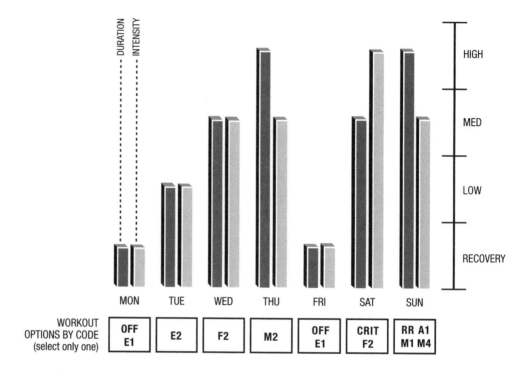

| WORKOUT OPTIONS BY CODE (select only one) | OFF E1 | E2 | F2 | M2 | OFF E1 | CRIT F2 | RR A1 M1 M4 |

BUILD 1

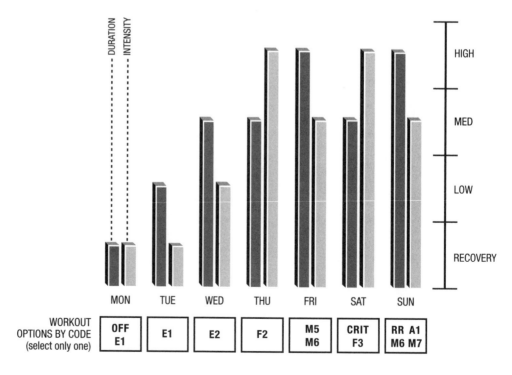

| WORKOUT OPTIONS BY CODE (select only one) | OFF E1 | E1 | E2 | F2 | M5 M6 | CRIT F3 | RR A1 M6 M7 |

BUILD 2

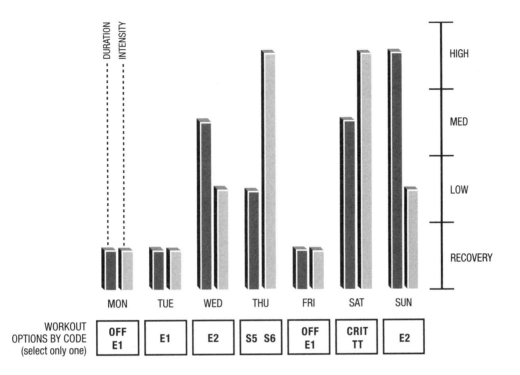

Figure 10.1
continued

R & R

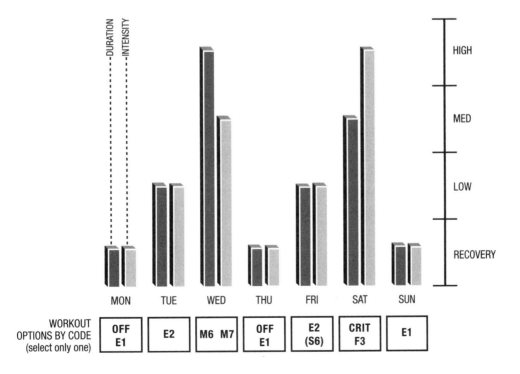

PEAK

Following the stage race, while the glow of the accomplishment is still fresh, take one or two weeks to transition back into normal training. You've just had a major physiological crash and the body needs to recover from it fully. As always, a Transition period should be a break from structured training that allows the mind and body to recover, rest, and refresh.

If you don't reduce training to allow the body to "catch up" with all of the stress it has experienced, you are likely to wind up overtrained or burned out. Stage races must be treated with respect.

If your endurance was good going into the stage race, you're likely to find that once returning to training your fitness is greater than it was before. That's the super-compensation kicking in again. If you finished all the stages, despite questionable endurance, recovery is likely to be longer than two weeks, and you may feel as if you lost fitness. That's called overtraining. This is a good reason not to attempt a stage race until you know you're ready.

References

Borysewicz, E. "Bicycle Road Racing." *VeloNews*, 1985.

Costill, D., et al. "Effects of Repeated Days of Intensified Training on Muscle Glycogen and Swimming Performance." *Medicine and Science in Sports and Exercise* 20, no. 3 (1988): 249–254.

Fry, R.W., et al. "Biological Responses to Overload Training in Endurance Sports." *European Journal of Applied Physiology* 64 (1992): 335–344.

Jeukendrup, A.E., et al. "Physiological Changes in Male Competitive Cyclists after Two Weeks of Intensified Training." *International Journal of Sports Medicine* 13, no. 7 (1992): 534–541.

Snell, P., et al. "Changes in Selected Parameters During Overtraining." *Medicine and Science in Sports and Exercise* 18 (1986): abstract #268.

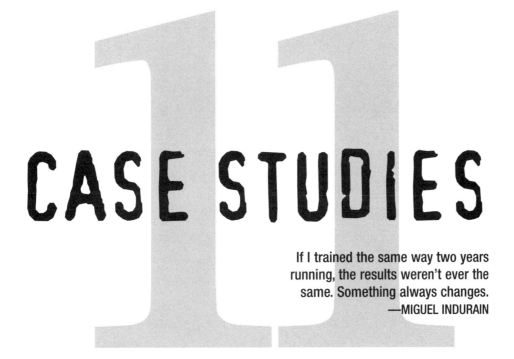

CASE STUDIES

If I trained the same way two years running, the results weren't ever the same. Something always changes.
—MIGUEL INDURAIN

By now it should be clear that there is no single training plan for all athletes. Not only do individual abilities and limiters vary, but so do goals, time available, race schedules, experience, and on and on. By the time all of these variables are mixed, the resulting schedule can not be readily used by another rider. Training must match the individual's unique needs. The Annual Training Plan you've been developing is for your use only.

While it may have seemed easy to design a schedule, there is more to it than that. As I said earlier, training is as much an art as a science. What I've described so far is the science. The schedule you've written is largely based on scientific principles, and will undoubtedly serve your needs well. As you become more experienced at writing your own schedules, however, it will become apparent that bending or even breaking the rules is sometimes necessary to better fit your needs. This chapter provides examples of designing the plan to match the individual rider's unique needs. The following plans were developed for four very different cyclists. The same steps you used were applied, but each of these athletes had a unique set of circumstances that required bending the rules in some way.

Case Study 1: Single Peak Season

Profile

Tom Brown, 39, is a sales manager for an electronics retail store. He works six days weekly, averaging over fifty hours a week. Married with two daughters, ages 8 and

10, Tom is in his third year of racing. He races with masters, mostly in road races, as he is uncomfortable with the high-speed cornering of criteriums. In his first two years, he was satisfied with simply finishing road races, but at the end of last season he began to see improvement, probably due to increased endurance.

Tom's greatest limiter for cycling is endurance, due primarily to many missed workouts in the past two years. His job promises to place fewer demands on his time this season, and he has a greater commitment to riding consistently now. With regular training, his endurance will undoubtedly improve.

The Mental Skills Profile pointed out that lack of confidence is a serious limiter for Tom. Even though he set goals around three of the biggest races he could participate in, he lacks confidence when talking about them. Testing revealed that he has the ability to achieve the goals, which seemed to bolster his self-esteem. He has been asked to read books on mental skills training for athletes and apply the techniques. In August, he will repeat the Mental Skills Profile.

His maximum power tested high, but his power at lactate threshold was relatively low. He is limited by low muscular endurance, a major weakness when it comes to road racing.

Plan

Due to the weather in Regina, Saskatchewan, where Tom lives, training in the winter is difficult at best. He prefers to cross-country ski from October through February rather than ride an indoor trainer. He participates in a few ski races, mostly in the late winter, which in Regina extends into March. Winter is also the busiest time of year for his business, so he has less time to train then. His Annual Training Plan, illustrated in Figure 11.1, projects a longer-than-normal Preparation period for these reasons.

I encouraged Tom to train more than the six-hour weeks scheduled through the winter Preparation period whenever he could. As this will be mostly on skis, I suggested he get on the trainer once or twice each week to do speed-skill drills.

Since the road racing season is so short in Regina, and all of Tom's A-priority races are clumped near the end of the season, there is only one Peak period. Notice that in weeks 33 and 35, his hours are increased and endurance workouts are added. This change to the usual Race period layout is to help maintain his endurance, which could easily erode with all of the races. This will better prepare him for a century in week 36. By that week his anaerobic endurance will be better suited for 50-mile road races than for 100-mile efforts, so the century will be done at a conservative speed.

Athlete: Tom Brown   **Annual Hours:** 350   **ANNUAL TRAINING PLAN**

Season Goals:
1. Top 50 finish in Masters Nationals Road Race.
2. Top 25 at Provincial Masters Road Race.
3. Top 15 G.C. for masters at Tumbler's Classic Stage Race.

Training Objectives:
1. Improve endurance: Start 90% of all workouts scheduled for season.
2. Improve confidence: Finish all races by August 4.
3. Read Mental Toughness... by March 3 and use skills.
4. Improve confidence: Higher score on Mental Skills Profile by August 4.
5. Improve muscular endurance: Increase power on LT test by May 25.

WORKOUTS

WK#	MON	RACE	PRI	PERIOD	HOURS	DETAILS		WEIGHTS	ENDURANCE	FORCE	SPEED SKILL	MUSCULAR ENDUR.	ANAEROBIC ENDUR.	POWER	TESTING
01	1/6			Prep	6:00	XC Ski	AA	X		X					
02	1/13							X		X					
03	1/20							X		X					
04	1/27							X		X					
05	2/3							X		X					
06	2/10							X		X					
07	2/17							MS	X		X					
08	2/24							X		X					
09	3/3			Base 1	7:00			X		X					
10	3/10				8:30			X		X					
11	3/17				9:30			X		X					
12	3/24				5:00	*ATT		X		X					*
13	3/31			Base 2	7:30		SM	X	X	X	X				
14	4/7				9:00			X	X	X	X				
15	4/14				10:00			X	X	X	X				
16	4/21	Regina RR	C		5:00	*Race #ATT		X		X		*			#
17	4/28			Base 3	8:00			X	X	X	X				
18	5/5				9:30			X	X	X	X				
19	5/12				10:30			X	X	X	X				
20	5/19	Saskatoon RR	C		5:00	*Race #LT Test		X		X	X	*			#
21	5/26			Build 1	9:00			X	X	X	X				
22	6/2							X	X	X	X				
23	6/9	Regina RR	C			*Race		X	X	X	*				
24	6/16				5:00	*TT Test		X		X					*
25	6/23	Race Across Saskatoon	B	Build 2	8:30	*Race		X	X			*	X		
26	6/30	Prince Albert SR	B			*Race		X				*	*		
27	7/7							X	X			X	X		
28	7/14				5:00	*TT Test		X		X					*
29	7/21	Canada Cup RR	C	Peak	7:30	*Race						*	X		
30	7/28				6:00							X	X		
31	8/4	Tumbler's Classic SR	A	Race	5:00	*Race						*	*		
32	8/11	Provincial RR	A			*Race						*	X		
33	8/18				7:00		SM	X	X				X		
34	8/25	Nationals RR	A		5:00	*Race			X				*		
35	9/1				6:00			X	X				X		
36	9/8	Harvest Century	B			*Race			X			*			
37	9/15			Tran											
38	9/22														
39	9/29														
40	10/6														
41	10/13			Prep	6:00	XC Ski		X		X					
42	10/20							X		X					
43	10/27							X		X					
44	11/3							X		X					
45	11/10							X		X					
46	11/17							X		X					
47	11/24							X		X					
48	12/1							X		X					
49	12/8							X		X					
50	12/15							X		X					
51	12/22							X		X					
52	12/29							X		X					

Figure 11.1
Tom Brown's training plan

Case Study 2: Lots of Time and Limiters

Profile

Lisa Harvey is a 27-year-old Category II who has been racing for four years. She works full-time as an engineer with an aeronautics company in the Phoenix, Arizona, area. She usually puts in forty-five hours per week on the job and has weekends off. She lives with a roommate, has few family or community-related commitments, and is able to ride with few restrictions on her time. Her training in the past was free form—she did what she wanted, when she wanted, *if* she wanted. As a result, many of the basic abilities are weak.

Lisa has good power due primarily to her ability to turn the cranks at high cadence. She has always been a good sprinter. Her limiters are force, climbing, and muscular endurance. Her endurance is not as bad as the other limiters, but nevertheless it needs improving as well.

Plan

While someone of Lisa's age with few restrictions on her time should be able to train on a 500-annual hour basis, she has broken down frequently over the past two years with colds and sore throats. It may be due to her habit of piling on too many hard workouts without adequate rest. Diet is also suspect. She trained about 400 hours last year, based on her records, so she will start at the same level. Her ability to cope with a structured training regimen that includes frequent recovery and rest should allow her to avoid such problems. At the end of Base 2, we will evaluate her capacity for handling the workload to that point and increase the volume if it seems manageable.

Lisa has two Race periods planned, the first in June with two A-priority races in five weeks, and the second in September with back-to-back A races. There will be a short Transition period following the first Race period to allow her to recover in order to reach a higher peak later on. It's possible that this Transition period will be only five days off the bike, as that should be adequate at her age to fully recover. With only seven weeks from the end of the transition to the start of the second peak, Build 2 was shortened by one week. The recovery week was, of course, not removed. Build 1 was left intact, as her basic abilities need more time to develop. We may even decide to go back to Base 3 at this point if her endurance and force are not responding to training to the extent that we would like them to.

In this seven-week Build period, there will undoubtedly be other races that weren't known of when she drafted the plan. She can substitute these for workouts. If a B race falls in a non-R & R week the volume will be reduced by about 20 percent so that she goes into these races fairly well-recovered.

Athlete: Lisa Harvey **Annual Hours:** 400 **ANNUAL TRAINING PLAN**

Season Goals:
1. Break 1:04 at State Time Trial.
2. Finish in top 20 at La Vuelta Stage Race.
3. Finish in top 15 at State Road Race.

Training Objectives:
1. Improve climbing: Climb S. Mountain in less than 32 minutes by May 25.
2. Improve muscular endurance: Complete 40-min. threshold workout by May 11.
3. Improve endurance: Complete at least five 10+ hour training weeks by Mar 16.
4. Improve strength: Increase all max lifts by at least 15% by Feb 16.

WORKOUTS

WK#	MON	RACE	PRI	PERIOD	HOURS	DETAILS	WEIGHTS	ENDURANCE	FORCE	SPEED SKILL	MUSCULAR ENDUR.	ANAEROBIC ENDUR.	POWER	TESTING
01	1/6			Base 1	10:30		MS	X		X				
02	1/13			↓	5:30	*ATT	↓	X		X				*
03	1/20			Base 2	8:30		SM	X	X	X	X			
04	1/27				10:00			X	X	X	X			
05	2/3			↓	11:00			X	X	X	X			
06	2/10				5:30	*Test Max		X		X				*
07	2/17			Base 3	9:00			X	X	X	X			
08	2/24				10:30			X	X	X	X			
09	3/3				11:30			X	X	X	X			
10	3/10			↓	5:30	*ATT		X		X				*
11	3/17			Build 1	10:00			X	X	X	X			
12	3/24	Arrowhead RR	C			*Race		X	X	X			*	
13	3/31			↓				X	X	X				
14	4/7			↓	5:30	*TT Test		X		X				*
15	4/14	Congress-Yarnell RR	C	Build 2	9:30	*Race		X	X		*	X		
16	4/21							X	X		*	X		
17	4/28	Fountain Hills RR	C	↓				X	X		*	X		
18	5/5	Festival RR	C	↓	5:30			X		X	*			
19	5/12			Peak	7:30				X	X	X	X		
20	5/19			↓	6:00		↓		X	X	X	X		
21	5/26	La Vuelta SR	A	Race	5:30	*Race			X	*	*			
22	6/2	Thunder Road TT	B	Build 2	9:30	*Race	SM	X	X		*	X		
23	6/9	Climb to the Stars TT	B	↓		*Race	↓	X	X		*	X		
24	6/16	Grand Canyon State RR	B	Peak	6:00	*Race	↓		X	X	*	X		
25	6/23	Wupatki	A	Race	5:30	*Race			X	*	*			
26	6/30			Tran	0:00									
27	7/7	High Country RR	C	Build 1	10:00	*Race	SM	X	X	X	*			
28	7/14			↓				X	X	X	X			
29	7/21			↓				X	X	X	X			
30	7/28				5:30	*TT Test		X		X				*
31	8/4			Build 2	9:30			X	X		X	X		
32	8/11	Falcon Field Crit	C	↓		*Race		X	X		X	*		
33	8/18	Road to Nowhere TT	B		5:30	*Race		X		X	*			
34	8/25			Peak	7:30			X	X		X			
35	9/1			↓	6:00		↓		X		X			
36	9/8	State TT	A	Race	5:30	*Race			X	*	X			
37	9/15	State RR	A	↓		*Race			X	*	X			
38	9/22				7:30		SM	X		X	X	X		
39	9/29				6:00			X		X	X	X		
40	10/6	Mt Graham RR	C	↓	5:30	*Race	↓		X	X				
41	10/13			Tran										
42	10/20						SM							
43	10/27													
44	11/3													
45	11/10													
46	11/17			↓			↓							
47	11/24			Prep	7:00		AA	X		X				
48	12/1							X		X				
49	12/8							X		X				
50	12/15			↓		*ATT	↓	X		X				
51	12/22			Base 1	8:00		MS	X		X				
52	12/29			↓	9:30		↓	X		X				

Figure 11.2
Lisa Harvey's training plan

The last Race period is five weeks finishing with a C race—the last race of the season. There's no reason with only three weeks remaining in the race season following the state road race in week 37 to try to build to a higher level of fitness. Therefore, Lisa's C race is being treated like an A race, except more endurance work is added in the preceding two weeks.

Case Study 3: Three Race Peaks

Profile

Sam Crooks, 37, is a dentist in Johnson City, Tennessee. He is married and has two children, by a former marriage, who sometimes spend the weekend with him and his wife. When the kids are visiting, Sam reduces his training and racing schedule in order to spend more time with them.

Sam is a Category III and has been racing for four years in both Category III and masters races. He competes mostly in criteriums. He is dedicated to racing and training and fits in workouts whenever he can around his busy schedule. This means training on lunch hours and before and after work. He rarely misses a workout.

Maximum power and speed skills are Sam's strong points, making him an excellent criterium racer, but his marginal endurance, climbing, and muscular endurance limit his performance when it comes to road races and time trials. He has what it takes to win the district masters criterium, but will be taken to his limits with his goals: a top-five finish in the Johnson City Stage Race and a top-twenty at the Greenville Road Race.

Plan

Sam has a long season with races starting in early March and extending into mid-October. His A-priority races are widely separated with one in late May, a pair in July, and the last in October. Because of this spread, I scheduled Sam for three Race periods. For his first race peak in late May, I decided to maintain his peak for the district time trial in week 21 since he needs to concentrate more on muscular-endurance training. A bit more focus on time trial training will help accomplish that.

The second Race period is followed by a one-week transition, which comes fairly late in the season. This Transition period may be extended by another three to five days if Sam loses enthusiasm after completing the Greenville Road Race. With a break in the racing and ten weeks until the next A race, that shouldn't present a problem.

In the second Race period, endurance workouts have been added to weeks 27 and 28, since he will be coming into two road races in weeks 29 and 30—one is an A race, and endurance is one of his limiters. If the week 27 and 28 criteriums are on Saturdays, he will ride long on the two Sundays. If they're Sunday races, he'll do

Athlete: Sam Crooks **Annual Hours:** 500

ANNUAL TRAINING PLAN

Season Goals:
1. Win District Masters Criterium.
2. Top 5 at Johnson County Stage Race.
3. Top 20 at Greenville Road Race.

Training Objectives:
1. Improve climbing strength: Increase squat by 20% by Jan 12.
2. Improve muscular endurance: Sub-57-minute 40k at District Time Trial.
3. Improve endurance: Train on a 500-annual-hour schedule.

WORKOUTS

WK#	MON	RACE	PRI	PERIOD	HOURS	DETAILS	WEIGHTS	ENDURANCE	FORCE	SPEED SKILL	MUSCULAR ENDUR.	ANAEROBIC ENDUR.	POWER	TESTING
01	1/6			Base 1	7:00	*ATT, Test squat	MS X		X					*
02	1/13			Base 2	10:30		SM X	X	X	X				
03	1/20			↓	12:30			X	X	X	X			
04	1/27			↓	14:00			X	X	X	X			
05	2/3			↓	7:00	*ATT		X	X					*
06	2/10			Base 3	11:00			X	X	X	X			
07	2/17			↓	13:30			X	X	X	X			
08	2/24	Crossville RR	C	↓	15:00	*Race		X	X	X	*			
09	3/3			↓	7:00	*TT		X	X				*	
10	3/10			Build 1	12:30	///1 St/wk///		X	X		X	X	X	
11	3/17	Anderson Crit	C	↓		*Race		X	X			*	X	
12	3/24			↓				X	X		X	X	X	
13	3/31	Korbel Crit	B	↓	7:00	*Race		X	X		X	*		
14	4/7			Build 2	12:00			X	X		X	X	X	
15	4/14	Raccoon Mtn RR	C	↓		*Race		X	*		X	X	X	
16	4/21	Athens Crit	C	↓		*Race		X	X		X	*	X	
17	4/28			↓	7:00	*TT		X	X					*
18	5/5	McMinnville Crit	B	Peak	10:30	*Race	↓	X			X	*	X	
19	5/12	Drummond Crit	C	↓	8:30	*Race					X	*	X	
20	5/19	Johnson Cty SR	A	Race	7:00	*Race				X	*	*		
21	5/26	District TT*	B	↓	7:00	*Race	SM			X	*	X		
22	6/2	Roann RR	C	Build 1	12:30	*Race		X	X		*		X	
23	6/19	Crossville Crit	B	↓	10:00	*Race		X	X		X	*	X	
24	6/16			↓	7:00	*TT		X	X				X	*
25	6/23	Charleston Crit	C	Peak	10:30	*Race		X			X	*	X	
26	6/30	Murfreesboro Crit	B	↓	8:30	*Race		X			X	X	X	
27	7/7	District Crit	A	Race	8:00	*Race		X			X	*		
28	7/14	Gaffney Crit	B	Peak	10:30	*Race		X			X	X	X	
29	7/21	Asheville RR	B	↓	8:30	*Race	↓				X	X	X	
30	7/28	Greenville RR	A	Race	8:00	*Race					X	*	X	
31	8/4			Tran	0									
32	8/11			Base 3	11:00		SM X	X	X	X				
33	8/18			↓	13:30			X	X	X				
34	8/25			↓	7:00	*TT		X	X					*
35	9/1			Build 2	12:30			X	X		X	X	X	
36	9/8	Carolina Cup	B	↓	10:00	*Race		X	X		X	X	X	
37	9/15			↓				X	X		X	X	X	
38	9/22	A to Z RR	B	↓	7:00	*Race		X	X		X	*		
39	9/29	Apple Dash	C	Peak	10:30	*Race		X			*	X	X	
40	10/6			↓	8:30		↓				X	X	X	
41	10/13	Michelin Classic Crit	A	Race	7:00	*Race					X	X	*	
42	10/20			Tran	0									
43	10/27			↓	7:00									
44	11/3			↓										
45	11/10			↓										
46	11/17			↓										
47	11/24			↓	↓									
48	12/1			Prep	8:30		AA X	X						
49	12/8			↓				X	X					
50	12/15			↓				X	X					
51	12/22			↓	↓			X	X					
52	12/29			Base 1	10:00		MS X	X						

Figure 11.3
Sam Crooks' training plan

endurance rides following the races. He has increased his hours for these two weeks to allow for the longer rides.

The last peak of the season (early October) will be preceded by a four-week Build 2 period because the last race is a group of criteriums and he will want to emphasize anaerobic endurance coming into them. By that point, Sam will have solidly established endurance and muscular endurance.

After such a long season, Sam may be in need of a longer transition starting in October, so it has been extended to six weeks.

Case Study 4: Summer Base Training

Profile

Randy Stickler, 25, is a college student living in Fort Collins, Colorado. He has been racing since age 14 and has been on the national team participating as a Category I in several high-profile races in the United States and in international competition. He carries a full load at Colorado State University, majoring in watershed management. Classes and studying limit his available riding time during the week, but on the weekends time is available to train. In the summer, he will be doing an internship that keeps his time to ride somewhat restricted on weekdays.

Randy's greatest abilities are endurance, force, muscular endurance, power, and climbing. With so much on his side, it's no wonder that he is a force to be reckoned with in every race he enters. He believes his limiter is anaerobic endurance, but since he determined that from early-winter testing, that concern is somewhat suspect. Nearly everyone has poor anaerobic endurance in the winter months. However, Randy's short sprint is excellent, but his longer sprints fade in races.

Plan

Randy is capable of training about 1,000 hours a year. However, with restrictions on his free time, his volume has been limited to only 800 hours. With the massive base he's built during eleven years of racing that should not present any problems. With his age and muscular strength as a strong ability, a primary emphasis on force training will end the last week of March. But it will be maintained throughout much of the remainder of the season.

The first A race of the season for Randy will be the Bisbee Stage Race in late April, a five-day event that attracts a strong field. He will train through the Boulder Criterium Series and other races in March and early April, using them in combination with a build-up of intensity to peak for Bisbee. A top-ten placement in the general classification is well within his reach.

ANNUAL TRAINING PLAN

Athlete: Randy Stickler **Annual Hours:** 800

Seasonal Goals:
1. Top 10 in G.C. at Bisbee Stage Race.
2. Top 3 at Stage Road Race Championships.
3. Top 3 in G.C. at Colorado Cyclist Stage Race.

Training Objectives:
1. Improve sprint: Average 800 W on Power Test by 4/20 and again by 9/14.
2. Improve anaerobic endurance: 5 min. anaerobic on LT test by 4/20 and 9/14.
3. Improve anaerobic endurance: Average 30 mph for 30 min. of AE intervals by 6/18.

WK#	MON	RACE	PRI	PERIOD	HOURS	DETAILS	WEIGHTS	ENDURANCE	FORCE	SPEED SKILL	MUSCULAR ENDUR.	ANAEROBIC ENDUR.	POWER	TESTING
01	1/6			Base 2	17:00		MS	X		X	X			
02	1/13				20:00		SM	X	X	X	X			
03	1/20			↓	23:00			X	X	X	X			
04	1/27				11:30	*ATT		X		X				*
05	2/3			Base 3	18:00			X	X	X	X			
06	2/10				21:30			X	X	X	X			
07	2/17			↓	23:30			X	X	X	X			
08	2/24				11:30	*LT, Power Tests		X		X				*
09	3/3	Boulder Crit Series	C	Build 1	20:30	*Race		X		X	*	X		
10	3/10	Boulder Crit Series	C	↓		*Race		X		X	*	X		
11	3/17				11:30	*TT		X		X				*
12	3/24	Boulder Crit Series	C	Build 2	20:30	*Race		X		X	*	X		
13	3/31	Boulder RR	B		16:30	*Race		X		X	*	X		
14	4/7			↓	11:30	*TT		X		X				*
15	4/14			Peak	13:30	*TT, LT, Power	↓	X			X	X		*
16	4/21	Bisbee SR	A	Race	11:30	*Race		*	*		*	*	X	
17	4/28			Build 1	20:30		SM	X		X	X	X		
18	5/5	Sunburst Circuit/Crit	C			*Race		X		X	*	X		
19	5/12	Pueblo Crit	C	↓		*Race		X		X	*	X		
20	5/19				11:30			X	X					
21	5/26	Ironhorse RR	B	Peak	17:00	*Race		X		X	*	X	X	
22	6/2	Meridian Crit	C	↓	13:30	*Race			X		X	*	X	
23	6/9	State RR Champs	A	Race	11:30	*Race					*	X	X	
24	6/16			Peak	13:30			X	X		X	X		
25	6/23	Mt Evans RR	A	Race	11:30	*Race			*		*	X	X	
26	6/30			Tran	0									
27	7/7	Peak to Peak RR	C	Base 3	18:00	*Race		X	*	X	*			
28	7/14	Grand Junct. RR/Crit	C		21:30	*Race		X	*	X	*	*		
29	7/21			↓	23:30			X	X	X	X			
30	7/28	Hummel Crit	C		11:30	*Race		X		X		*		
31	8/4	Coal Miner Crit	C	Build 1	20:30	*Race		X		X	*	X		
32	8/11	Black Forest RR	B		16:30	*Race		X		X	*	X	X	
33	8/18			↓	11:30	*TT		X		X				*
34	8/25			Build 2	19:00			X		X	X	X		
35	9/1	Deer Creek HC	C	↓		*Race		X	*	X	*	X	X	
36	9/8				11:30	*TT, LT, Power		X		X				*
37	9/15			Peak	17:00			X	X		X	X	X	
38	9/22			↓	13:30				X		X	X	X	
39	9/29	Colorado Cyclist SR	A	Race	11:30	*Race		*	*		*	X	X	
40	10/6			Tran	0									
41	10/13				0									
42	10/20				0									
43	10/27			↓	0		↓							
44	11/3			Prep	13:30		AA	X		X				
45	11/10							X		X				
46	11/17							X		X				
47	11/24							X		X				
48	12/1							X		X				
49	12/8			↓			↓	X		X				
50	12/15			Base 1	15:30		MS	X		X				
51	12/22				19:00			X		X				
52	12/29			↓	21:30		↓	X		X				

WORKOUTS

Figure 11.4
Randy Stickler's training plan

Following the Bisbee Stage Race, Randy will return to Build 1 as he is preparing for the Colorado State Road Race Championship in week 23. With this race coming so soon after Bisbee, he should be in excellent form.

The greatest challenge in Randy's race schedule is maintaining race form for the three-day Colorado Cyclist Stage Race at the very end of the season (week 39). With fourteen weeks separating his last two A races, it's best to re-establish his basic fitness by repeating Base 3 training in July, even though that may be seen as an unusual time to work on base. The events during this period are all C races, so he can either train through them or even skip a few.

With no races in the three weeks preceding the Colorado Cyclist Stage Race it's important that Randy make best use of dwindling group rides at that time of year and race-intense workouts to peak his fitness.

Not having done any strength training since March, six weeks of AA phase weight work will begin in week 44 following a four-week Transition period. During the six-week Preparation period Randy will mountain bike, run, and cross-country ski, as the weather allows.

I hope you noticed that in each of these case studies I occasionally changed the procedures for designing a training plan as discussed in Chapters 8, 9, and 10. Life rarely presents you with races, work, vacations, and other events spaced to neatly fit into annual plans. Don't be afraid to bend the rules a little so you can design a plan that exactly fits your needs.

PART FIVE

OTHER ASPECTS OF TRAINING

HISTORICAL PERSPECTIVES

Conditioning for Cycling
by Willie Honeman
As it appeared in *American Bicyclist Magazine*, June 1945

Sleep eight to nine hours daily and try to make it a point of retiring and arising at about the same hour every day. Of course, when one races at night this may break up the routine, but otherwise try to follow this rule.

The question of food and what to eat is one that would take much space to cover. A good rule is to eat whatever foods appeal to you, but be sure they are of good quality and fresh. Avoid too many starchy foods, such as white bread, potatoes, pies, pastries, etc. Eat plenty of green and cooked vegetables.

Before a race meet, or road race, eat at least three hours before. If your appetite is good, and it should be, a good quality steak, cooked rare (when and if it can be had), spinach, or lettuce, toast, prunes, or some other fruit, black coffee, with a small quantity of sugar, makes up a good pre-race meal. If the time before a meet or race is limited, two soft-boiled eggs, toast, fruit, and black coffee is another menu. Lamb chops may be a good substitute for the steak. Ovoid overeating. It is better to leave the table a little hungry than to overeat, which will interfere with the proper digestion of your food.

Physical culture and exercise should be indulged in each morning to develop the arms, chest, and to prevent getting too fat around the stomach. Small weights, or pulleys, can be used. Perform these exercises before an open window and practice deep breathing at the same time.

STRENGTH 12

Golf pros hit balls on the range, swimmers practice with wooden paddles on their hands, and athletes in other sports do other things that improve performance by enhancing muscle memory. Too many cyclists just ride their bikes.
—MIKE KOLIN, cycling coach

There are many factors that go into determining who gets to the finish line first, not the least of which is the condition of the athlete's connective tissues—muscles and tendons.

The human body has more than 660 muscles, making up some 35 to 40 percent of its mass. How strong and flexible these muscles are will contribute immensely to the athlete's race performance. Developing the ability to produce great force while maintaining a wide range of motion means greater racing speeds and a reduced risk of injury. If the muscles are even a bit weak or inflexible, the rider never realizes his or her full potential, as power for climbing and handling the bike is too low and muscle pulls and strains are likely. Developing the muscles will provide the potential to significantly improve racing at all levels. Every successful athlete I have trained has lifted weights for at least part of the season. Those with a force limiter have improved their race performances the most. And, as we have seen, muscular force is a major component in time trialing, climbing, and sprinting. The rider who can apply the greatest force to the pedal has a leg up on the competition.

There was a time when endurance athletes avoided strength training like the plague. Today there are still reasons why some don't strength train. Many riders have a great fear of gaining weight. While there are those who have a tendency to increase their muscle mass, very few cyclists have a genetic predisposition to become hulking monsters, especially on an endurance-based program. If three or four extra pounds result from weight training, however, the increased power typically more than offsets the mass to be carried. For most riders, strength training does not cause appreciable weight changes. But since it's winter when most of them are lifting, and they are riding infrequently while eating as much as they do during the racing season, fat accumulates and they blame it on weight training. By spring when the mileage goes back up, this excess blubber will disappear.

Strength Training Benefits

Research has demonstrated positive gains in cycling-endurance performance resulting from strength increases, but no change in aerobic capacity (VO$_2$max). A possible reason for this apparent contradiction is that the greater strength of the slow-twitch, endurance muscles allows them to carry more of the burden of powering the bike, thus relying less on the fast-twitch muscles. Since the fast-twitch muscles fatigue rather quickly, reducing their contribution to the total force created means greater endurance.

One study done at the University of Maryland showed that improved strength from weight lifting was associated with a higher lactate threshold. Since lactate threshold is a major determiner of performance in an event such as bike racing, anything that elevates it is beneficial. This finding may have resulted from the athletes using more slow-twitch and less fast-twitch muscle to power the bike. Since fast-twitch muscles produce abundant amounts of lactic acid, using them to provide less of the pedaling force means there will be less lactate in the blood at any given power output, therefore raising lactate threshold.

Lifting weights also has the potential to increase the total amount of force that can be applied to the pedal in every stroke. As you may recall from Chapter 4, as force rises at any given cadence, power increases. Greater power outputs are always associated with faster riding.

Nearly all the studies show that subjects enjoy an increased "time to exhaustion"—meaning the subjects could ride farther at a given intensity level—after following a leg-strength program for a few weeks. The endurance improvements have typically ranged from 10 to 33 percent, depending on the intensity of the effort. It should be pointed out, however, that the subjects in these tests are seldom experienced cyclists. It is more likely they are moderately to poorly trained college students, and weight training will typically provide this endurance enhancement to those who are newest to the sport rather than to the more experienced riders in a given group.

The weakest point in a muscle is where it attaches to the tendon. Most muscle tears occur at this point. Increasing the load capacity of these muscle-tendon unions reduces the risk of pulled muscles during a sudden change in power, as when accelerating quickly or sprinting.

Strength training also has the potential to improve muscle imbalances. These may be gross imbalances, such as a weak upper body and a strong lower body, or they may be relative imbalances between muscle groups that have opposing effects on a joint. Again, such enhancements reduce the chances of an injury.

Whatever the mechanism of improvement may be, there is a high probability that strength work will make you a better racer. Even if you were to improve your pedal force by only a few percentage points, think how much better you could race. You would be able to ride faster or feel stronger at the end of a long road race.

Getting Started

There are two challenges for the rider determined to improve his or her racing with greater strength. The first is that there are as many strength programs as there are athletes, coaches, weight training and cycling books. The average rider does not know which to follow.

The second challenge is time. Many of the weight programs suggested include an unrealistic number of exercises to complete, often a dozen or more. Given jobs, family, and life in general, most riders just can't afford huge blocks of time in the gym. The program below is pared down to fit into the "normal" athlete's busy lifestyle. While you might be able to squeeze in more gym time, the racing benefits would not be much greater.

The sport of bodybuilding has had an unusually heavy influence on strength training in the United States. But for cyclists, using resistance exercise the same way bodybuilders do is likely to *decrease* endurance performance. Bodybuilders organize training to maximize and balance muscle mass while shaping their physiques for display. Function is not a concern. Endurance athletes' goals are far different, but all too often they learn the bodybuilder's methods at their gym and follow them for lack of a better way.

The purpose of strength training for cycling is the application of force to the pedals for a prolonged period of time. To accomplish this, the cyclist must improve the synchronization and recruitment patterns of muscle groups—not their size and shape. This means that resistance work must not only develop the muscles, but also the central nervous system that controls muscle use.

Rules to Lift By

Based on comments from the athletes who I train and their results over the years, I have slowly refined the weight training program that I recommend. The basic rules of my program have stayed the same. Whatever program you follow as far as sets, reps, and load, be sure to lift by these rules.

Rule 1: Focus on prime movers.

Prime movers are the big muscle groups that do the major work on the bike. Cycling's prime movers are the quadriceps, hamstrings, and gluteals. While having well-developed deltoids may look nice, they're only good for lifting your bike—not a common movement in road racing.

Rule 2: Prevent muscle imbalances.

Some of the injuries common to riders result from an imbalance between muscles that must work in harmony to produce a movement. For example, if the lateral quadriceps on the outside of the thigh is overly developed relative to the medial quadriceps above and inside the knee, a knee injury is possible.

Rule 3: Use multi-joint exercises whenever possible.

Biceps curls are a single-joint exercise, involving only the elbow joint. This is the type of muscle-isolation exercise bodybuilders do. Squats, a basic cycling exercise, include three joints—the hip, knee, and ankle. This comes closer to simulating the dynamic movement patterns of the sport of cycling and also reduces time in the gym.

Rule 4: Mimic the positions and movements of cycling as closely as possible.

Position your hands and feet when lifting weights so they are in similar positions to when you are on the bike. On a leg-press sled, for example, the feet should be placed about the same width as the pedals. You don't ride with your feet spread 18 inches (45 cm) and your toes turned out at 45 degrees. Another example: When holding the bar for seated rows, position your hands as as you would on handlebars.

Rule 5: Always include the "core"—abdominals and lower back.

The forces applied by your arms and legs must pass through the core of your body. If it is weak, much of the force is dissipated and lost. As you climb or during a sprint, it takes a strong core to transfer more of the force generated by pulling against the handlebars to the pedals. Weak abdominal and back muscles make for wimpy climbing and sprinting.

Rule 6: As the race season approaches make strength training more specific and less time intensive.

While a crucial period in developing force is during the winter Maximum Strength phase, the strength developed then must be converted to power and muscular endurance later—forms of strength usable in road racing. These conversions are best accomplished on the bike while max strength is maintained in the weight room. If you read the earlier editions of this book you will notice that this is the area where I have made significant changes to my recommendations for using weights to improve cycling performance.

Rule 7: Keep the number of exercises low.

In order to concentrate on improving specific movements, put greater focus on sets and reps rather than the number of exercises. Following the initial Anatomical Adaptation phase, gradually reduce the number of exercises. The idea is to spend as little time in the weight room as possible and yet still improve race performance.

Rule 8: Strength training fitness precedes on-bike training within each season period.

Specific exercise demands in the weight room must come before the same or similar demands on the bike. For example, the Maximum Strength training phase should occur in the weeks just prior to the start of hill training on the bike. In this way your muscles and tendons have been prepared for the workloads that you will experience on the bike, and you will be able to start stressful workouts such as hill repeats at higher levels of performance with a lower risk of injury.

The following suggested strength program complies with the above guidelines. I designed it specifically for road cyclists. If you have been training like a body-builder before, you may feel guilty at times using lighter weights, higher repetitions, and only a few exercises. Stay with the program and I think you'll see improvements in your racing. You won't look much better in the mirror. But then again, that is not what you are after.

Strength Training Phases

There are three phases through which the cyclist should progress in approaching the most important races of the year.

Preparation Period: Anatomical Adaptation (AA) and Maximum Transition (MT)

Anatomical Adaptation is the initial phase of strength training that usually is included in the late fall or early winter. Its purpose is to prepare the muscles and tendons for the greater loads of the next phases—Maximum Transition and Maximum Strength. More exercises are done at this time of year than at any other, since improved general body strength is a goal. There is less time spent on the bike at this time of year so more time is available for weight training.

Weight machines are convenient, but you should also use free weight training during this period. Circuit training, involving continuous movement from one station to the next, doing several circuits in a workout, can add an aerobic element to the AA phase.

The Maximum Transition phase is just that—a phase that provides a transition from the light loads and high reps of the AA phase to the heavy loads and low reps of MS. With only a few of these workouts with the loads increasing slightly each time, you will be ready to begin MS. Always be conservative when increasing loads, especially in the MS phase.

In the AA and MS phases the athlete should be able to increase loads by about 5 percent every four or five workouts.

Base 1 Period: Maximum Strength (MS)

As resistance is gradually increased and repetitions decreased, more force is generated. This phase is necessary to teach the central nervous system to easily recruit high numbers of muscle fibers. If you are new to weight training, omit this phase the first year and focus just on the MT phase throughout Base 1 and following. This is the most dangerous phase of training and injury, possibly severe, is likely. Be particularly careful during this phase, especially with free weight exercises such as the squat. If there is any question about whether or not you should do the squat exercise due to a questionable back, knees or any other joints, leave it out and do one of the alternatives (leg press or step-up).

Sidebar 12.1

ANATOMICAL ADAPTATION (AA) PHASE

Total sessions/phase	8–12
Sessions/week	2–3
Load (% 1RM)	40–60
Sets/session	2–5
Reps/set	20–30
Speed of lift	Slow
Recovery (in minutes)	1–1.5

EXERCISES (IN ORDER OF COMPLETION):
1. Hip extension (squat, leg press, or step-up)
2. Lat pull-down
3. Hip extension (use a different exercise than in #1)
4. Chest press or push-ups
5. Seated row
6. Personal weakness (hamstring curl, knee extension, or heel raise)
7. Standing row
8. Abdominal with twist

Sidebar 12.2

MAXIMUM TRANSITION (MT) PHASE

Total sessions/phase	3–5
Sessions/week	2–3
Load	Select loads that allow only 10–15 reps*
Sets/session	3–4
Reps/set	10–15*
Speed of lift	Slow to moderate, emphasizing form
Recovery (in minutes)	1.5–3*

* Only **bold** exercises listed below follow this guideline. All others continue AA guidelines.

EXERCISES (IN ORDER OF COMPLETION):
1. **Hip extension** (squat, leg press, or step-up)
2. **Seated row**
3. Abdominal with twist
4. Upper body choice (chest press or lat pull-down)
5. Personal weakness (hamstring curl, knee extension, or heel raise)
6. **Standing row**

Sidebar 12.3

MAXIMUM STRENGTH (MS) PHASE

Total sessions/phase	8–12
Sessions/week	2–3
Load (% 1RM)	BW goals*
Sets/session	2–6
Reps/set	3–6+*
Speed of lift	Slow to moderate
Recovery (in minutes)	2–4*

* Only **bold** exercises listed below follow this guideline. All others continue AA guidelines.

EXERCISES (IN ORDER OF COMPLETION):

1. **Hip extension** (squat, leg press, or step-up)
2. **Seated row**
3. Abdominal with twist
4. Upper body choice (chest press or lat pull-down)
5. Personal weakness (hamstring curl, knee extension, or heel raise)
6. **Standing row**

Sidebar 12.4

MS PHASE LOAD GOALS BASED ON BODY WEIGHT (BW)

NOTE: The goal is to complete three sets of six repetitions each at these loads by the end of the MS phase. If a goal is achieved early, maintain the load and increase the repetitions beyond six for the remainder of the MS phase.

Freebar squat	1.3–1.7 x BW
Leg press (sled)	2.5–2.9 x BW
Step-up	0.7–0.9 x BW
Seated row	0.5–0.8 x BW
Standing row	0.4–0.7 x BW

Don't take any risks during the MS phase. Be conservative. This includes selecting your loads conservatively at the start of this phase and in the first set of each workout. You can gradually increase the loads throughout this phase.

Loads are gradually increased throughout MS up to certain goal levels based on your body weight (BW). These are summarized in Sidebar 12.4. Generally, women will aim for the lower ends of the ranges and men the upper ends. Those new to the MS phase of training should also set load goals based on the lower ends of the ranges.

It is tempting for some athletes to extend this phase beyond the recommended ranges in the table. Don't do it. Continuing this phase for several weeks is likely to result in muscle imbalances, especially in the upper leg, which may contribute to hip or knee injuries.

All Other Periods: Strength Maintenance (SM)

Carefully limited high-intensity lifting maintains the raw strength needed for racing. Stopping all resistance training once the Base 2 period starts may cause a gradual loss of strength and performance throughout the season unless serious strength training on hills is incorporated. Maintenance of strength is particularly important for women and those over the age of forty.

Hip extension training (squats, step-ups, or leg presses) is optional during the maintenance phase. If you find hip extension exercises help your racing, continue doing them. However, if working the legs only deepens your fatigue level, cut them out. Continuing to work on core muscles and personal weakness areas will maintain your strength needs.

To properly time your peak, eliminate all strength training for the seven days leading up to A-priority races.

Determining Load

Perhaps the most critical aspect of lifting weights is the load you select during each phase. While it suggests a load based on the maximum you can lift for a single repetition (1RM), that is not always the best way to determine weight due to the possibility of injury, especially to the back, and of prolonged soreness reducing most, if not all, training for two or three days.

Another way to decide how much weight to use is to initially estimate the load and then adjust as the phase progresses. Always start with less than you think is possible for the number of reps indicated. You can add more later, if you do it cautiously.

You can also estimate one-repetition maximums based on a higher number of reps done to failure. Start by doing a warm-up set or two. Select a resistance you can lift at least four times, but no more than ten. You may need to experiment for a couple of sets. If you do, rest for at least five minutes between attempts. To find your predicted one-repetition maximum, divide the weight lifted by the factor below that corresponds with the number of repetitions completed (see Table 12.1).

Another way of estimating your 1RM from a multiple lift effort is described in Appendix A.

During the Maximum Strength phase, free weights are likely to bring greater results than machines, but if you use free weights also include them in the MT phase. Again, be cautious whenever using barbells and dumbbells, especially with rapid movement.

Miscellaneous Guidelines

In carrying out a strength-development program there are several other factors that you will want to consider.

Sidebar 12.5

STRENGTH MAINTENANCE (SM) PHASE

Total sessions/phase	Indefinite
Sessions/week	1
Load (% 1RM)	60, 80 (last set)*
Sets/session	2–3
Reps/set	6–12*
Speed of lift	Moderate
Recovery (in minutes)	1–2*

* Only **bold** exercises listed below follow this guideline. All others continue AA guidelines.

EXERCISES (IN ORDER OF COMPLETION):
1. **Hip extension** (squat, leg press, or step-up)
2. **Seated row**
3. Abdominal with twist
4. Upper body choice (chest press or lat pull-down)
5. Personal weakness (hamstring curl, knee extension, or heel raise)
6. **Standing row**

Table 12.1
Estimating One-Repetition Maximums

# OF REPS	FACTOR
4	.90
5	.875
6	.85
7	.825
8	.80
9	.775
10	.75

Experience Level

If you are in the first two years of strength training, emphasis must be on building efficient movement patterns and bolstering connective tissue—not on heavy loads. Experienced athletes are ready to do more maximum strength development.

Days per Week

The weight phase tables suggest a range of days per week to lift weights based on the phase. The period of the season you are in will help you to further refine this number. During Base 3, Build 1, and Build 2, reduce the number of days of strength training per week by one. In the Peak and Race periods cut back to the minimum listed on the table. The week of A races, eliminate strength training altogether.

Warm-up and Cool Down

Before an individual strength workout, warm up with about ten minutes of easy aerobic activity. This could be running, rowing, stair-climbing, or cycling. Following a weight session, spin with a light resistance at a cadence of 90 or higher for ten to twenty minutes on a stationary bike. Allow your toes to relax. Do not run immediately following a strength workout, as this raises your risk of injury.

Phasing In

As you move into a new phase of strength training be cautious with load progression. This is as important at the start of the AA phase as you return to weight training after some time off as it is to the MS phase as you progress to heavy loads. If you do it right, soreness will be minimal and there will be little or no need to modify any other workouts that week. If you do it wrong you are likely to be quite sore for several days and be forced to cut back on other forms of training.

Exercise Order

Exercises are listed in the phase tables in the order of completion to allow for a smooth progression and for recovery. In the AA phase you may want to use "circuit" training to give this phase an aerobic component. To do this complete the first set of all exercises before starting the second sets, moving rapidly between stations with little time for recovery. For example, in AA, do the first set of squats followed by the first set of seated rows. In the other phases, all sets of each exercise are done to completion before progressing to the next exercise. This is called "horizontal progression."

In some cases, you may do two exercises as a "superset" in the MS phase—alternate sets between two exercises to completion. Supersetting will make better use of your time in the gym since you'll spend less time waiting for recovery of a specific neuromuscular group. This does not eliminate the need to stretch following each set, however.

Recovery Intervals

On the tables, notice that the recovery time between sets is specified. During this time the muscle burn fades away, your heart rate drops, and breathing returns to a resting level as lactate is cleared and energy stores are rebuilt in preparation for the next set. These recovery periods are important, especially as the weight loads increase, if you expect to derive any benefit from strength work. Some phases require longer recovery intervals than others. During the recovery time stretch the muscles just exercised. See Chapter 13 for illustrations of stretches listed here.

Recovery Weeks

Every third or fourth week is a time of reduced training volume coinciding with your recovery weeks scheduled on the annual training plan. Reduce the number of strength workouts that week, or reduce the number of sets within workouts. Keep the loads the same as in the previous week.

Strength Exercises

Hip Extension: Squat

(Quadriceps, Gluteus, Hamstrings)

The squat improves force delivery to the pedals. For the novice, the squat is one of the most dangerous exercise options in this routine. Great care is necessary to protect the back and knees.

1. Wear a weight belt during the Maximum Strength (MS) phase.
2. Stand with the feet pedal-width apart, about 10 inches, center to center, with the toes pointed straight ahead.
3. Keep the head up and the back straight.
4. Squat until the upper thighs are just short of parallel to floor—about the same knee bend as at the top of a pedal stroke.
5. Point the knees straight ahead, maintaining their position over the feet at all times.
6. Return to the start position.
7. Stretches: Stork Stand and Triangle

Figure 12.1
Squat

Hip Extension: Step-up

(Quadriceps, Gluteus, Hamstrings)

Improves force delivery to the pedals. The step-up closely mimics the movement of pedaling, but the exercise takes more time than the squat or leg press, since each leg is worked individually. Caution is necessary to ensure a stable platform and overhead clearance. The platform should be a height equal to twice the length of your cranks. That's approximately 14 inches (35cm). A higher platform puts great stress on the knee and raises the possibility of injury.

Figure 12.2
Step-up

1. Use either a barbell on the shoulders or dumbbells in the hands. Use wrist straps with dumbbells.
2. Place the left foot fully on a sturdy platform with the toes pointing straight ahead.
3. With the back straight and the head erect, step up with the right foot, touching the top of the platform, and immediately return to the start position.
4. Complete all left-leg reps before repeating with the right leg.
5. Stretches: Stork Stand and Triangle

Figure 12.3
Leg press

Hip Extension: Leg Press

(Quadriceps, Gluteus, Hamstrings)

Improves force delivery to the pedals. It is probably the safest of the hip-extension exercises and generally takes the least time. Be careful not to "throw" the platform, since it may damage knee cartilage when it drops back down and lands on legs with locked knees.

1. Center the feet on the middle portion of platform about 10 inches (25 cm) apart, center to center. The feet are parallel, not angled out. The higher the feet are placed on the platform, the more the gluteus and hamstrings are involved.
2. Press the platform up until the legs are almost straight, but with the knees short of locking.

3. Lower the platform until the knees are about 8 inches (20 cm) from the chest. Going lower places unnecessary stress on the knees.

4. The knees remain in line with the feet throughout the movement.

5. Return to the start position.

6. Stretches: Stork Stand and Triangle

Seated Row

(Upper and Lower Back, Lower Lats, Biceps)

This simulates the movement of pulling on the handlebars while climbing a hill in a seated position. Strengthens the core—the lower back.

1. Grasp the bar with the arms fully extended and the hands about the same width as when gripping the handlebar.

2. Pull the bar toward the stomach, keeping the elbows close to the body.

3. Keep movement at the waist to a minimum, using the back muscles to stabilize the position.

4. Return to the start position.

5. Stretch: Pull-down and Squat Stretch

Chest Press

(Pectorals and Triceps)

The chest press, along with the lat pull-down and the standing row, helps support the shoulders in the event of a crash. With free weights, a spotter is necessary in the MS phase.

1. Grasp the bar with the hands above the shoulders and about as wide apart as when holding the handlebars.

2. Lower the bar to the chest, keeping the elbows close to the body.

3. Return to the start position without raising the butt off the bench.

4. Stretch: Pull-down

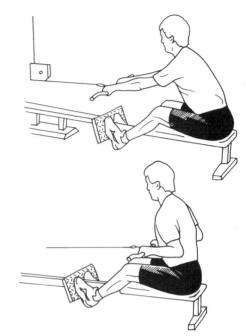

Figure 12.4
Seated row

Figure 12.5
Chest press

Figure 12.6
Push-up

Figure 12.7
Heel raise

Push-up

(Pectorals and Triceps)

The push-up provides the same benefits as the chest press. The advantage is that no equipment is necessary, so it can be done anywhere.

1. Place the hands slightly wider than the shoulders.
2. Keep the back straight and the head up.
3. Maintaining a straight-line, rigid body position, lower the body until the chest is within about 4 inches (10 cm) of the floor. This may be done with the knees on the floor as strength is developing.
4. Return to the start position.
5. Stretch: Twister

Heel Raise

(Gastrocnemius)

This is a "personal weakness" exercise for athletes who experience calf and Achilles tendon problems. The heel raise may reduce susceptibility to such injuries, but be careful to use very light weights when starting, as it may also cause some calf or Achilles tendon problems initially. Progress slowly with this exercise. Never attempt a 1RM test with this exercise if the lower leg is an area of personal weakness.

1. Stand with the balls of the feet on a 1- to 2-inch (2.5 to 5 cm) riser, with the heels on the floor.
2. The feet are parallel and pedal-width apart.
3. With straight knees, rise up onto the toes.
4. Return to the start position.
5. Stretch: Wall Lean

Knee Extension

(Medial Quadriceps)

If you are plagued by a kneecap tracking injury, this exercise may help by improving balance between the lateral and medial quadriceps, keeping the injury under control.

1. Start with the knee fully extended and the toes pointing slightly to the outside. Work one leg at a time.
2. Lower the ankle pad only about 8 inches (20 cm)—do not go all the way down, as this may increase internal knee pressure, making the underside of the kneecap sore.
3. Return to the start position.
4. Stretch: Stork Stand

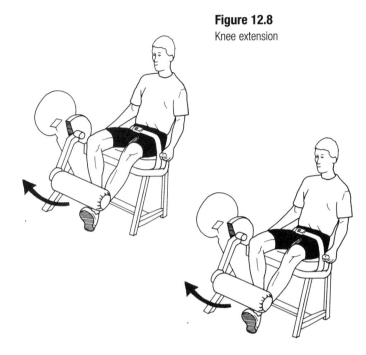

Figure 12.8
Knee extension

Leg Curl

(Hamstrings)

Hamstring injuries may result from an imbalance between the quadriceps and hamstrings. By strengthening the hamstrings, the strength ratio between these two major movers is improved. Leg curls can be done on either prone or standing machines.

1. Bend the leg to about a 90-degree angle at the knee.
2. Return to the start position.
3. Stretch: Triangle

Figure 12.9
Leg curl

Figure 12.10
Abdominal with twist

Abdominal with Twist
(Rectus Abdominus, External Oblique)

This is a core exercise to improve the transfer of energy from the upper to the lower body.

1. Sit on a decline board with the knees bent at about 90 degrees and the ankles held firmly in place.
2. The arms are crossed over the chest and may hold a weight plate.
3. Lower the upper body to about a 45-degree angle from parallel with the floor.
4. Return to the start position with a twist. With each repetition, alternate looking over the right and left shoulders as the torso twists to the right and left.
5. Stretch: Arch the back and extend the arms and legs.

Figure 12.11
Lat pull-down

Lat Pull-down
(Latissimus Dorsi, Biceps)

Just as with the chest press, the lat pull-down stabilizes the shoulder.

1. Grasp a straight bar with the arms fully extended and the hands placed about as wide as they would be on the handlebars.
2. Pull the bar toward the upper chest (not behind the head).
3. Minimize both movement at the waist and rocking back and forth to start the weight moving. Keep the body still, using the back muscles to stabilize this position.
4. Return to the start position.
5. Stretch: Pull-down

Standing Row

(Deltoids, Trapezius, Biceps)

The standing row stabilizes the shoulder and improves the ability to lift the front wheel when clearing obstacles.

1. At the low-pulley station, or with a barbell or dumbbells, grasp the bar at thigh height with the hands handlebar grip–width apart.

2. Pull the bar to the chest.

3. Return to the start position.

4. Stretch: Grasp a stationary object, such as a pole, behind your lower back with the hands as high up as possible. Lean away from the pole, allowing your body to sag while relaxing.

Figure 12.12
Standing row

References

Bompa, T. *Periodization of Strength*. Veritas, 1993.

Bompa, T. *Power Training for Sports*. New York: Mosaic Press, 1993.

Bompa, T. *Theory and Methodology of Training*. Dubuque, IA: Kendall/Hunt Publishing, 1994.

Brzycki, M. "Strength Testing—Predicting a One-Rep Max from Reps to Fatigue." *Journal of Physical Education, Recreation and Dance* 64 (1993): 88–90.

Hickson, R.C., et al. "Potential for Strength and Endurance Training to Amplify Endurance Performance." *Journal of Applied Physiology* 65 (1988): 2285–2290.

Hickson, R.C., et al. "Strength Training Effects on Aerobic Power and Short-term Endurance," *Medicine and Science in Sports and Exercise* 12 (1980): 336–339.

Hortobagyi, T., et al. "Effects of Simultaneous Training for Strength and Endurance on Upper- and Lower-body Strength and Running Performance." *The Journal of Sports Medicine and Physical Fitness* 31 (1991): 20–30.

Johnston, R.E., et al. "Strength Training for Female Distance Runners: Impact on Economy." *Medicine and Science in Sport and Exercise* 27, no. 5 (1995): S47.

Kraemer, W.J., et al. "Compatibility of High-Intensity Strength and Endurance Training on Hormonal and Skeletal Muscle Adaptations." *Journal of Applied Physiology* 78, no. 3 (1995): 976–989.

Marcinik, E.J., et al. "Effects of Strength Training on Lactate Threshold and Endurance Performance." *Medicine and Science in Sports and Exercise* 23, no. 6 (1991): 739–743.

McCarthy, J.P., et al. "Compatibility of Adaptive Responses with Combining Strength and Endurance Training." *Medicine and Science in Sports and Exercise* 27, no. 3 (1995): 429–436.

Nelson, A.G., et al. "Consequences of Combining Strength and Endurance Training Regimens." Physical Therapy 70 (1990): 287–294.

Sale, D.G., and D. MacDougall. "Specificity in Strength Training: A Review for the Coach and Athlete." *Canadian Journal of Applied Sciences* 6 (1981): 87–92.

Sale, D.G., et al. "Comparison of Two Regimens of Concurrent Strength and Endurance Training." *Medicine and Science in Sports and Exercise* 22, no. 3 (1990): 348–356.

Stone, M.H., et al. "Health- and Performance-Related Potential of Resistance Training." *Sports Medicine* 11, no. 4 (1991): 210–231.

Zatiorsky, V.M. *Science and Practice of Strength Training*. Champaign, IL: Human Kinetics, 1995.

STRETCHING

It doesn't get any easier; you just get faster.
—GREG LEMOND

Physiologically speaking, cycling is not a perfect sport. But then again, no sport is. The repetitive movements of cycling cause a shortening and tightening of certain muscles. Pedaling leg muscles lose elasticity since they don't go through a full range of motion—the leg stops both before reaching a full extension and complete flexion. Muscular tension affects the back, neck, arms, and shoulders on rides lasting several hours with little change of position. Such tightness can hold you back.

A good example of how tight muscles limit your performance involves the hamstring muscle on the back of the upper leg. Of all the tightness that can result from cycling, this may be the most debilitating. Tight hamstrings restrain the leg during the down stroke. In this condition they work to prevent the leg from straightening, and in doing so, reduce the force produced by the leg. In an attempt to alleviate the tension felt in the back of the leg, the affected cyclist will often lower his or her saddle. A saddle that is set too low further reduces force generation, which in turn reduces power output.

Benefits of Stretching

Tight hamstrings can also contribute to a tight lower back, which haunts some riders on long rides as they wonder when it might lock up, forcing them to abandon a hard workout or race. Off the bike, this low-back tightness may become lower-back pain. A consistent and effective program of stretching can prevent, or, at the least, alleviate such problems. Prevention is always more comfortable, less time consuming, and cheaper than treatment.

A study of 1,543 runners in the Honolulu Marathon found that those who stretched regularly following workouts had fewer injuries than those who didn't. It is noteworthy that in this same study those who stretched only before workouts had the highest rate of injuries.

Stretching after workouts appears to aid the recovery process by improving muscle cells' uptake of amino acids. This promotes protein synthesis within muscle cells, which is necessary for full and quick recovery, and maintains the integrity of muscle cells.

Stretching after a workout takes less than fifteen minutes, and you can do it while downing a recovery drink and chatting with your training partners. This is the optimum time to work on flexibility, as the muscles are warm and supple.

Another important time to stretch is during strength workouts. The act of forcefully contracting muscles against resistance creates extreme tightness. As described in the previous chapter, following each strength set in the weight room you should stretch the muscles that were just used. Correctly doing a strength workout means spending more time stretching in the gym than lifting weights.

Stretching a little bit throughout the day is also beneficial to long-term flexibility and performance. While sitting at a desk working or reading, you can gently stretch major muscle groups such as the hamstrings and calves. Work on flexibility while watching television, standing in line, talking with friends, and first thing in the morning while still in bed. After a while, you may make it such an integral part of your life that you no longer even think about stretching. It just happens. That's when your flexibility will be at its peak.

Stretching Models

Over the past forty years, four stretching methods have gained (and sometimes lost) popularity.

Ballistic

When I was in college in the 1960s, ballistic stretching was common. Bouncing movements were thought to be the best way to make muscles longer. Later we learned that this technique had just the opposite effect—muscles resisted lengthening and could even be damaged by overly motivated stretchers. Today almost no one stretches this way.

Static

In the 1970s, Californian Bob Anderson refined a stretching method and in 1980 released a book called *Stretching*. Anderson's approach involved static stretching with little or no movement at all: Stretch the muscle to a level of slight discomfort and then hold it in that position for several seconds. Static stretching remains the most popular style today.

PNF

Another method also surfaced about the same time as static stretching, but never received much exposure or support until the 1990s. Several university studies going back to the early 1970s found it to be 10 to 15 percent more effective than static stretching. This approach, called "proprioceptive neuromuscular facilitation," has started to catch on over the last few years.

There are many variations on PNF stretching, some being quite complex. Here are the steps in one easy-to-follow version:

1. Static-stretch the muscle for about eight seconds.
2. Contract the same muscle for about eight seconds. (Leave out the contraction step when stretching between sets of strength training. Instead, hold static stretches for about fifteen seconds.)
3. Static-stretch the muscle again for about eight seconds.
4. Continue alternating contractions with stretches until you have done four to eight static stretches. Always finish with a static stretch.

You should find that the static stretches become deeper with each repeat as the muscles seem to loosen up.

Using this PNF method, a stretch would take one to two minutes. The time is well worth it for the benefit received.

Active-Isolated

A relatively new arrival on the fitness scene, active-isolated stretching involves brief, assisted stretches that are repeated several times. Here is a typical routine:

1. Contract the opposing muscle group as you move into a stretching position.
2. Use your hands, a rope, or a towel to enhance the stretch.
3. Stretch to the point of light tension.
4. Hold for two seconds and then release.
5. Return to the starting position and relax for two seconds.
6. Do one or two sets of eight to twelve repetitions of each two-second stretch.

Cycling Stretches

The following are a few of the many possible stretches for cyclists. You may find that some are more important for you than others. These are the ones to focus on every day and every time you ride. You should also blend some of these with your strength training in the gym. Those combinations are indicated here and also with the strength exercise drawings in the last chapter. I recommend following this stretching order at the end of a workout. You can do most of these stretches while holding your bike for balance.

Stork Stand

(Quadriceps)

1. While balancing against your bike or a wall, grasp your right foot behind your back with your left hand.
2. Static-stretch by gently pulling your hand up and away from your butt.
3. Keep your head up and stand erect—do not bend over at the waist.
4. Contract by pushing against your hand with your foot, more gently at first.
5. Repeat with other leg.

Use this stretch in the weight room during the hip extension and seated knee extension exercises.

Triangle

(Hamstrings)

1. Bend over at the waist while leaning on your bike or a wall.
2. Place the leg to be stretched forward with the foot about 18 inches from the bike.
3. The other leg is directly behind the first. The farther back you place this leg, the greater the stretch.
4. With your weight on the front foot, sag your upper body toward the floor. You should feel the stretch in the hamstring of your forward leg.
5. Contract the forward leg by trying to pull it backward against the floor. There will be no movement.
6. Repeat with other leg.

Use this stretch in the weight room during the hip extension and leg curl exercises.

Figure 13.1
Stork stand

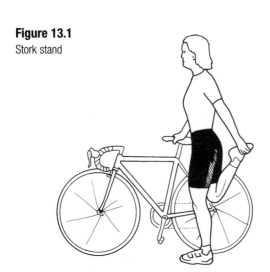

Figure 13.2
Triangle

Pull-down

(Latissimus Dorsi, Trapezius, Pectoralis, and Triceps)

1. Hold onto your bike or a railing for balance, with your weight resting on your arms.
2. Allow your head to sag deeply between outstretched arms to create a stretch in your lats.
3. To contract, pull down with your arms.

In the weight room do this stretch with seated lat pulls to chest, chest press, and seated rows.

Squat

(Low Back, Calves, Quadriceps, Gluteus)

1. Using your bike for balance, squat down keeping your heels on the floor. (This is easier with cycling shoes off.)
2. Allow your butt to sag close to your heels as you rock forward. Hold this position for about thirty seconds. (There is no contraction for this stretch.)

Do this stretch during back extension strength exercises in the weight room.

Wall Lean

(Calves)

1. Lean against a wall with the leg to be stretched straight behind you and the other forward holding most of your weight.
2. Keep the heel of the rear foot on the floor with the toe pointed forward.
3. The farther forward your hips move the greater the stretch in your calf.
4. To contract the calf, push against the wall as if trying to push it away using your leg.
5. Repeat with other leg.

Use this stretch in the weight room during the heel raise exercise.

Figure 13.3
Pull-down

Figure 13.4
Squat

Figure 13.5
Wall lean

References

Alter, M.J. *Sport Stretch*. Champaign, IL: Human Kinetics, 1998.

Anderson, B. *Stretching*. Bolinas, CA: Shelter Publications, 1980.

Avela, J., et al. "Altered Reflex Sensitivity after Repeated and Prolonged Passive Muscle Stretching." *Journal of Applied Physiology* 84, no. 4 (1999): 1283–1291.

Fowles, J.R., and D.G. Sale. "Time Course of Strength Deficit after Maximal Passive Stretch in Humans." *Medicine and Sciences in Sport and Exercise* 29, no. 5 (1997): S155.

Gleim, G.W., and M.P. McHugh. "Flexibility and Its Effects on Sports Injury and Performance." *Sports Medicine* 24, no. 5 (1997): 289–299.

Goldspink, D.F. "The Influence of Immobilization and Stretch on Protein Turnover of Rat Skeletal Muscle." *Journal of Physiology* 264 (1977): 267–282.

Holly, R.G., et al. "Stretch-Induced Growth in Chicken Wing Muscles: A New Model of Stretch Hypertrophy." *American Journal of Physiology* 7 (1980): C62–C71.

Kokkonen, J., et al. "Acute Muscle Stretching Inhibits Maximal Strength Performance." *Research Quarterly for Exercise and Sport* 69 (1998): 411–415.

Schatz, M.P. "Easy Hamstring Stretches." *Physician and Sports Medicine* 22, no. 2 (1994): 115–116.

Vanderburgh, H., and S. Kaufman. "Stretch and Skeletal Myotube Growth: What is the Physical to Biochemical Linkage?" *Frontiers of Exercise Biology*, K. Borer, D. Edington, and T. White (eds.). Champaign, IL: Human Kinetics, 1983.

Wallin, D., et al. "Improvement of Muscle Flexibility: A Comparison between Two Techniques." *The American Journal of Sports Medicine* 13, no. 4 (1985): 263–268.

UNIQUE NEEDS

I'm a 42-year-old in a 20-year-old's body.
—KENT BOSTICK,
Olympian at age 42 and again at age 46

Wouldn't it be easy if there was a "training formula?" Sometimes I wish there was. Every day I get questions from athletes asking how they should do this or that in their training. They typically tell me their ages, how long they have been in the sport, and their categories. Then they present a training problem to me along with a question of how they should deal with it. I guess most athletes believe there is a body of information out there someplace that allows me to simply answer these questions much as a skilled auto mechanic might do when asked about a 1993 Chevy Caprice that burns oil. It isn't that easy.

On the other hand, I think it's good that we don't have such a one-size-fits-all training formula. That would take all of the fun out of the individualized experience of training. As I've said throughout this book: Training is as much an art as a science. A unique blending of personal experiences with research produces an "art form" called performance. While science can postulate and predict a lot of what to expect when certain elements of human physiology and exercise are combined, it is not even close to being able to state with certainty the outcomes of a given training program for a given individual. In the final analysis, we are each unique and must experiment to find what works best. That makes it fun.

Much of what is presented in this chapter is based on my experiences as a coach and not just on scientific research. I have coached male and female athletes, both young and old and with widely varying experience levels, since 1971. With each of those athletes I've had to make some adjustments in training—no two followed exactly the same program. Some of the adjustments were small, while others were significant. This chapter summarizes the most important changes to what you have read in the previous chapters when it comes to the training of women, masters, and juniors.

Women

Throughout most of the twentieth century there were few sports that women were officially allowed to compete in on a scale even approaching that of men. They were "protected." The most popular—and "ladylike"—sports throughout most of this period were tennis, golf, gymnastics, and figure skating. At about mid-century, women began challenging the restrictions placed on them, especially when it came to endurance sports. As a result, women made considerable progress toward full acceptance in endurance sports in the latter years of the previous century.

The change was quite evident in the sport of track and field. In the 1928 Olympic Games in Amsterdam, for example, the longest race in which women were allowed to compete was the 800-meter run. In that Olympiad, three female runners broke the world record for the distance, but finished in "such a distressed condition" that officials were horrified and dropped the event from future competition. "Women just weren't meant to run that far," was the position of many male officials and even scientists. It wasn't until the 1964 Tokyo Games that the women's 800-meter run was resurrected in the Olympics.

Cycling has had its ups and downs when it comes to equality of the sexes but has generally reflected the same attitudes. In the 1890s, the "Golden Age" of cycling, at a time when society often closeted and sheltered the "weaker sex," women were nonetheless accepted into mass-start races alongside men. It wasn't until many years later that this attitude of near-equality changed and women were discouraged from racing bikes. Then, in the last few decades of the twentieth century, attitudes began to shift again.

Unique Considerations

A couple of years ago, a particularly thorough female professional cyclist was interviewing me as a potential coach. One of the questions she asked was a good one: Is there any difference between the way men and women should train? My answer was simple: No. Perhaps it was *too* simple. There are some things women could do differently than men to improve their performance.

There is no getting around the obvious male-female differences. Hip width, short torsos relative to leg length, and a low center of gravity all certainly affect the equipment a woman uses. There are other differences. Numerous studies have demonstrated that elite women athletes have aerobic capacities somewhat below that of elite men. The highest VO_2max ever recorded for a man was 94 ml/kg/min while the highest woman's aerobic power measured was 77 ml/kg/min—both Nordic skiers. Absolute muscular power outputs of women are also well below those of men. In comparison with male athletes, women riders carry a higher percentage of body weight as fat and can generate less absolute force due to their smaller muscle mass. These differences result in about a 10-percent variance in the results of world-class competitions involving males and females, in events ranging from weight lifting to sprinting to endurance sports like bike racing.

In the real world of racing, there are actually more similarities between male and female athletes at comparable levels of sport than there are differences. Women are capable of training at the same volume levels as men, and they respond to training in essentially the same ways. Except for absolute magnitude of workload, there is not much difference in the way the two sexes should train. But there are a few opportunities for individual women to improve relative to their competition that men seldom, if ever, have. Here are five that may give you an edge.

Quantity versus Quality

Even though women are fully capable of training at the same volume as men, do they need to? Women's races typically evolve in a way unlike men's. First of all, women's road races aren't as long—sometimes no more than half the men's distance. I have no hard evidence to back this up, but it seems that women's races are, therefore, more likely to end in a pack sprint. But then a rider, or better, a couple of riders, who are strong enough to break from the women's field early in the race, are more likely to stay off the front and finish ahead of the field than in a men's race.

What all of this means is that women road racers should concentrate more on the quality of their training than on their mileage. Not that building an aerobic base with long, steady rides is unimportant—it certainly is. A woman, however, must place more emphasis on developing her muscular endurance, power, and anaerobic endurance for the unique demands of her shorter and relatively faster race. Somewhat shifting the emphasis of training from volume to these abilities is likely to produce better results in women's road races.

Strength

The average woman's total body strength is about a third less than the average man's, but that difference isn't distributed equally. Women are relatively stronger in their legs and weaker in the abdominal region and arms. While women do not race against men, this comparison makes it apparent where a woman's greatest opportunity for improvement lies. By increasing the strength of her arms and abdominal region, a woman can improve her climbing and sprinting relative to her competition. Powerful riding out of the saddle requires strength to stabilize the upper body against the torque applied by the legs. Spaghetti arms and an accordion abdominal muscle dissipate the force produced by the legs.

Upper-body strength work to improve this relative weakness involves pushing and pulling exercises that use all the arm joints plus the back and the abdominals. Abdominal strength also needs emphasizing due to the size and shape of the female pelvis. Whenever possible, work the arms in conjunction with the abdominal and back muscles, rather than in isolation. The seated-row exercise described in Chapter 12 is a good example of a multi-joint exercise that benefits cycling. This station builds the arms and back in a way similar to climbing on a bike. The chest press will also provide muscular balance.

I generally recommend that women riders continue to lift weights year-round, even in the summer racing months. Otherwise, strength may soon be lost after a winter of focused weight room work.

Psychology

Society expects less of women in sports and offers less—less media coverage, less prize money, less crowd support, and less time to train due to greater family responsibilities. That women make it in sport is a testament to their perseverance and dedication.

Despite the socio-cultural obstacles, I have found that women have a somewhat healthier view of winning and losing than do men. Since women typically strive to attain personal standards and are less preoccupied with defeating other riders, they are less devastated by losing and recover faster emotionally. Men take losing, when they feel they should have won, as a mark against their "manhood."

Women, however, carry even heavier and deeper psychological baggage than men in another area. Women are more likely to associate poor performance with lack of ability. After all, society taught most women that sport was for boys, and girls were not particularly good at it. When men have a bad race, they tend to view the problem as a lack of effort—ability is not the issue.

Confidence is as important for success in sport as physical ability. No matter how talented you are, if you don't believe you can, you won't. A good example of this is a female cyclist I once coached. She frequently had reasons why she couldn't achieve her high goals and generally thought of herself as inferior to the other women she raced with. She often commented on her limitations and failures. A lack of confidence was her greatest limiter.

I suggested that every night after turning the lights off and before falling asleep, she should use those few minutes in bed to review and relive the major success of her day, no matter how small it seemed. It could simply be that she finished a tough workout feeling strong, or that she climbed one hill particularly well, or that one interval felt especially good. She would recapture that experience in her mind and go to sleep feeling good about her ability.

I also told her to act as if she was the best rider in the peloton. Look at the best riders in your group. How do they sit on their bikes, talk with others, and generally behave? Mimic their behaviors by sitting proudly and confidently on the bike, by looking others in the eye when talking with them, and by acting as if you are the best woman in the field. It's amazing how the mind reacts when the body says, "I'm confident."

I knew that she had a voice in her head that was frequently telling her she was not any good. We all hear this voice from time to time. I told her that when she heard the voice starting to put her down to regain control of her mind by immediately mentally reliving her latest, greatest success. Never let the voice take control of the mind.

That year she had her best season ever, winning a national championship and finishing fifth at the world championship. It's hard to know exactly what the impetus for her obviously improved confidence was, but I believe part of it came from simply looking for success in her daily rides, acting as if she were the top rider and taking control of her mind.

Diet

Due to a greater propensity to store body fat, women athletes tend to restrict their caloric intake, especially from foods high in fat and protein. And yet high protein intake has been shown as more necessary for endurance athletes than for the population at large. A low-protein diet can easily cause a decline in aerobic capacity, while producing fatigue and anemia in women cyclists.

Many women cyclists consume fewer than 2,000 calories a day but often require more than 3,000. With an average of 5 milligrams of iron per 1,000 calories in the typical American diet, a female athlete may only be getting 10 milligrams daily, but she needs 15 milligrams. Vegetarian diets, favored by many women, are even lower in iron and provide a less absorbable type of iron. Exercise and menstruation further decrease iron levels. Over the course of several weeks, borderline iron deficiency or even anemia can creep up on a female athlete. Owen Anderson, Ph.D., the publisher of *Running Research News*, estimates that 30 percent of women athletes have an iron deficiency. One study even linked low iron with an increase in running injuries in high school girls.

Eating more calories or including red meat are ways to solve these dilemmas, although not popular ones for many women. There are other ways to improve iron intake and absorption including eating high-iron-content foods with orange juice or vitamin C, eating certain foods such as spinach, and cooking in iron skillets with acidic tomato sauces. It may also be a good idea to talk with a health-care provider about supplementing with iron. Don't supplement iron without medical guidance. It is also wise to avoid food products that hinder iron absorption such as tea, wheat bran, antacids, and calcium phosphate supplements. Women, indeed all riders, should have their blood tested in the winter to establish an iron-level baseline.

Also frequently restricted in the female diet are foods high in fat. Dietary fat is necessary for peak performance. A body deprived of essential fats is in danger of being run-down and susceptible to illness, due to a weakened immune system. If sick, injured, or tired, you can't perform at your best. Include fat in your diet every day from good sources such as nuts, nut spreads, avocados, and canola and olive oil. Continue to avoid saturated fat and trans fatty acids, which are found in foods with hydrogenated fat, such as snack foods and prepackaged meals. Chapter 16 provides more details on the athlete's diet.

Contraceptives and Performance

A study at the University of Illinois showed that women who are on the pill may have an advantage in endurance sports such as cycling. During long endurance runs at a low intensity, women taking oral contraceptives showed an increase in growth hormone. They used significantly find carbohydrates and more fat for fuel than those women not taking the pill. This suggests that using oral contraceptives may improve a woman's capacity for burning fat, may allow her to get into shape faster, and may extend her endurance range in races. I am not aware of any other studies that have tested this finding, so the results should be taken with some reservation.

If you are not currently using an oral contraceptive, talk with your health-care provider before starting. Don't take the pill only for race-performance reasons.

Masters

A few years ago I spoke at an American College of Sports Medicine workshop in New York City. The topic for the workshop was masters athletes—those over the age of 40. For two hours before my presentation I listened as one doctor after another talked about "normal" performance declining with aging.

When I finally got my turn to speak, I was beginning to think we were all supposed to give up sports as we got older. I told the audience not to believe half of what they had been hearing. The reason people slow down so much after age 40 is not as much physiology as it is psychology. We think we should be slower.

I reminded the audience of 41-year-old Eamonn Coghlan, the first person over 40 to run under four minutes for the mile. He didn't do this by reading statistics on what is supposed to happen with age. I pointed to 40-year-old Dave Scott, who was planning a comeback at that year's Ironman—not to just finish, but to win (he finished second). And Mark Spitz, who took a serious shot at making the 1992 U.S. Olympic swim team twenty years after his seven gold medals in Munich. Then there was Carlos Lopes who, at age 37, won the Olympic marathon. And Kent Bostick, 42, who surprised everyone by qualifying for the 1996 Olympics by defeating 28-year-old Mike McCarthy by nearly one second in the 4,000-meter pursuit (Bostick qualified again for the 2000 Olympics at age 46).

These aging athletes are just the tip of the iceberg. There are hundreds of masters in the world of sport who are within seconds or inches of their best performances of all time. In the last ten years, there has been tremendous growth in the number of USCF members who are over 40. Between 1984 and 1993 there was a 75-percent increase in the number of members in their forties. In 1996, 20 percent of USCF racers were over 40. What just fifteen years ago was a young man's sport has become a sport for both sexes and all ages.

Ability and Age

There's no denying that there's a loss of ability for racing with advancing age. The best indicators of this in road cycling are age group records for the individual time trial (ITT). The 40k records reveal an average slowing of twenty seconds per year, about 0.6 percent, after the age of 35. For the 20k, ITT times slow about 12 seconds per year from age 20 to 65—a 0.7-percent decline per decade of life.

These small drops in performance result from continuing losses of the three basic abilities—endurance, force, and speed skills. While longitudinal studies of highly-trained athletes are few and far between, it appears that the decline of each of these abilities is similar to what the ITT records show—about 6 percent per decade. That is well below the expected decline of 10 percent per decade that's found in the "normal" population after age 25.

Since the 1930s, scientists have studied the link between aging and physiological function. One inescapable conclusion has come from this research: Getting older inevitably means some degree of reduced function. Aerobic capacity (VO_2max) decline is a good example of what the studies show.

You may recall from Chapter 4 that aerobic capacity is a measure of how much oxygen the body uses to produce energy at a maximal workload. The higher one's aerobic capacity, the greater his or her potential for performance will be in an event like bike racing. Studies show that starting at about age 20, aerobic capacity begins to drop in the general population, in part because maximum heart rate decreases. A lowered maximum heart rate means less oxygen delivery to the muscles, and therefore a lowered aerobic capacity. The usual rate of decline measured in such research is in the range of six to ten beats per decade.

Similar results have come from aging studies on the pulmonary, nervous, muscular, thermal regulatory, immune, and anaerobic systems: Sometime in the third and fourth decades of life (ages 20 to 39), functional decreases begin, with losses of up to 10 percent per decade. Compounding the problem is what appears to be a normal increase in body fat after the early twenties, obviously made worse by a sedentary lifestyle. Again, this is for the general population—not those who race bikes or are highly active.

Flexibility is also lost with age. This is in part due to a drop in the amount of body fluids the body can store in later life. An aging immune system doesn't work as well as it once did, either—a good reason to take antioxidants. Then there's heat. Getting older means not sweating as much in hot, dry conditions, yet our urinary systems are more effective at flushing water, thus decreasing blood volume. To make matters worse, the thirst mechanism isn't as sensitive as it once was. All of this means a greater likelihood of overheating and dehydrating.

The Aging Myth

A little skepticism is a healthy thing when it comes to research. Most studies of aging are based on "cross-sectional" analysis. This means, for example, that a group of 30-year-olds and a similar group of 40-year-olds are tested for some parameter of fitness, and the difference is assumed as the normal loss.

The alternative is "longitudinal" research, which involves following a group of subjects for several years, testing regularly to see how they change. This method has many benefits. Time is an obvious downside, however, so there are few longitudinal studies of athletes.

Research on aging also raises the question of who the subjects are. Many studies characterize the subjects as "trained endurance athletes." This vague description is usually based on measures of training volume, such as years of activity, or hours of training in a week. Definitions vary. One study's trained endurance athlete may be another study's novice. Seldom is the intensity of training used to categorize the groups studied, as it is hard to quantify. But since it appears that intensity is the key to maintaining race fitness, this is a crucial issue.

The few longitudinal studies that have been done show that when the intensity of training is maintained, aerobic capacity and other selected measures of fitness decline as little as 2 percent per decade. This is roughly a third to a fifth of what is usually discovered in sedentary subjects, or even in those who maintain their health and continue exercising at low intensities.

The "normal" decline in performance of 6 to 10 percent per decade is probably more a result of self-imposed training and lifestyle limitations than it is of human physiology. Aging may actually only account for a fourth of the losses, while disuse takes the bigger bite.

Beating the Curve

While slowing down with age to some extent may be inevitable beyond some number of years, many riders have found that the rate of decline can be dramatically reduced by a willingness to train with the same high intensity and volume as they did when they were younger. In fact, some of the top masters riders are even doing more now than in previous decades. One scientific study has shown that it's possible to maintain aerobic capacity, a good indicator of fitness, for ten years past your youth. Another has demonstrated that aerobic capacity drops of 2 percent or less can be accomplished well into an athlete's fifties.

The bottom line is that intense training keeps the heart, nerves, muscles, lungs, and other systems all working to their genetic potential. If you never exercise at high intensity, you will lose fitness, and possibly health, more rapidly than is necessary. For those beyond the age of 40, the following training guidelines will help to keep fitness high and, for some, even improving.

Training Implications

How willing and able are you to train as much as you did when younger—or even more? Here are some suggestions for improving your racing even as you get older.

- Strength train year-round. While younger and more naturally muscular athletes may stop strength training in the late winter, masters should continue throughout the year. The stronger you are, the more force you can apply to the pedal. Greater strength means lower perceived exertions at all levels of power output.

- Train a minimum of seven to ten hours a week on average throughout the year. That means an annual volume of at least 350 to 500 hours.

- Take a full twelve weeks in the Base period. Don't cut it short. You must maximize your endurance, force, and speed skills before upping the intensity. Be sure to stay proficient at spinning at high cadences.

- Once you have established your base fitness, put less emphasis than younger riders do on endurance and more on power, anaerobic endurance, and muscular endurance. That means greater attention to jumps, sprints, intervals, and time trialing than to long workouts. Your longest ride should be only as long as your longest race time.

- After you have established your base, allow for more recovery time between workouts than you had in the past. Few masters can handle more than two or three high-quality workouts a week and get away with it for long. Many masters have found it is possible to race quite well on two breakthrough workouts a week. For example, in the Build period, at mid-week combine a muscular-endurance workout with anaerobic endurance or power, doing the faster portion first. Then recover for two or three days and complete a high-intensity group ride or tune-up race on the weekend. Take a day off the bike every week. If you find recovery to be especially difficult, change the pattern of weekly training hours in Table 8.5, so that there are only two weeks between recovery weeks instead of three. Omit the first week in each case. You may find that with only two weeks of hard training, you need only five days or so of recovery before starting the next cycle. So consider training with a pattern of sixteen days of hard training, followed by five days of R & R. Or maybe you'll find that a 15-6 pattern works best at certain times of the season. This will take some experimentation.

- Train in the heat once or twice a week during the summer, including higher-intensity workouts on hot days once you feel adapted. Be especially cautious with your levels of hydration. Drink a 16-ounce bottle of sports drink every hour during a ride whether you feel like it or not. Sip water throughout the day even if you don't feel thirsty.

- Stretch after every workout and again later in the day. Try to become more flexible now than you've been in years. You can do it if you are dedicated.

- In road races, stay in the front third from the start. Due to the wide range in abilities and experience levels at masters races, the groups tend to break up sooner than senior races do.

Diet, Aging, and Muscle

Popeye was right: Eating spinach can make you stronger and more muscular, especially if you're over age 50. Let me explain.

It's apparent that as we grow older muscle mass is lost. Although this loss is slowed somewhat by weight lifting and vigorous aerobic exercise, it still happens. Even athletes in their sixties typically demonstrate considerably less muscle than they had in their forties.

Now there is research that shows why. Nitrogen, an essential component of muscle protein, is given up by the body at a faster rate than it can be taken in as we get older. This is due to a gradual change in kidney function that comes with aging, ultimately producing an acidic state in the blood. Essentially, we are peeing off our muscles as we pass the half-century mark in life.

Also, with a net loss of nitrogen, new muscle cannot be formed. This same acidic state of the blood also explains why calcium is lost with aging resulting in osteoporosis for many, especially women, with advanced age.

The key to reducing, or even avoiding, this situation is to lower the blood's acid level and increasing its alkalinity. There are studies demonstrating that taking a supplement called potassium bicarbonate daily for as few as eighteen days increases the blood's alkaline level by balancing nitrogen in the body. While it can be purchased relatively inexpensively in laboratory supply shops, potassium bicarbonate is not currently available as an over-the-counter supplement, and there are no long-term studies of its effects on health. There is some evidence that it contributes to irregular ECG readings.

But there is also a natural way of achieving this same result through diet by eating foods that naturally increase the blood's alkalinity—fruits and vegetables. Fats and oils have a neutral effect on blood acid. In other words, they don't make it either more acidic or more alkaline. All other foods, including grains, meats, nuts, beans, dairy, fish, and eggs, increase the blood's acidity. If your diet is high in these latter foods but low in fruits and vegetables, you can expect to lose muscle mass and bone calcium as you age.

A study by T. Remer and F. Manz ranks foods in terms of their effect on blood acidity and alkalinity. For example, the food that has the most acidic effect, therefore contributing to a loss of nitrogen and ultimately muscle, is parmesan cheese. The food Remer found to have the greatest alkaline effect thus reducing nitrogen and muscle loss is raisins. Among vegetables, spinach was the most alkaline food. See what I mean? Popeye was right.

Table 14.1 ranks common foods (per 100-gram portions) and their effect on alkalinity and acidity taken from Remer's study. The higher a food's positive acidic ranking, the more likely it is to contribute to a loss of muscle mass and bone-mineral levels. The more negative the food's alkaline ranking, the more beneficial is the effect is on these measures.

Juniors

In 1982, my son Dirk competed in his first bicycle race at age 12. On that cold September day, he raced three laps around the block in baggy windpants with a big smile on his face and finished dead last. But he was hooked. From this inauspicious start, Dirk went on to win the junior Colorado Road Race Championship, make the U.S. national team, race as an amateur in Europe for five years, turn pro at age 22 and continue racing as a pro into his thirties.

Table 14.1
Acidic Ranking of Common Foods

ACID FOODS (+)		ALKALINE FOODS (–)	
GRAINS		**FRUITS**	
Brown rice	+12.5	Raisins	–21.0
Rolled oats	+10.7	Black currants	–6.5
Whole wheat bread	+8.2	Bananas	–5.5
Spaghetti	+6.5	Apricots	–4.8
Corn flakes	+6.0	Kiwi fruit	–4.1
White rice	+4.6	Cherries	–3.6
Rye bread	+4.1	Pears	–2.9
White bread	+3.7	Pineapple	–2.7
DAIRY		Peaches	–2.4
Parmesan cheese	+34.2	Apples	–2.2
Processed cheese	+28.7	Watermelon	–1.9
Hard cheese	+19.2	**VEGETABLES**	
Gouda cheese	+18.6	Spinach	–14.0
Cottage cheese	+8.7	Celery	–5.2
Whole milk	+0.7	Carrots	–4.9
LEGUMES		Zucchini	–4.6
Peanuts	+8.3	Cauliflower	–4.0
Lentils	+3.5	Potatoes	–4.0
Peas	+1.2	Radishes	–3.7
MEATS, FISH, EGGS		Eggplant	–3.4
Trout	+10.8	Tomatoes	–3.1
Turkey	+9.9	Lettuce	–2.5
Chicken	+8.7	Chicory	–2.0
Eggs	+8.1	Leeks	–1.8
Pork	+7.9	Onions	–1.5
Beef	+7.8	Mushrooms	–1.4
Cod	+7.1	Green peppers	–1.4
Herring	+7.0	Broccoli	–1.2
		Cucumber	–0.8

How to Improve

As a junior, Dirk was an exceptional athlete, one in whom I saw a great deal of promise. I wanted to coach him, but knew that would not work. A father is a young athlete's worst possible mentor, so I hired Pat Nash, a local coach who specialized in juniors, to work with my son. Dirk's early and continuing success was largely due to Pat's careful nurturing. I was not interested in how many races Dirk could win as a teenager. My major concern, which I expressed to Pat, was that Dirk still be enthusiastically riding, racing, and improving at age 25. A good coach helped to make that possible.

If you are a junior and new to racing, try to find a coach who has a local team and rides along on workouts. You and the coach will get to know each other better that way, and he or she will be better able to help you grow as a racer. Avoid coaches and teams more concerned about winning the next race than in developing the team tactics, skills, and fitness that come from a long-term approach.

Another way to speed up your progress is by attending a camp for juniors. These are usually staffed with one or more coaches and, perhaps, with elite riders. In a few days you can learn a lot about training and racing. Check in the advertising sections at the backs of cycling magazines and on the Web for camps that may be available in your area. If the only camps available in your area are for senior riders, call the camp director and ask if it would be appropriate for you to attend.

Cycling clubs are also good for providing support, expertise, racing experience, and the camaraderie of other juniors. Join a club if there is one in your region, and try to ride with the members as often as you can. You'll learn a lot just from being around more experienced athletes. Also ask the club to provide events for juniors at their sponsored races, if they don't already do so.

On a slightly different note, you and your parents have probably come to realize that cycling is an expensive sport. Don't be concerned with having the latest and greatest frame, wheels, and pedals. Instead, concentrate on becoming the best motor and the most knowledgeable and skilled rider in your category. When it's time to replace a bike you've outgrown, talk with other juniors about purchasing a bike for which they've also gotten too big. In the same way, see if younger athletes can use your old bike. Regardless of what you may read in the magazines and what others say, the key to improvement is not equipment, but fitness, bike-racing savvy, and skills.

Training

When your school sports end for the year and bike training starts, it's necessary to keep things in perspective. Remember that you're not an accomplished cyclist yet; there is a lot of room for improvement, and steady growth is necessary to eventually achieve your potential. Professional cyclists didn't start off training with huge volumes and lots of intense workouts. They progressed steadily from year to year, a little at a time. Following are suggested guidelines for maintaining a healthy perspective and steady growth.

By age 17, you and your coach should develop an Annual Training Plan like that described in Part IV. Prior to age 17, your training should be mostly centered on the basic abilities of force, endurance, and speed skills with occasional races. In your early years as a cyclist, it is best that you participate in at least one other sport. Even the top champions such as Miguel Indurain and Lance Armstrong did this. Lance was a world-class junior triathlete before he took up bike racing. Don't specialize in cycling before the age of 17—your long-term development will be greater because of this.

In the first two years of riding, when you are participating in other sports, an annual training volume of 200 to 350 hours is best. By age 17, you should be able to increase the volume, if you have been handling that level without difficulty. But do so gradually. More is not always better, and often worse.

Each year the number of races you enter should increase a little until, by age 18, you are racing as often as seniors. When you begin to race, emphasize team tactics more than winning. Learn what it takes to break away, to legally block, to work with other riders in a break, to lead out a teammate, and to sprint. Cycling is much like football or basketball in this respect—teamwork produces greater results than everyone riding only for themselves.

Regardless of your age when you begin to do weight room strength workouts, the first year should include only the Anatomical Adaptation (AA) phase. Working both with machines and free weights, perfect your lifting form for each exercise in this first season. In the second year of strength training, it's okay to start the Maximum Strength (MS) phase in the weight room. The first time you do the MS phase use a weight no greater than 80 percent of your estimated one-repetition maximum. Don't worry about finding a one-repetition max. Use the guidelines for estimating it from multiple reps as described in Chapter 12. The most common injury that occurs in juniors starting to lift weights is to the lower back. Be careful. By the third year you should be ready to move into more serious weight work, assuming you are at least 17 by then.

Before the start of each season get a complete physical from your doctor. This is something even the pros do. It will allow you and your coach to start the year with a "clean bill of health."

When you purchase a handlebar computer, look for one that displays cadence. This is useful for helping you improve leg speed.

Patience

Always try to remember that you are in bicycle racing for the long haul. That's easy to say, but there will be times when you want to accelerate the program and do more because one of your friends is. Before you change the plan, talk with your coach.

In his book, *Greg LeMond's Complete Book of Bicycling*, LeMond describes how when he was 15 he wanted to ride even more since one of his friends was putting in twice as much mileage. He was smart, however, and held back. The next year his friend was out of cycling, and LeMond went on to become one of America's greatest cyclists. Be patient.

Have Fun

Always remember why you race. It certainly isn't for money or glory—these are far more abundant in sports like football and basketball. You're probably racing bikes for the personal challenge, for the enjoyment of having exceptional fitness, and, most of all, for fun. Keep that perspective. Win with humility, lose with dignity, congratulate those who beat you without offering excuses, and learn from mistakes.

References

Bemben, D.A., et al. "Effects of Oral Contraceptives on Hormonal and Metabolic Responses during Exercise." *Medicine and Science in Sport and Exercise* 24, no. 4 (1992).

Bompa, T. *From Childhood to Champion Athlete*. Veritas Publishing, 1995.

Brown, C., and J. Wilmore. "The Effects of Maximal Resistance Training on the Strength and Body Composition of Women Athletes." *Medicine and Science in Sports* 6 (1974): 174–177.

Chamari, K., et al. "Anaerobic and Aerobic Peak Power and the Force-Velocity Relationship in Endurance-Trained Athletes: Effects of Aging." *European Journal of Applied Physiology* 71, no. 2-3 (1995): 230-234.

Child, J.S., et al. "Cardiac Hypertrophy and Function in Masters Endurance Runners and Sprinters." *Journal of Applied Physiology* 57 (1984): 170–181.

Cohen, J., and C.V. Gisolfi. "Effects of Interval Training in Work-Heat Tolerance in Young Women." *Medicine and Science in Sport and Exercise* 14 (1982): 46–52.

Cunningham, D.A., et al. "Cardiovascular Response to Intervals and Continuous Training in Women." *European Journal of Applied Physiology* 41 (1979): 187–197.

Dill, D., et al. "A Longitudinal Study of 16 Champion Runners." *Journal of Sports Medicine* 7 (1967): 4–32.

Drinkwater, B.L. (ed.). *Female Endurance Athletes*. Champaign, IL: Human Kinetics, 1986.

Drinkwater, B.L. "Women and Exercise: Physiological Aspects." *Exercise and Sports Sciences Reviews* 12 (1984): 21–51.

Ekblom, B. "Effect of Physical Training in Adolescent Boys." *Journal of Applied Physiology* 27 (1969): 350–353.

Frassetto, L.A., et al. "Effect of Age on Blood Acid-Base Composition in Adult Humans: Role of Age-Related Renal Function Decline." *American Journal of Physiology* 271, no. 6-2 (1996): F1114–1122.

Frassetto, L.A., et al. "Potassium Bicarbonate Reduces Urinary Nitrogen Excretion in Postmenopausal Women." *Journal of Endocrinology and Metabolism* 82, no. 1 (1997): 254–259.

Frontera, W.R., et al. "Aging of Skeletal Muscle: A 12-Year Longitudinal Study." *Journal of Applied Physiology* 4 (2000): 1321–1326.

Heath, G. "A Physiological Comparison of Young and Older Endurance Athletes." *Journal of Applied Physiology* 51, no. 3 (1981): 634–640.

Kent-Braun, J.A., et al. "Skeletal Muscle Oxidative Capacity in Young and Older Women and Men." *Journal of Applied Physiology* 89, no. 3 (2000): 1072–1078.

Legwold, G. "Masters Competitors Age Little in Ten Years." *The Physician and Sports Medicine* 10, no. 10 (1982): 27.

LeMond, G., and K. Gordis. G*reg LeMond's Complete Book of Bicycling.* New York: Perigee Books, 1988.

Mayhew, J., and P. Gross. "Body Composition Changes in Young Women and High Resistance Weight Training." *Research Quarterly* 45 (1974): 433–440.

Parizkova, J. "Body Composition and Exercise during Growth and Development." *Physical Activity: Human Growth and Development* (1974).

Pate, R.R., et al. "Cardiorespiratory and Metabolic Responses to Submaximal and Maximal Exercise in Elite Women Distance Runners." *International Journal of Sports Medicine* 8, no. 2 (1987): 91–95.

Pollock, M., et al. "Effect of Age and Training on Aerobic Capacity and Body Composition of Master Athletes." *Journal of Applied Physiology* 62, no. 2 (1987): 725–731.

Pollock, M., et al. "Frequency of Training as a Determinant for Improvement in Cardiovascular Function and Body Composition of Middle-aged Men.*" Archives of Physical Medicine and Rehabilitation* 56 (1975): 141–145.

Remer, T., and F. Manz. "Potential Renal Acid Load of Foods and Its Influence on Urine pH." *Journal of the American Dietetic Association* 95, no. 7 (1995): 791–797.

Rogers, et al. "Decline in VO$_2$max with Aging in Masters Athletes and Sedentary Men." *Journal of Applied Physiology* 68, no. 5 (1990): 2195–2199.

Roth, S.M., et al. "High-Volume, Heavy-Resistance Strength Training and Muscle Damage in Young and Older Men." *Journal of Applied Physiology* 88, no. 3 (2000): 1112–1119

Seals, D.R., et al. "Endurance Training in Older Men and Women." *Journal of Applied Physiology* 57 (1984): 1024–1029.

Sebastian, A., et al. "Improved Mineral Balance and Skeletal Metabolism in Postmenopausal Women Treated with Potassium Bicarbonate." *New England Journal of Medicine* 330, no. 25 (1994): 1776–1781.

Shangold, M.M., and G. Mirkin (eds.). *Women and Exercise: Physiology and Sports Medicine*. Philadelphia: F.A. Davis, 1988.

Shasby, G.B., and F.C. Hagerman." The Effects of Conditioning on Cardiorespiratory Function in Adolescent Boys." *Journal of Sports Medicine* 3 (1975): 97–107.

Wells, C.L. *Women, Sport, and Performance: A Physiological Perspective*. Champaign, IL: Human Kinetics, 1991.

Wilmore, J., et al. "Is There Energy Conservation in Amenorrheic Compared with Eumenorrheic Distance Runners?" *Journal of Applied Physiology* 72 (1992): 15–22.

Wilmore, J., and D. Costill. *Physiology of Sport and Exercise*. Champaign, IL: Human Kinetics, 1994.

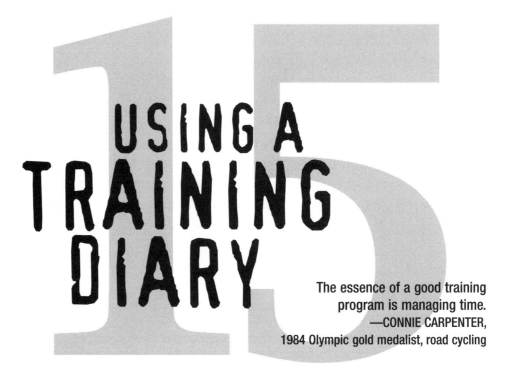

USING A TRAINING DIARY

The essence of a good training program is managing time.
—CONNIE CARPENTER,
1984 Olympic gold medalist, road cycling

Each athlete responds to training in a unique way. If two cyclists who test similarly do exactly the same workouts day after day, one will eventually become more fit than the other. One may even become *overtrained* on a regimen that the other thrives on. So it is critical that you follow a program designed just for you. To do otherwise is to place limits on your potential.

How can you determine what constitutes the optimum training method for your unique needs? While races and testing reveal how you're doing, learning the causes of your performance improvements or declines can be discovered in training records. Keeping a journal is your third most important task when not working out. It ranks right behind eating and resting.

In addition to offering the opportunity for keener analysis, a journal also helps you grow by increasing motivation. Motivation comes from recording successes such as training goals accomplished, higher levels of training, subjective feelings of achievement, and personal race performance records.

Be forewarned: Training diaries can be abused. I have known athletes who realized on Sunday afternoon they were a few miles or minutes short of their weekly goal and so they went out for a short ride to reach the magic number. This is how you go about building "junk" miles. Becoming overly invested in the numbers that you record causes problems. Instead of using your journal as a score card, think of it more as a diary—a place for important and personal information.

Planning with a Training Diary

The training diary is the best place to record your weekly training plan. Chapters 9 and 10 offered guidance in how to determine what workouts should be done each day. Figures 9.1 and 10.1 recommended specific daily training structure. The training diary pages provided in Appendix D bring the final pieces of the training plan together by providing a space to outline your planned workouts each day. Figure 15.1 is a sample diary to demonstrate how to log the critical information.

It is a good idea to plan the next week's training regimen at the end of each week. After reviewing how the preceding week went, sit down with your Annual Training Plan and jot down what you'll do and when you'll do it. Using the workout codes from Chapter 9 and the workout durations from Table 9.1 makes this quick and easy. Once you get used to it, planning an entire week in detail takes about ten minutes.

You don't have to use my training diary. Many athletes, indeed most elites, prefer to use a simple blank notebook in which they can record as much data as they want in any way they want. The only problem with such a system is that it makes recall and analysis laborious since you may have to search every page for the critical information. A standardized form makes these tasks much easier.

You can also choose to track and monitor your progress online. The Web-based training software available at www.TrainingBible.com offers a free daily workout log to record your workouts and graph your progress. The program also allows you to upload data from training devices such as heart rate monitors and powermeters.

At the top of Figure 15.1, there are spaces to write in three weekly goals. These are specific actions you need to accomplish in order to stay on track with your training objectives, which are in turn tied to season goals. Consistent success in achieving short-term, weekly goals brings long-term success.

Weekly goals should focus on what the BT workout and race objectives are for that week. If you properly selected weekly workouts based on your limiters and strengths, depending on what period of the season you're in, achieving their scheduled outcomes brings you one step closer to the season's goals. For example, if you've scheduled AE intervals (workout code A2) to include 5 x 4 minutes building to zone 5b on each, a weekly goal may be "twenty minutes of AE intervals." When you accomplish that goal check it off. By periodically scanning weekly goals, you have a quick check of how you're doing throughout the year.

What to Record

If you've never kept a journal, you may find record keeping a bit scattered at first. I ask the athletes I coach to record data in their journals in five categories.

Figure 15.1　　**WEEK BEGINNING:** *April 28*　**PLANNED WEEKLY HOURS/MILES:** *13:30*
~ 240 mi

NOTES

MON
3 sets of ME
felt strong

TUES
On trainer at 7 a.m.,
hard to get going.
Felt strong in zones
1-3, 4 was hard.
Good Workout

MONDAY			*4/28/03*
1 Sleep	*2* Fatigue	*2* Stress	*1* Soreness

Resting heart rate *64*　Weight *152*

WORKOUT 1 *Weights 3 x ME*

Weather

Route

Distance

Time *1:00*		Total *1:00*	
Time by zone	**1**		**2**
3	**4**		**5**

WORKOUT 2

Weather

Route

Distance

Time		Total	
Time by zone	**1**		**2**
3	**4**		**5**

TUESDAY			*4/29/03*
1 Sleep	*1* Fatigue	*1* Stress	*2* Soreness

Resting heart rate *62*　Weight *152*

WORKOUT 1 *M2, 4x6' (2' RI)*

Weather *36 F*

Route *Trainer*

Distance *29 mi*

Time *1:30*		Total *1:30*	
Time by zone	**1** *25:00*	**2** *42:00*	
3 *2:10*	**4** *18:20*	**5** *2:30*	

WORKOUT 2 *E1*

Weather *52 F*

Route *Trainer*

Distance *7 mi*

Time *0:30*		Total *0:30*	
Time by zone	**1** *0:30*		**2**
3	**4**		**5**

NOTES

WED
Tired all day.
Stressful day at
work. Rode w/ Bill.
Nice and easy to
unwind.

THURS
Only did 3 intervals.
Haven't fully recovered
from Tuesday and work
problems. Power
still pretty good.

WEDNESDAY			*4/30/03*
3 Sleep	*2* Fatigue	*3* Stress	*1* Soreness

Resting heart rate *67*　Weight *151*

WORKOUT 1 *E1*

Weather *68 F*

Route *Frontage Road*

Distance *46 mi*

Time *3:00*		Total *2:52*	
Time by zone	**1** *2:39*	**2** *0:13*	
3	**4**		**5**

WORKOUT 2

Weather

Route

Distance

Time		Total	
Time by zone	**1**		**2**
3	**4**		**5**

THURSDAY			*5/ 1/03*
3 Sleep	*5* Fatigue	*4* Stress	*1* Soreness

Resting heart rate *69*　Weight *150*

WORKOUT 1 *A2, 5x3' (3' RI)*

Weather *62 F, windy*

Route *Hwy 1*

Distance *20 mi*

Time *1:00*		Total *1:09*	
Time by zone	**1** *18:00*	**2** *30:00*	
3 *10:00*	**4** *3:10*	**5** *7:50*	

WORKOUT 2 *E1*

Weather *56 F, raining*

Route *Trainer*

Distance *6 mi*

Time *0:30*		Total *0:20*	
Time by zone	**1** *20:00*		**2**
3	**4**		**5**

WEEK'S GOALS (Check off as achieved)

X   24 minutes of cruise intervals

    15 minutes of SE intervals

X   Good effort for club ride

FRIDAY   5/ 2/03

2 Sleep 5 Fatigue 5 Stress 5 Soreness

Resting heart rate 68   Weight 151

WORKOUT 1 OFF

Weather

Route

Distance

Time   Total

Time by zone	1		2	
3		4		5

WORKOUT 2

Weather

Route

Distance

Time   Total

Time by zone	1		2	
3		4		5

SATURDAY   5/ 3/03

1 Sleep 3 Fatigue 2 Stress 1 Soreness

Resting heart rate 64   Weight 152

WORKOUT 1 A1

Weather 75 F

Route Big Loop

Distance 58 mi

Time 2:30   Total 2:40

Time by zone	1	22:00	2	36:00
3	35:00	4	42:40	5	24:20

WORKOUT 2

Weather

Route

Distance

Time   Total

Time by zone	1		2	
3		4		5

NOTES

Needed to take Fri. off. Came at the right time.

SAT
Club ride, big crowd. Everyone rode hard today.

SUNDAY   5/ 4/03

2 Sleep 3 Fatigue 1 Stress 3 Soreness

Resting heart rate 67   Weight 151

WORKOUT 1 E2

Weather 77 F

Route to Lyons

Distance 63 mi

Time 3:30   Total 3:32

Time by zone	1	1:44	2	1:48
3		4		5

WORKOUT 2

Weather

Route

Distance

Time   Total

Time by zone	1		2	
3		4		5

WEEKLY SUMMARY

	Weekly total	Year to date
Bike miles	229	2,800
Bike time	12:33	215:25
Strength time	1:00	29:30
Total	13:33	244:55

Soreness Quad's were sore, probably from Saturday's ride

Notes   Club ride was my first race effort of the year—a real eye opener! Long way to go. Stress didn't help. Feel great about Tuesday's intervals.

NOTES

SUN
Nice day for a long ride. Feeling yesterday's workout in my quad's. Will get massage tomorrow.

- Morning warnings
- Workout basics
- Time by zone
- Physical comments
- Mental comments

Morning Warnings

Every morning on waking your body "whispers" what it can handle that day. The problem is, most of us refuse to listen. A journal helps the body be heard if certain indicators of readiness are studied. These are sleep quality, fatigue, stress level, muscle soreness, and heart rate. The first four should be rated on a scale of 1 to 7, with 1 being the best situation (for example, an excellent night's sleep) and 7 the worst (for example, extremely high stress).

Take your pulse while still lying quietly in bed and record it in beats per minute above (positive number) or below (negative number) your average morning pulse rate that was found during a R & R week. If you record a 5, 6, or 7 for any of the first four indicators or a positive or negative 5 or greater for heart rate, consider that a warning that something is wrong.

Another way of taking resting heart rate that has been shown as a more reliable indicator with some athletes, is to take lying-down pulse as described above and then to stand for twenty seconds and take the pulse again. A heart rate monitor is best in this case. The variance in difference between the two is the indicator. An example may better explain this method:

Lying-down heart rate	46
Standing heart rate	72
Difference	26

Record your variance from a normal difference in the "HR above/below normal" box. For example, if your average difference over several days is found to be 26, but one day the difference is 32, record a variance of +6—a warning sign for that day. This may be a better warning method for you than simply tracking the lying-down heart rate. You may be able to determine which method is better for you by doing both for three to four weeks during a period of hard training.

Two morning warning scores of 5 or higher mean reduce training intensity today. Three or more morning warnings means your body is telling you to take the day off— you need more recovery. Failure to heed the morning warnings your body is whispering to you forces it to eventually "shout" by giving you a cold or by leaving you too exhausted to work out for several days. Ratings of 4 or less are generally good signs that your body is ready for serious training. The lower the scores, the harder the workout can be any given day.

A study at the University of Queensland in Australia showed these indicators to be relatively reliable measures of overtraining and burnout. But they are not necessarily the best for everyone. You may find others that work better for you. If so, record them in the same manner.

Checking and recording body weight every morning after visiting the bathroom and before eating can also reveal the state of your body. Short-term weight loss is a measure of fluid levels, so if your weight is down a pound from the previous day, the first thing you should do is drink water. A pint of water weighs about one pound. A study done in Oregon found that afternoon weight loss is also a good indicator of overtraining and may be the easiest-to-measure initial indicator. (Chapter 17 discusses overtraining in greater detail.)

Workout Basics

This is the detail stuff that will help you remember the workout months later. Specify any changes made to your training plan in the Notes section. Record the distance, weather, route, and other varables such as equipment used (for example, mountain bike or fixed gear bike).

Time by Zone

Each day of the training journal has space to record data for two workouts. The first workout section provides spaces to write in the time spent in each training zone for the first workout of the day. This could be heart rate or power data and serves as a good check of how the workout profile went in relation to the plan. A few weeks or even a year later you can compare this information following a repeat of the same workout.

Fill in the actual duration of your workout to the right of your planned time. This should be about the same as the planned duration.

The second workout section is completed in the same way for the second daily workout. If you worked out just once, leave it blank.

Physical Comments

Observing how you are performing in workouts and races is critical to measuring progress. After each workout, record such information as average heart rate, heart rate at the end of work intervals, highest heart rates observed, and average speed. If you have sophisticated equipment, you may record average power, maximum power, and lactate levels. Later, you may use any or all of this data for comparisons under similar conditions. Also record aches or pains no matter how trivial they may seem at the time. Season-wrecking injuries often start as insignificant discomforts. Later, it may be helpful to trace when, why, and how they occurred.

Women should record their menstrual periods to help them get a clearer picture of how they affect training and racing.

For races, you may want to record warm-up, key moves, limiters, strengths, gearing, results, and notes for future reference. Race information may also be recorded using Sidebar 15.1, Season Results. This will come in handy when you need to seek sponsors or change teams. Putting together a race resumé is much easier when all of the information is in one location.

Mental Comments

Here is where most journal keepers fail. Training and racing are usually thought of as strictly physical, deeming what's happening inside the head as unimportant. Sometimes emotions are the most telling aspect of physical performance.

Always include your perception of how hard or easy the workout or race was. It's not necessary to be overly scientific about this. Just say something such as "A tough workout," or "Felt easy." These tell a lot about your experience. Commenting on how enjoyable the workout was is also revealing. Repeated remarks about training being a "drag" is a good sign that burnout is imminent, just as frequent "Fun workout" comments speak volumes about your mental state.

From the Mental Skills Profile completed in Chapter 5, you should have a good idea of what needs work. If, for example, confidence is lacking, look for and record the positive aspects of the workout or race. What did you achieve that was at the limits of your ability? What were your successes today? Remembering and reliving accomplishments is the first step in becoming more confident.

Mental comments should also include unusual stresses in your life off the bike. Visiting relatives, working overtime, illness, sleep deprivation, and relationship problems all affect performance.

Week's Summary

At the end of the week, complete a short summary of how things went for you. Total your training time. This will come in handy later in the year when it's time to decide training volumes for the new season. Check how you felt physically this week. It's not a good idea to frequently feel "on the edge" of overtraining, though that feeling is inevitable whenever you're trying to become more fit. The third week of a four-week training block is when this typically happens. If you never feel on the edge, you are not working hard enough. This is seldom a problem for serious riders.

Sidebar 15.1

SEASON RESULTS					YEAR_____
DATE	RACE	DISTANCE	TIME	PLACE (STARTERS)	COMMENTS

Indicate any soreness felt during the week no matter how trivial it may seem at the time. There may be a pattern developing that will be easier to find if you noted it here.

Summarize how the week went, noting the successes, the areas needing work, racing and training revelations, and notes for the future, such as how to deal with a problem you experienced this week. For example, you may have had a head cold coming on and discovered something that helped you fight it off.

Analysis

Training Analysis

When training and racing aren't going so well, looking back in the journal to what was happening in more positive times can sometimes get you back on track. In addition, you'll find that by comparing recent workouts to what you were doing a year or more ago provides a solid gauge of improvement. When trying to regain the top form from an earlier period, look for patterns such as types of workouts done, morning warning levels, stress, recovery between BT workouts, equipment used, training volume, training partners, and anything else that may provide a clue. Become a detective.

Here's an example of detective work. An athlete once asked me to review her training journal. She was training hard, putting in lots of quality miles, and was very focused on her goals. Yet she wasn't in top form at the A-priority races, and sometimes even had trouble finishing.

The first thing I noticed in her journal was that she ignored her warning signs. She faithfully took her resting heart rate every day and recorded hours of sleep and fatigue level. Yet she always did the planned workout regardless of what the morning warnings said. She was so driven to succeed that she let nothing get in her way—not even her own body. I told her about a 1968 study in which rats were forced to swim six hours a day, six days a week. After 161 hours of swimming, they showed great improvement in their aerobic capacities. But after 610 hours, their aerobic powers were no better than the untrained, control-group rats. She was an "overtrained rat," I told her.

We also talked about how to peak and taper for a big race. It was obvious that she was not rested on race days. She trained through the A-priority races as if they were the same as her C-priority races. We discussed how backing off in the days and even weeks before an important event allows the body to absorb all of the stress that has been placed on it and grow stronger.

The next time I talked with this rider was several weeks later, and she was riding well and pleased with her results. Had it not been for the detailed journal she kept, I would have never been able to so exactly determine the causes of her lackluster performance.

Racing Analysis

Want to improve your race performances? After cooling down, ask yourself: Why did it turn out as it did? Was there any particular aspect of it that was especially strong or weak? What role did the pre-race meal, warm-up, start, pacing, power, technical skills, endurance, refueling, and mental skills play in the outcome? Did I have a sound strategy and follow through on it? The answers to such questions come from nothing more than your memory and conversations with other riders following the race. The longer you wait to answer such questions, the more your memory erodes. To enhance recall, and especially to create a record for the future when you return to this same race, it will help to write down what happened as soon as possible after finishing. The Race Evaluation form suggested in Sidebar 15.2 helps with this.

Race days on which you felt really good or bad deserve special attention. Examine the preceding days to determine what may have led to this high or low. Perhaps it was a certain pattern of workouts, a period of good rest or excessive stress, or a particular diet that contributed to your results. If such trends are identified, you

Sidebar 15.2

RACE EVALUATION FORM

Race name:

Date and start time:

Location:

Type/distance:

Competitors to watch:

Weather:

Course conditions:

Race goal:

Race strategy:

Pre-race meal (foods and quantities):

Warm-up description:

Start-line arousal level (circle one):   Very low   Low   Moderate   High   Very high

Results (place, time, splits, etc.):

What I did well:

What I need to improve:

Aches/pains/problems afterward:

Comments on or description of how race developed:

are one step closer to knowing the secret of what does and doesn't work for you. Reproducing the positive factors while minimizing the negative is valuable for race peaking and performance.

A diary helps you see the bigger picture by keeping all the details in focus. When used effectively, it serves as an excellent tool for planning, motivating, and diagnosing. It also provides a personal history of training and racing accomplishments. A well-kept diary ranks right up there with training, rest, and nutrition when it comes to developing a competitive edge.

References

Abraham, W.M. "Factors in Delayed Muscle Soreness." *Medicine and Science in Sports and Exercise* 9 (1977): 11–20.

Berdanier, C.D. "The Many Faces of Stress." *Nutrition Today* 2, no. 2 (1987): 12–17.

Brown, R.L. "Overtraining in Athletes: A Round Table Discussion." *The Physician and Sports Medicine* 11, no. 6 (1983): 99.

Czajkowski, W. "A Simple Method to Control Fatigue in Endurance Training." *Exercise and Sport Biology, International Series on Sport Sciences* 10 (1982): 207–212, P.V. Komi (ed.), Human Kinetics.

Dressendorfer, R., et al. "Increased Morning Heart Rate in Runners: A Valid Sign of Overtraining?" *The Physician and Sports Medicine* 13, no. 8 (1985) 77–86.

Galbo, H. *Hormonal and Metabolic Adaptations to Exercise.* Stuttgart: Georg Thieme Verlag, 1983.

Hooper, S.L., et al. "Markers for Monitoring Overtraining and Recovery." *Medicine and Science in Sport and Exercise* 27 (1995): 106–112.

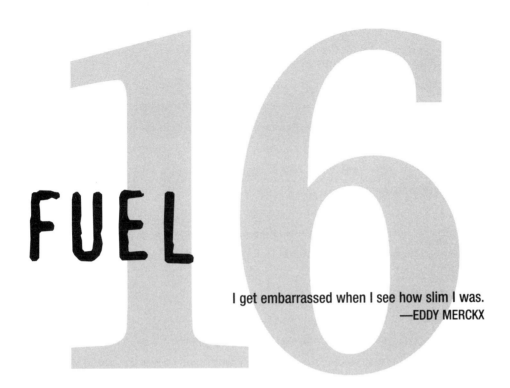

FUEL 16

I get embarrassed when I see how slim I was.
—EDDY MERCKX

The focus of this book is training, not diet, but there is no denying the complex connections between nutritional practices and exhaustive exercise. Eating foods to which the human body is optimally adapted will reduce body fat, improve recovery, decrease down time due to illness, and generally enhance athletic performance. The older you are, the more important diet is for performance. At age 20, you can make some dietary mistakes and get away with it. At age 50 everything is crucial, especially diet. Age is not the only individual variable for which diet is critical. For many female athletes who are chronically low in iron stores and fighting a seemingly endless battle to keep off excess pounds, getting their diet right is crucial to athletic success. For the athlete who eats a junk food diet low in micronutrients, recovery and performance will ultimately suffer due to illness and constant fatigue. Even something as seemingly innocuous as eating the right foods but at the wrong times relative to training will prolong recovery and reduce performance levels. Other than training and rest, nothing is as important for your race results as what you eat and when you eat it.

So what should you eat? Suppose you were a zookeeper and in charge of selecting food for the animals. It wouldn't be too difficult to figure out that the lions thrive on a diet made up primarily of the protein in meat and the giraffes do best when allowed to graze on vegetation. You wouldn't feed leaves and grass to the lions. Nor would you feed the giraffes meat. Their health and well-being would decline if you did. So there are foods that are optimal for different types of animals. Why are these particular foods optimal for these animals? Because they evolved eating such foods.

For as long as lions and giraffes have been on the planet they have eaten these foods. As the zookeeper, you will not change that. It's best to accept it.

So what would you do if the zoo received an exotic animal that no other zoo has and for which the diet is unknown? Well, the obvious answer would be to study that animal in its natural environment to see what it eats there, and then feed it the same foods in your zoo. That would be the optimal food for that animal. Seems simple enough.

So what foods are optimal for Homo sapiens—you and me? One way to answer that question would be through the science of paleontology—the study of man before the advent of farming and civilization. Why would we not want to study human eating patterns after the introduction of farming? The reason has to do with time and evolution.

The evolutionary process is slow, taking hundreds of thousands of years to bring 1-percent changes. Homo sapiens have been on the planet for about five million years. Farming was introduced in the Middle East some 10,000 years ago. Dairy is even younger with its roots going back about 5,000 years. In the big picture these developments are "recent." If our five million years on the planet were represented by a twenty-four-hour clock, farming would have been with us for only the last two minutes and fifty-two seconds. Dairy would have been around less than ninety seconds. These time spans are simply not long enough for humans to evolve and adapt to the foods that are unique to farming and dairy production.

So what did humans eat prior to farming? What are the optimal foods for humans? Paleontology tells us those foods were vegetables, fruits, and lean meats (fish, poultry, and other wild or free-ranging game). Nuts, some seeds, berries, and honey are also foods that humans have eaten for millions of years, although in far smaller amounts than those listed above. Non-optimal foods are those we have eaten only for the last 10,000-or-so years such as grains, milk, and cheese. Does this mean humans should never eat these non-optimal foods? No, it merely means that we will thrive on a diet made up primarily of vegetables, fruits, and lean meats. The more of these nutrient-dense foods you eat the better your health and athletic performance will be. The scientific evidence in support of the optimal foods as health-promoting is overwhelming. Replace them with non-optimal foods and, just as with the exotic animal in your zoo, your health and vitality will diminish. Fitness will also suffer.

Paleontology also tells us that our Homo sapien ancestors in the distant past would never have considered putting in multi-hour bouts of exercise, much of it at high intensity, day after day, week after week. This was unheard of until relatively recent times. Man evolved to do only what is necessary to provide food, shelter, and safety and nothing more. We are meant to be lazy, making our couch potato friends the true descendants of earliest man, at least philosophically. Serious athletes are an anomaly.

Because of this latter point my experience has taught me that we must "break the rules" to some extent when it comes to eating. Certain non-optimal foods, such as grains and other starches, are energy-dense. While this is a disadvantage to our friend the couch potato, one that helps to explain his being so overweight and unhealthy, it has the potential to be quite advantageous to the athlete seeking quick restoration of glycogen stores following a hard workout. This does not contradict the concept that the athlete's diet should be primarily composed of optimal foods; it merely suggests that there are small windows of time when non-optimal foods may well be beneficial to recovery.

The details of how to blend all of these elements into the "athlete's diet" is the focus of this chapter. To learn more about the concept of optimal foods read *The Paleo Diet* by Loren Cordain (2002).

Food as Fuel

While the human genetic code has changed very little, dietary recommendations change often. In the mid-twentieth century, endurance athletes were advised to avoid starchy foods such as bread and potatoes, and to eat more vegetables and meats instead. In the 1970s, a dietary shift away from protein began with an increase in carbohydrates, especially starchy grains. The 1980s brought concerns for fat in the diet, and low-fat and fat-free foods boomed, with an accompanying increase in sugar consumption. Now the pendulum is swinging back the other way, with the realizations that certain fats are beneficial and that some carbohydrates are deleterious in large quantities.

The crux of your daily dietary decisions is the relative mix of the four macronutrients you consume—protein, fat, carbohydrates, and water. How much of each you include in your diet has a great deal to do with how well you train and race.

Protein

The word protein is derived from the Greek word *proteios*, meaning "first" or "of primary importance." That's fitting, because determining macronutrient balance begins with protein intake.

Protein has a checkered history in the world of athletics. Greek and Roman competitors believed that the strength, speed, and endurance qualities of animals could be gained by merely eating their meat. Lion meat was in great demand. In the 1800s, protein was considered the major fuel of exercise, so athletes also ate prodigious quantities of meat. In the early part of the twentieth century, scientists came to understand that fat and carbohydrates provide most of our energy for movement. By the 1960s, athletic diets began to change, reflecting this shift in knowledge. In fact, little interest was paid to the role of protein in sports fuel throughout most of the

1970s and 1980s. That changed in the latter years of the twentieth century as more research was done on this almost forgotten macronutrient.

Protein plays a key role in health and athletic performance. It is necessary to repair muscle damage, maintain the immune system, manufacture hormones and enzymes, replace red blood cells that carry oxygen to the muscles, and produce up to 10 percent of the energy needed for long or intense workouts and races. It also stimulates the secretion of glucagon, a hormone that allows the body to use fat for fuel more efficiently.

Protein is so important to the athlete that it may even determine the outcome of races. For example, a study of Olympians by the International Center for Sports Nutrition in Omaha, Nebraska, compared the diets of medal winners and non-medalists. The only significant difference found was that the winners ate more protein than those who did not medal.

Performance is dependent on dietary protein because the body is unable to produce all it needs from scratch. And, unlike carbohydrates and fat, protein is not stored in the body at fuel depot sites for later use. The protein you eat is used to meet immediate needs, with excess intakes converted to the storage forms of carbohydrates or fat.

Dietary protein is made up of twenty amino acids useable by the human body as building blocks for replacing damaged cells. Most of these amino acids are readily produced by the body when a need arises, but there are nine that the body cannot manufacture. These "essential" amino acids must come from the diet in order for all the protein-related functions to continue normally. If the diet is lacking in protein, your body is likely to break down muscle tissues to provide what is necessary for areas of greater need, thus resulting in muscle wasting. This was evidenced in 1988 by the 7-Eleven cycling team during the Tour de France. It was discovered that the circumferences of the riders' thighs decreased during three weeks of racing. After studying their diets, the team doctor determined that they were protein deficient.

Protein is more important for endurance athletes than for those in power sports such as American football, baseball, and basketball. An intense, one-hour criterium can cause the depletion of up to 30 grams of protein, about equal to the amount of protein in a 3-ounce can of tuna. Replacing these losses is critical to recovery and improved fitness. Without such replenishment, the endurance athlete's body is forced to cannibalize protein from muscle.

Unfortunately, there is not a general agreement within the nutritional field regarding the recommended protein intake for endurance athletes. The U.S. recommended daily allowance (RDA) for protein is 0.013 ounces per pound of body weight (0.8gm/kg), but that is likely too low for an athlete. Peter Lemon, a noted protein researcher at Kent State University, suggests athletes eat about 0.020 to 0.022 ounces of protein per pound of body weight each day (1.2–1.4 gm/kg). During a period of heavy weight lifting, such as in the MS phase described in Chapter 12, Lemon recommends a high of 0.028 ounces per pound (1.8 gm/kg). The American Dietetic Association suggests a high-end protein intake of 0.032 ounces per pound (2.0 gm/kg) each day. A non-scientific survey of sports scientists from around the world found a rather broad range of 0.020 to 0.040 ounces per pound (1.2–2.5 gm/kg) suggested for endurance athletes daily. Applying these recommendations for a 150-pound (68-kilogram) athlete, the possible range, excluding the U.S. RDA, would be 3 to 6 ounces (84 to 168 grams) of protein each day. Table 16.1 shows how much protein is found in common foods.

Protein is found in both vegetable and animal forms, and the quantity required, regardless of the source, can be difficult to consume unless you closely watch your diet. To get 127 grams of protein from vegetable sources would mean eating 17 cups of spaghetti, 14 cups of yogurt, or 21 bagels. The same 127 grams could also come from 15 ounces of chicken or lean steak, or 17 ounces of tuna. This is a lot of food from either type, but there is an added benefit in getting protein from animal sources: All of the necessary amino acids in the right proportions, easily absorbable iron, zinc, calcium, and vitamin B-12 are present and the protein is more absorbable due to less fiber in the meat.

So what happens if you fail to get your daily need for protein when training hard? Occasionally missing out on your daily protein intake probably has no measurable impact on performance, but regular avoidance of high quality protein accompanied by a volume of high-intensity exercise can have a significant impact on training

ANIMAL SOURCES	PROTEIN OZ.	(g)	PLANT SOURCES	PROTEIN OZ.	(g)
Sirloin steak (broiled)	1.05	(30.0)	Almonds (12 dried)	0.71	(20.0)
Chicken breast	1.05	(30.0)	Tofu (extra firm)	0.39	(11.0)
Swiss cheese	1.01	(29.0)	Bagel	0.38	(11.0)
Pork loin	0.92	(26.0)	Kidney beans	0.30	(9.0)
Hamburger	0.92	(26.0)	Rye bread	0.29	(8.0)
Cheddar cheese	0.85	(24.5)	Cereal (corn flakes)	0.28	(8.0)
Tuna	0.82	(23.0)	Refried beans	0.22	(6.0)
Haddock	0.82	(23.0)	Baked beans	0.17	(5.0)
Venison	0.73	(21.0)	Hummus	0.17	(5.0)
Cottage cheese (low-fat)	0.43	(12.0)	Soy milk	0.10	(3.0)
Egg (whole)	0.42	(12.0)	Brown rice (cooked)	0.09	(2.5)
Egg white	0.36	(10.0)	Tomato (red)	0.03	(1.0)
Milk (skim)	0.12	(3.0)			

Table 16.1
Protein Content of Common Foods per 3.5-ounce (100 g) Serving

and racing. Besides being a minor fuel source during strenuous exercise, protein is responsible for building muscle, making hormones that regulate basal metabolic rate, and for fighting off disease.

There's no doubt that during prolonged, high-intensity exercise, the body turns to stored protein, eventually resulting in the loss of muscle. A 1992 study of sixteen hikers who spent twenty-one days in the Andes Mountains traveling five hours a day on foot with an average elevation gain of 2,500 feet per day, found significant loss of muscle mass. This may explain why some endurance athletes have a gaunt look during several weeks of rigorous training with low intake of protein.

Without meat in the diet, the risk of low iron levels is also high. One study linked low iron levels with injuries in runners. Those lowest in iron had twice as many injuries as those highest in iron. Besides providing protein, lean red meat is also a good source of easily absorbed iron.

Are you getting enough protein? One way to determine this is to evaluate your physical and mental well-being. Indicators that you need more protein in your diet include:

- Frequent colds or sore throats
- Slow recovery following workouts
- An irritable demeanor
- Poor response to training (slow to get in shape)
- Slow fingernail growth and easily broken nails
- Thin hair or unusual hair loss
- Chronic fatigue
- Poor mental focus
- Sugar cravings
- Pallid complexion
- Cessation of menstrual periods

Note that none of these indicators is certain proof of the need for more protein, as each may have other causes. A dietary analysis by a registered dietitian, or by the use of a computer software program such as DietBalancer, may help make the determination if you have concerns. Increasing your protein intake to see how it affects you is another simple option. It's unlikely that you will eat too much protein. Even at 30 percent of daily calories, as recommended in some diets, the excess, if any, will be converted to glycogen or fat and stored. There is no research suggesting that moderately high protein diets pose a health risk for otherwise healthy individuals, as long as plenty of water is consumed each day to help with the removal of nitrogen, a by-product of protein metabolism.

ARE YOU REALLY OVERTRAINED?

Low dietary intake of the mineral iron may be the most common nutritional deficiency for serious multisport athletes, especially women. Unfortunately, it goes undetected in most.

A 1988 university study of female high school cross-country runners found 45 percent had low iron stores. In the same study, 17 percent of the boys were low. Other research conducted on female college athletes showed that 31 percent were iron deficient. Up to 80 percent of women runners were below normal iron stores in a 1983 study.

Commonly accepted, although still debated, causes of iron depletion include high-volume running, especially on hard surfaces; too much anaerobic training; chronic intake of aspirin; travel to high altitude; excessive menstrual flow; and a diet low in animal-food products. Athletes most at risk for iron deficiency, in the order of their risk, are runners, women, endurance athletes, vegetarians, those who sweat heavily, dieters and those who have recently donated blood.

The symptoms of iron deficiency include loss of endurance, chronic fatigue, high exercise heart rate, low power, frequent injury, recurring illness and an attitude problem. Since many of these symptoms are the same as in overtraining, the athlete may correctly cut back on exercise, begin feeling better, and return to training only to find an almost immediate relapse. In the early stages of iron depletion, performance may show only slight decrements, but additional training volume and intensity cause further declines. Many unknowingly flirt with this level of "tired blood" frequently.

If a deficiency is suspected, what should you do? Once a year have a blood test to determine your healthy baseline levels of serum ferritin, hemoglobin, reticulocytes and haptoglobin. This should be done during the Transition, Prep, or Base training periods when training volume and intensity are low. This blood test should be done in a fasted state with no exercise for fifteen hours prior. Your health-care provider will help you understand the results. Then, if the symptoms of low iron appear, a follow-up test may support or rule this out as the culprit. Your blood indicators of iron status may be "normal" based on the reference range, but low in relation to your baseline. Many exercise scientists believe that even this obvious dip may adversely affect performance.

Should the blood test indicate an abnormally low iron status, an increased dietary intake of iron is necessary. You may want to have a registered dietitian analyze your eating habits for adequate iron consumption. The RDA for women and teenagers is 15 mg per day. Men should consume 10 mg. Endurance athletes may need more. The normal North American diet contains about 6 mg of iron for every 1,000 calories eaten, so a female athlete restricting food intake to 2,000 calories a day while exercising strenuously can easily create a low-iron condition in a few weeks.

Dietary iron comes in two forms—heme and non-heme. Heme iron is found in animal meat. Plant foods are the source of non-heme iron. Very little of the iron you eat is absorbed by the body regardless of source, but heme iron has the best absorption rate at about 15 percent. Up to 5 percent of non-heme iron is taken up by the body. So the most effective way to increase iron status is by eating meat, especially red meat. Humans probably developed this capacity to absorb iron from red meat as a result of our omnivorous, hunter-gatherer origins. Plant sources of iron, although not very available to the human body due to their accompanying phytates, are raisins, leafy green vegetables, dates, dried fruits, lima beans, baked beans, broccoli, baked potatoes, soybeans and brussels sprouts. Other sources are listed in Table 16.1.

Iron absorption from any of these foods, whether plant or animal, is decreased if they are accompanied at meals by egg yolk, coffee, tea, wheat, or cereal grains. Calcium and zinc also reduce the ability of the body to take up iron. Including fruits, especially citrus fruit, in meals enhances iron absorption.

Don't use iron supplements unless under the supervision of your health-care provider. Some people are susceptible to iron overload, a condition called hemochromatosis marked by toxic deposits in the skin, joints, and liver. Other symptoms, including fatigue and malaise, may mimic iron deficiency and overtraining. Also note that ingesting iron supplements is the second leading cause of poisoning in children. Aspirin is first.

Carbohydrates

Carbohydrates are critical for performance in endurance events, as they provide much of the fuel in the forms of glycogen and glucose that is converted to useable energy by the body. Low carbohydrate stores are likely to result in poor endurance and lackluster racing.

The zealous athlete who learns this often overeats carbohydrates at the expense of protein and fat. A day in the life of such a person may find that breakfast is cereal, toast, and orange juice; a bagel is eaten as a midmorning snack; lunch is a baked potato with vegetables; sports bars or pretzels are eaten in the afternoon; and supper is pasta with bread. Not only is such a diet excessively high in starch with an overemphasis on wheat, but it is also likely to provide dangerously low protein and fat levels. Such a dietary plan could be improved by replacing the cereal with an egg-white omelet and including fresh fruit, topping the potato with tuna, snacking on mixed nuts and dried fruit, and eating fish with vegetables for supper.

When you eat a high-carbohydrate meal or snack, the pancreas releases insulin to regulate the level of blood sugar. That insulin stays in the blood for up to two hours, during which time it has other effects, such as preventing the body from utilizing stored fat, converting carbohydrates and protein to body fat, and moving fat in the blood to storage sites. This may explain why, despite serious training and eating a "healthy" diet, some athletes are unable to lose body fat.

Some carbohydrates enter the bloodstream quicker than others, producing an elevated blood-sugar response and quickly bringing about all the negative aspects of high insulin described above. These rapidly digested carbohydrates are high on the glycemic index—a food rating system developed for diabetics. Foods with a low glycemic index produce a less dramatic rise in blood sugar, and help avoid the craving for more sugary food that comes with eating high-glycemic carbohydrates. Table 16.2 lists some common high-, moderate-, low-, and very low-glycemic foods.

HIGH GLYCEMIC INDEX (OVER 80%)

Bread, French	Molasses	Potatoes, baked	Rice Chex	Rice, white
Corn flakes	Parsnips	Potatoes, instant	Rice, instant	Tapioca
Grapenuts	Pasta, rice	Rice cakes	Rice Krispies	Tofu frozen dessert

MODERATE GLYCEMIC INDEX (50–80%)

All-Bran cereal	Bread, rye	Doughnuts	Pea soup	Pumpkin
Apricots	Bread, wheat	Ice cream	Pineapple	Raisins
Bagels	Bread, white	Mango	Popcorn	Rice, brown
Bananas	Corn chips	Muesli	Potato chips	Rye crisps
Barley	Cornmeal	Muffins	Potatoes, boiled	Soft drinks
Beets	Corn, sweet	Oat bran	Potatoes, mashed	Taco shells
Black bean soup	Couscous	Oatmeal	Potatoes, sweet	Watermelon
Bread, pita	Crackers	Orange juice	PowerBar	Yams

LOW GLYCEMIC INDEX (30–49%)

Apple	Beans, black	Grapefruit juice	Pasta	Rye
Apple juice	Beans, lima	Grapes	Pears	Tomato soup
Apple sauce	Beans, pinto	Kiwifruit	Peas, black-eyed	Yogurt, fruit
Beans, baked	Chocolate	Oranges	Peas, split	

VERY LOW GLYCEMIC INDEX (LESS THAN 30%)

Barley	Cherries	Lentils	Peaches	Plums
Beans, kidney	Grapefruit	Milk	Peanuts	Soy beans

Table 16.2
Glycemic Index of Common Foods

How a carbohydrate food is prepared and what other foods it is eaten with affects its glycemic index. Adding fat to a high-glycemic-index food lowers its glycemic index by slowing down digestion. An example of this is ice cream, which has a moderate glycemic index despite the presence of large amounts of sugar. In the same way, adding fiber to a meal that includes a high- or moderate-glycemic-index carbohydrate reduces the meal's effect on your blood sugar and insulin levels and turns it into timed-release energy.

Notice in Table 16.2 that many of the foods that have a moderate- to high-glycemic index are the ones we have typically thought of as "healthy" and therefore eaten liberally. These include the starchy foods—cereal, bread, rice, pasta, potatoes, crackers, bagels, pancakes, and bananas. No wonder so many endurance athletes are always hungry and have a hard time losing excess body fat. Their blood sugar levels are routinely kept at high levels, causing regular cascades of insulin. Not only do high insulin levels produce regular and frequent food cravings and excess body fat, they are also associated with such widespread health problems as high blood pressure, heart disease, and adult-onset diabetes.

But moderate- and high-glycemic-index foods have an important role in the athlete's diet. During long and intense training sessions and races it is necessary to replenish carbohydrate stores in the muscles and liver. That's why sports drinks and gels are used during exercise. The thirty minutes immediately following a hard training session is when moderate- to high-glycemic-index carbohydrates and insulin are also beneficial. This is the time to use a commercial recovery drink or starchy food. Combining protein with a high-glycemic-index food at this time has been shown to effectively boost recovery. For very hard workouts, this recovery window during which higher glycemic carbohydrates are eaten may extend as long as the duration of the preceding workout. So if you do a very intense two-hour ride, continue taking in high-glycemic foods for two hours post-workout.

Except for during and immediately after exercise, sports drinks, gels, and soft drinks should be avoided, however. Other high- and moderate-glycemic-index foods should be consumed in quite limited quantities throughout the day, also.

Eating a diet extremely high in carbohydrates is not unanimously supported by the sports science literature. A high-carbohydrate diet may cause your body to rely heavily on glycogen for fuel during exercise, with an associated increase in blood lactate levels, while reducing your use of fat as a fuel for exercise.

Fat

In the 1980s, Western society painted dietary fat as such a terrifying specter that many athletes still see all types of fat as the enemy and try to eliminate it entirely from their diet. Indeed, there are some types of fat that should be kept at low levels. These are saturated fat, found in prodigious quantities in feedlot cattle, and trans fatty acids, the man-made fats found in many highly processed foods and called "hydrogenated" on the label. Hydrogenated fats lead to artery clogging the same as the saturated variety.

Don't confuse these "bad" fats with all types of fat. There are, in fact, "good" fats that not only prevent dry skin and dull hair, but more importantly help maintain a regular menstrual cycle in women and prevent colds and other infections common to serious athletes. Such fats also assist with the manufacture of hormones, such as testosterone and estrogen, and nerve and brain cells, and are important for carrying and absorbing the vitamins A, D, E, and K. Fat is also the body's most efficient source of energy. Every gram of fat provides nine calories, compared with four each for protein and carbohydrates. You

may find that eating these essential fats improves your long-term recovery and capacity to train at a high level, if you previously have been low in them.

After three decades of believing that very high-carbohydrate eating is best for performance, there is now compelling evidence, albeit in the early stages, that increasing fat intake while decreasing and properly timing carbohydrate consumption may be good for endurance athletes, especially in events lasting four hours or longer. Several studies reveal that eating a diet high in fat causes the body to preferentially use fat for fuel, and that eating a high-carbohydrate diet results in the body relying more heavily on limited stores of muscle glycogen for fuel. Theoretically, even the skinniest athlete has enough fat stored to last for forty hours or more at a low intensity without refueling, but only enough carbohydrates for about three hours at most.

A study at State University of New York illustrates the performance benefits of fat. Researchers had a group of runners eat a higher-than-usual fat diet consisting of 38-percent fat and 50-percent carbohydrate calories for one week. The second week they ate a more typical high-carbohydrate diet with 73 percent of calories coming from carbs and 15 percent from fat. At the end of each week the subjects were tested for maximum aerobic capacities and then ran themselves to exhaustion on a treadmill. On the higher-fat diet their VO_2max was 11 percent greater than when they were on the high-carbohydrate diet and they lasted 9 percent longer on the run to exhaustion. One confounding element of the study, however, was that the subjects were glycogen-depleted before starting the endurance run.

A 1994 study conducted by Tim Noakes, M.D, Ph.D., author of *The Lore of Running* (1991), and colleagues at the University of Cape Town in South Africa found that after cyclists ate a diet of 70 percent fat for two weeks, their endurance at a low intensity improved significantly compared with cycling after consuming a diet high in carbohydrates for two weeks. At high intensities, there was no difference in the performances—fat did just as well as carbohydrates.

Other research has shown that our greatest fears associated with dietary fat—risk for heart disease and weight gain—do not occur when eating a diet that includes what might be called "good" fats. The good fats are monounsaturated and omega-3, polyunsaturated fatty acids, which were plentiful in our Stone Age ancestors' diets according to paleontology. The oils and spreads of almonds, avocado, hazelnuts, macadamia nuts, pecans, cashews, and olives are high in these fats. Other good sources are the oils of cold-water fish such as tuna, salmon, and mackerel. The red meat of wild game also provides significant amounts of monounsaturated and omega-3 fats. Canola oil is another good source.

The bottom line on fat is to select the leanest cuts of meat (wild game or free-range cattle, if possible); trim away all visible fat from meat, including fish and fowl;

eat low- or non-fat dairy in small quantities; avoid trans fatty acids in packaged foods; and regularly include monounsaturated and omega-3 fats in your diet. Eating 20 to 30 percent of your calories from fat, with an emphasis on the good fats, is not harmful, and may actually be helpful for training and racing if your fat intake has been low.

Water

Many athletes don't drink enough fluids, leaving them perpetually on the edge of dehydration. In this state, recovery is compromised and the risk of illness rises. Drinking throughout the day is one of the simplest and yet most effective means of boosting performance for these athletes. Since sports drinks and most fruit juices are high to moderate on the glycemic index, the best fluid replacement between work-outs is water.

Dehydration results in a reduction of plasma, making the blood thick and forcing the heart and body to work harder moving it. Even with slight dehydration, exercise intensity and duration are negatively affected. A 2-percent loss of body weight as fluids will slow a racer by about 4 percent—that's nearly five minutes in a two-hour race. When race intensity is high, you must stay well hydrated to keep up.

A 150-pound (68 kg) adult loses a little more than a half-gallon (2 liters) of body fluids a day just in living, not including training. Up to half of this loss is through urine at the rate of about 2 ounces (30 ml) per hour. Heavy training or a hot and humid environment can increase the loss to 2 gallons (8 liters) daily through heavy sweating.

Unfortunately, the human thirst mechanism is not very effective. By the time we sense thirst, dehydration is already well under way. Following prolonged and intense training or racing, it may take twenty-four to forty-eight hours to rehydrate if thirst is the controlling factor. In contrast, a dog will drink up to 10 percent of its body weight immediately following exercise, replacing all lost water. It's important to drink water steadily throughout the day when you are training whether you are thirsty or not.

Get in 8 to 12 cups (1 to 1.5 liters) a day, depending on your body size and training load. For every pound (450 g) lost during exercise, an additional 2 cups (500 ml) of water is needed. You can also use your rate of urination and urine color as a guide. You should need to visit the toilet at least once every two hours during the day and your urine should be clear to straw-colored. If you aren't achieving these standards, drink more.

Periodization of Diet

The optimal diet for peak performance must vary with the athlete just as the optimal training protocol must vary from person to person. We can't all eat the same things in the same relative amounts and reap the same benefits. Where your ancestors originated on the planet, and what was available for them to eat for the last 100,000 years or so, is important for what you should eat now.

So the bottom line is that you must discover what mix of foods works best for you. If you have never experimented with this, don't automatically assume you have found it already. You may be surprised at what happens when changes are made at the training table. A word of caution: Make changes gradually and allow at least three weeks for your body to adapt to a new diet before passing judgment based on how you feel and your performance in training. It usually takes at least two weeks to adapt to significant changes before seeing any benefit. During the adaptation period you may feel lethargic and train poorly. For this reason, changes in diet are best done in the Transition and Preparation periods early in the season. Also, be aware that as you age, changes may occur in your body chemistry requiring further shifts in the diet.

That said, an optimal diet to enhance training, racing, and recovery involves not only eating moderate amounts of protein, carbohydrates, and fat, but also varying the mix of these macronutrients throughout the year. In other words, diet should cycle just as training cycles within a periodization plan. Protein serves as the anchor for the diet and stays relatively constant throughout the year as fat and carbohydrates rise and fall alternately with the training periods. Figure 16.1 illustrates this "see-saw" effect of the periodized diet. Note that the numbers used in this figure are merely an example, and the diet right for you may vary considerably.

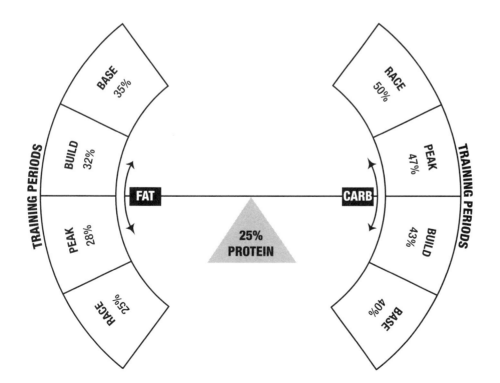

Figure 16.1
The dietary periodization "seesaw"
The percentages are for illustration only and will vary between athletes.

Antioxidant Supplements

Generally it's a good idea to meet your nutritional needs with real foods and use food supplements sparingly. Scientists and supplement designers just aren't as smart as Mother Nature when it comes to deciding what to include and what to leave out of foods. Real food provides everything needed for health and fitness. Adding lots of pills and potions to your diet is usually not wise. The exception is antioxidant supplements. Here's why.

The process of metabolizing food and oxygen for exercise releases free radicals that cause damage to healthy cells. This is much like the rusting of metal—a breakdown caused by oxidation. Hard training produces large numbers of free radicals, which threaten your health and ability to recover following workouts.

For example, one study measured by-products of free radical damage in highly trained athletes, moderately trained athletes, and a sedentary group. The researchers found that the highly trained athletes had the highest levels of damage, while the moderately trained subjects had the least. The sedentary group was in the middle. A little exercise appears to be a healthy thing when it comes to free radicals, but extensive exercise or none at all causes problems.

In recent years, studies have shown that vitamins C and E reduce damage and prevent colds associated with extreme physical exertion by combining with the free radicals to stop the oxidative process. The research studies typically use large doses of each of these micronutrients—usually hundreds of times the RDA. Because the calculation involves variables such as age, sex, diet, body fat, size, and training load, it is difficult to determine the necessary amounts for each individual. Recommended daily intakes based on these studies generally fall into the following ranges:

Vitamin E	400–800 IU
Vitamin C	300–1,000 mg

The problem is that in order to get even the lowest of these dosages you would have to eat all of the following foods every day:

Asparagus	15 spears
Avocados	31
Broccoli	4 cups
Peaches	33
Prunes	30
Tomato juice	12 ounces
Spinach	17 cups
Wheat germ	1/4 cup

While some cyclists I know put away 3,000 to 4,000 calories a day, none eat such foods in these volumes.

While eating a wholesome diet from a wide-ranging menu is absolutely necessary for optimal health and fitness, few people, including athletes, achieve the recommended standards. For example, it has been estimated that the minimum goal of eating five fruit and vegetable servings per day is accomplished by less than 10 percent of the American population.

While it is true that serious athletes tend to eat more than average citizens, they seldom eat enough of the right foods. A 1989 study of triathletes who competed in the national championship; the Hawaii Ironman®; or the Huntsville, Alabama, Double Ironman® found that as a group they had inadequate caloric intakes due to unusual eating habits. They also demonstrated poor food selection resulting from rigorous training schedules and limited time for eating.

Athletes often rely on daily multiple vitamins, but these seldom provide vitamins C and E in large enough volumes. Highly-trained athletes may need to supplement their diets with individual dosages, especially vitamin E. It appears that these supplements should be taken with meals twice a day for best results.

Vitamin C has a low level of risk associated with usage at the above level, but high dosages of vitamin E can cause problems for those who are deficient in vitamin K. Check with your health-care provider before starting supplementation.

Ergogenic Aids

Several years ago university researchers asked a group of elite athletes to answer a question: "If you could take a pill that would ensure a gold medal in the next Olympics, but you would die within five years, would you take it?" The overwhelming answer was "Yes!"

Such attitudes have led elite athletes to experiment with anabolic steroids, erythropoietin (EPO), amphetamines, and other banned ergogenic aids. Some have consequently died in their quest for athletic excellence. Others have simply wasted their money on products that have no benefit beyond a placebo effect and have not withstood scientific investigation.

There is no magic pill that will guarantee an Olympic medal—or even a better-than-average race performance in your local crit. Training is still the single most important component of athletic excellence. There are, however, a few products that go beyond a normal diet and which science has generally found effective. I say "generally," because as with the scientific study of almost anything, there are often contradictory results. Also, not all ergogenic aids have the same benefits for everyone. Individualization applies here just as it does in training.

Before deciding upon the use of certain ergogenic aids, the following five questions should be answered:

1. **Is it legal?** Products are often promoted to athletes despite the fact that they contain a banned substance. There have been many instances of blind trust resulting in a disqualification or worse for an elite athlete. To check on a specific product, visit the U.S. Olympic Committee's Anti-Doping Policies link at the Web site at www.olympic-usa.org.

2. **Is it ethical?** Only you can answer this question. Some believe that sport must be conducted in its purest form with absolutely no artificial assistance. But once we begin to ponder such ergogenic aids as carbohydrate loading and vitamin and mineral supplements, it becomes clear that drawing a line in the sand is difficult.

3. **Is it safe?** Studies on the effects of various sports aids are often limited to a few weeks, as most subjects don't want to donate their entire lives to science. Such short periods of observation may not produce observable effects that might otherwise occur with long-term use. There is also the outside possibility that using multiple substances simultaneously or in combination with common medications may produce undesirable side effects. Another complication is that the U.S. Food and Drug Administration (FDA) safety regulations for supplements are more lenient than for food products. It's always a good idea to check with your family physician before supplementing.

4. **Is its use supported by the research?** There may be an isolated study on any product that demonstrates a benefit, but does the bulk of the literature agree? To search the scientific journals for studies, point your browser at the government's PubMed Web site (www.ncbi.nlm.nih.gov/PubMed/), enter the substance of interest, and select "search." You'll be presented with a list of archived studies and their abstracts. Have fun reading the list—it could be a thousand or more items long. Better yet, ask a knowledgeable and trusted coach, trainer, registered dietitian, or medical professional for their insights on the product in question.

5. **Will it help in my race?** Even if generally supported by the research, not all ergogenic aids benefit all people in all events. There are many individual differences that may affect the use of a given product. It may not work well for you because of some combination of your age, sex, health status, medications used, and years of experience in the sport. Some aids have been shown to provide a benefit for short events such as the 100-meter dash, but not for events lasting for several hours.

The following is a discussion of several currently popular and legal ergogenic aids that are probably safe for most athletes and beneficial at some level in cycling. Before using any of these, consult with your health-care provider. Never use a product immediately before or in an important race without having first tried it in training or in a C-priority event.

Branched-Chain Amino Acids

During workouts lasting longer than about three hours, the body turns to protein to provide fuel—perhaps as much as 10 percent of the energy requirement. Three essential amino acids—ones that must be present in the diet since the body can't synthesize them—make up about a third of muscle. These are leucine, isoleucine, and valine. Collectively they are called branched chain amino acids (BCAA).

Those who eat little protein, especially from animal sources, are likely to get the most benefit from using BCAA. Since vegetarians are often deficient in protein intake levels, BCAA supplementation may prove especially helpful for them.

BCAA may be purchased in health food stores and drug stores that sell food supplements. They should come in a brown bottle to protect the capsules from light, and the label should indicate each of the individual amino acids, preceded by an "L" as in "L-valine." This ensures adequate absorption.

Research on the use of BCAA is inconclusive. Some studies have shown that supplementing the diet with BCAA enhances endurance performance in long events, especially those lasting three hours or longer. A few have found that it even helps in events of one-hour duration. When benefits are seen in research they typically fall into these categories:

- High workloads and exhaustive workouts and races are likely to weaken the immune system and lead to illness. BCAA help to maintain the immune system following exhaustive workouts and races, reducing the likelihood of training breakdowns. Thus they have the potential to speed recovery.
- Some studies have shown BCAA to maintain muscle mass, power, and endurance during exhaustive, multi-day endurance events such as stage races or crash training (see Chapter 10).
- BCAA may help to reduce central nervous system fatigue, thus maintaining performance late in a race. This is a recent theory that is still under investigation in the sports science community.
- BCAA promote the use of fat for fuel while conserving glycogen.

There are four times in your training season when using BCAA may be beneficial: during the Maximum Strength (MS) phase, in the Build and Peak training periods, for long and intense races, and while training intensely at high altitudes. It is important to observe the following guidelines for supplementing with BCAA.

- Take about 35 mg of BCAA for each pound of body weight daily, but only at the times indicated above. A 150-pound (68 kg) cyclist would take 5,250 milligrams, or about five grams daily. A 120-pound cyclist could consume 4,200 milligrams or about four grams a day.
- One to two hours before an MS strength workout, a high-intensity workout in the Build or Peak periods, or an A-priority race, take one-half of your daily dose. Then, one to two hours before bedtime the same day, take the other half.
- During a stage race, double your normal dosage taking one-third before the race, one-third an hour or two before your post-race nap, and one-third before turning in for the day.

One potential negative side effect of taking BCAA has to do with imbalances in dietary intakes of amino acids. When eating meat, all of the amino acids are present in the proper ratios, but excessive supplementation with BCAA may upset the balance between them. Some scientists and nutritionists are concerned that this may have long-term health implications.

Medium-Chain Triglycerides

Medium-chain triglycerides (MCT) are processed fats that are metabolically different from other fats in that they are not readily stored as body fat and are quickly absorbed by the digestive system like carbohydrates, thus offering quick energy. They also provide about twice the calories per gram when compared to carbohydrates. Some studies have shown that mixing MCT and carbohydrates in sports drinks can improve endurance and maintain the pace in the latter stages of races lasting two hours or longer.

In a 1990s study at the University of Capetown in South Africa, six experienced cyclists rode for two hours at about 73 percent of maximum heart rate. Immediately after this steady, but low-intensity ride, they time trialed 40 kilometers at maximum effort. They did this three times over a ten-day period using a different drink for each attempt. One drink was a normal carbohydrate sports drink. Another was an MCT-only beverage. The third ride used a sports drink spiked with MCT.

With the MCT-only drink their average 40k time was 1:12:08. The carbohydrate sports drink produced a 1:06:45. With the mixed MCT-carbohydrate beverage their time was 1:05:00—a significant improvement. The study's authors believe that the MCT spared glycogen during the two-hour steady ride, allowing the riders to better utilize carbohydrates during the more intense time trial late in the season.

An MCT–sports drink mix may benefit your performance late in races that last three hours or longer. You can create such a long-race drink for yourself by mixing 16 ounces of your favorite sports drink with four tablespoons of MCT. You can purchase liquid MCT at a local health food store. There are no known side effects for MCT used in this manner.

Creatine

Creatine is one of the most recent additions to the ergogenics field, having its first known usage in athletics in 1993. Since then, the number of creatine studies has steadily increased, but a lot of questions remain unanswered.

Creatine is a substance found in dietary meat and fish, but can also be created in your liver, kidneys, and pancreas. It is stored in muscle tissue in the form of creatine phosphate, a fuel used mostly during maximum efforts of up to about twelve seconds and, to a lesser extent, in intense efforts lasting a few minutes.

The amount of creatine formed by the human body is not enough to boost performance for endurance events, but scientists have found that by supplementing the diet for a few days preceding the event, certain types of performance can be enhanced. In order to get an adequate amount of creatine from the diet to improve performance, an athlete would have to eat up to five pounds of rare meat or fish daily. Supplementing appears to be quite effective in increasing stored creatine.

A few years ago, scientists from Sweden, Britain, and Estonia tried creatine supplements on a group of runners. Following a creatine-loading period the subjects ran a 4 x 1,000-meter interval workout at maximum effort. Compared with the pre-test results, the creatine-supplemented subjects improved their total 4,000-meter times by an average of 17 seconds while the placebo-control group slowed by one second. The relative advantage the creatine users experienced increased as the workout progressed. In other words, they experienced less fatigue and were faster at the end. Be aware, however, that a few other studies using swimmers and cyclists found no performance enhancement from creatine supplmentation in repeated short, anaerobic efforts.

There is still not a lot known about creatine supplementation, but the benefits are probably greatest for maximizing the gains from interval and hill repeat workouts, in races on the track, and in short races on the road such as criteriums. Some users believe that it decreases body fat, but it may only appear that way since body weight increases due to water retention as fat stays the same. Body-weight gains have been in the range of two to five pounds (0.9 to 2.3 kg). Also, creatine does not directly build muscle tissue. Instead it provides the fuel so more power training is possible within a given workout, thus stimulating muscle fiber growth. The use of creatine by endurance athletes is equivocal. The best times to supplement with creatine for an endurance athlete, if at all, are during the Maximum Strength weight training phase and the higher-intensity Build period of training. Athletes who are low in force and power qualities stand to benefit the most at these times. It is best to avoid its use in the Peak period, when water-weight gains may be difficult to reduce prior to important races. About 20 to 30 percent of those who take creatine experience no measurable physiological changes. Vegetarians may stand to realize greater gain from using creatine since they typically have low levels.

Most studies have used huge dosages, such as 20 to 30 grams of creatine a day taken in four to five doses during a four- to seven-day loading phase. One found the same muscle levels, however, on as little as 3 grams daily for thirty days. After loading, muscle creatine can be maintained at high levels for four to five weeks with 2 grams taken daily. Dissolving creatine in grape or orange juice seems to improve absorption. In these studies, not all the subjects experienced an increase in muscle creatine levels despite high dosages.

According to scientists who have been working with creatine, there appears to be little health risk since it is passively filtered from the blood and puts no extra workload on kidneys, but the longest study is only ten weeks. Scientists do know that once you stop short-term use, your natural production of creatine is regained. The only well-established side effect is the addition of body weight during the loading phase, which soon disappears. A greater concern is that creatine may give you a false positive in a urine test for kidney problems. There have also been anecdotal accounts of muscle spasm and cramping in power athletes using creatine on a long-term basis, perhaps due to a lowered concentration of electrolytes in the muscles. Talk with your health-care provider before supplementing with creatine.

Creatine can be purchased at health food stores and will probably cost $2–$3 a day during the loading phase. It is wise to talk with your health-care provider before supplementing with creatine.

Sodium Phosphate

The German Army used sodium phosphate in World War I, and even in the 1930s, German athletes knew of its worth. It has not received a great deal of publicity in recent years, though some athletes have known about it for years, but kept the secret.

Sodium phosphate has the potential to improve a 40k time trial significantly, allow you to hang on when the pace would normally have you off the back and make high-intensity efforts feel much easier.

In 1983, researchers working with elite runners found that sodium phosphate increased aerobic capacity by 9 percent and improved ventilatory threshold (like lactate threshold) by 12 percent. A more recent study of cyclists in Florida showed that using phosphate improved low-level endurance time significantly, lowered 40k time trial times by 8 percent, and raised lactate threshold by 10 percent, while lowering perceived effort. These results seem a bit extreme, but there is limited research on sodium phosphate.

It appears to produce benefits by causing the hemoglobin in the red blood cells to completely unload their stores of oxygen at the muscle. A greater supply of oxygen allows the muscles to operate aerobically at higher speeds and power outputs that would normally cause an anaerobic state.

Supplementation is similar to creatine loading. Take 4 grams of sodium phosphate for three days before an A-priority race. To prepare your gut for the change, take 1 or 2 grams for one or two days before starting the loading procedure. Spread out the daily dosage by taking one-third of it with each meal. Don't take it on an empty stomach. It's best not to continue using it more than three or four times each season, as continued supplementation reduces the benefits. In studies, the gains from sodium phosphate were still apparent one week after the loading stopped, meaning that consecutive races over two weeks can reap the benefits.

A side effect many athletes experience when sodium phosphate loading is an upset stomach. This may not appear until several days into the routine. Feeling sick right before a race is not good for your confidence, so it's best to try the loading procedure for the first time before an early-season C-priority race or workout. If you find it upsets your stomach, try the loading procedure shown in Table 16.3. Twin Labs, Inc. makes a product called Phos Fuel that works well. Take one capsule with a meal on each dosage day.

Table 16.3
Sodium Phosphate Loading

DAYS BEFORE A-PRIORITY RACE	DAILY DOSAGE (g)
16–19	1–1.5
14–15	none
9–13	1–1.5
7–8	none
6–race day	1–1.5

If you have a low dietary intake of calcium, sodium phosphate can cause a calcium deficiency. In this case, you'd be advised not to use it. Better yet, increase your intake of dietary calcium. Do not use calcium phosphate, as no performance benefits have been linked with it.

Caffeine

This is one of the oldest and most popular ergogenic aids. Caffeine has been shown to increase fatty acids in the blood, thus reducing the reliance on limited glycogen stores in the muscles. It also stimulates the central nervous system, decreasing the perception of fatigue, and may enhance muscle contractions. Most studies show benefits for intense events lasting an hour or longer when 300 to 600 milligrams of caffeine (two to four cups of coffee) are consumed forty-five minutes to an hour prior to the start. Table 16.4 lists the caffeine content of common products.

Numerous scientific studies of caffeine's effects over the past twenty years have produced many contradictions. Most have shown benefits for endurance athletes. A recent English study, however, found no benefits for marathon runners, but

Table 16.4

Caffeine Content in
6 ounces (180 ml)
of Common Products

PRODUCT	CAFFEINE CONTENT
Drip coffee	180 mg
Instant coffee	165 mg
Percolated coffee	149 mg
Brewed tea	60 mg
Mountain Dew	28 mg
Chocolate syrup	24 mg
Coca-Cola	23 mg
Pepsi Cola	19 mg

significant aid for milers. The majority of studies have suggested that caffeine only helps in events lasting longer than ninety minutes, but others have shown improvement in sixty- and even forty-five-minute competitions.

While the author of one study concluded that caffeine causes a complex chemical change in the muscles that stimulates more forceful contractions during a longer period of time than without it, most have found that caffeine simply spares muscle glycogen during endurance exercise. The beneficial effects peak at about one hour after consumption and seem to last three to five hours.

Glycogen is an energy source stored in the muscles. When glycogen runs low, the rider is forced to slow down or stop. Anything that causes the body to conserve this precious fuel, as caffeine appears to do, allows a cyclist to maintain a fast pace for a longer time. For example, a study of cyclists reported a 20-percent improvement in time to exhaustion following two cups of coffee one hour before testing.

The IOC's illegal limit requires about six to eight 5-ounce cups of coffee in an hour, depending on the athlete's size. While that's quite a bit to drink, it's certainly possible. It's interesting to note that other recent research suggested that caffeine at the illegal level actually had a negative effect on performance.

Most studies find that 1.4 to 2.8 milligrams of caffeine per pound of body weight taken an hour before exercise benefits most subjects engaged in endurance exercise. That's about two or three cups of coffee for a 154-pound person. Athletes have also been known to use other products high in caffeine before and during competition.

While caffeine may sound like a safe and effective aid, be aware that there are possible complications. Most studies have shown it to have a diuretic effect on non-exercisers, although one using athletes found little increased fluid losses during exercise. In people not used to caffeine, it may bring on anxiety, muscle tremors, gastrointestinal cramps, diarrhea, upset stomach, and nausea. These are not good things to experience before a race. Caffeine also inhibits the absorption of thiamin, a vitamin needed for carbohydrate metabolism, and several minerals, including calcium and iron.

If you normally have a cup or two of coffee in the morning, you'll probably have no side effects if it's used before a race. It appears that the benefits are greater for non-coffee drinkers than for regular users. If you don't drink coffee but are considering using it before a competition, try it several times before workouts to see how it affects you.

Glycerol

Do you wither in the heat? In long, hot races do you cramp up in the last few miles? Do you dread riding on days when the temperature reaches the 90s? If so, glycerol may be just what you need.

As your body loses fluid there is a corresponding drop in performance. As pointed out earlier, even a 1-percent drop in body weight due to dehydration reduces maximum work output by about 2 percent. This reduction is a result of decreased blood volume, since the plasma in blood supplies sweat. A 5-percent loss of body weight is common in hot, long races. Losing 7 percent of body weight due to fluid depletion is dangerous to health and may even require hospitalization. Some athletes suffer the effects of heat more than others.

Other factors besides heat may cause you to dehydrate. Sometimes all it takes is a missed feed during a race or a dropped bottle. Beyond these problems, there are also physiological limits on how much fluid the human digestive tract can absorb during high-intensity racing. All of this can lead to disaster in what might have otherwise been an exceptional race.

Glycerol, a syrupy, sweet-tasting liquid, turns your body into a water-hoarding sponge. Used prior to a race, it causes the body to hold on to 50 percent more fluid than when using water alone. Because of this, fluid losses through urination are decreased and there is more water available for sweat.

In one study using cyclists, body temperatures increased 40 percent less when using glycerol, compared with water only. Also, heart rate increased 5 percent less with glycerol, and there was a 32-percent improvement in endurance. These are tremendous advantages that could take you from the DNF listing to the top 10. Who would not want these benefits?

In recent years, glycerol products for endurance athletes have become available in running stores, bike shops, heath food and specialty stores, and through catalog sales. Simply mix and drink the product according to the instructions on the label. Using more will not help you and may even cause problems.

As with anything new, you should experiment with glycerol before a workout—not a race. It has been known to cause headaches and nausea in some athletes. Better to find that out in training rather than in the most important race of the season.

There have been no long-term studies on the effect of large doses of glycerol, but it is generally considered safe as it is found naturally in dietary fats.

The supplement industry in the United States is not closely regulated by the government, and consequently product purity may be an issue if any of the above products are purchased from unscrupulous manufacturers. For example, a recent analysis of a widely advertised category of dietary supplements found unidentifiable impurities in most of the products. Some of these have turned out to be banned substances that have cost athletes their eligibilities for several months. Buy only from reputable companies whose products are well-established in the marketplace. Don't take anything unless you are sure that it does not contain banned substances.

Also, no studies have been done on how any of the ergogenic aids described here may interact if all of them are used together, with other supplements, or even with many of the medications commonly used by athletes such as ibuprofen or aspirin. It's always a good idea to talk with your health-care provider before taking any supplement, all the more so if you are on any medications.

When using an ergogenic aid, it's important that you assess the benefits, if any, for your performance. Not only does using several concurrently increase your risk of side effects, it also clouds the issue of which one provided the most performance gain—or prevented it. In addition, you should always be skeptical of better race performances as a result of supplementation. Was it really the pill, or was it the placebo effect? While many athletes probably don't care, coming to understand what helps you and what doesn't will ultimately lead to your best races.

In the final analysis, training and diet provide 99.9 percent of the impetus for performance improvements. Supplements offer only a small benefit. If your training and diet are less than desirable, there is no reason to add any ergogenic supplement to the mix.

References

"Altering Cardiorespiratory Fitness." *Sports Medicine* 3, no. 5 (1986): 346–356.

Anderson, O. "Carbs, Creatine and Phosphate: If the King had Used these Uppers, He'd Still Be Around Today." *Running Research News* 12, no. 3 (1996): 1–4.

Angus, D.J., et al. "Effect of Carbohydrate or Carbohydrate Plus Medium-Chain Triglyceride Ingestion on Cycling Time Trial Performance." *Journal of Applied Physiology* 88, no. 1 (2000): 113–119.

"Antioxidants and the Elite Athlete." Proceedings of Panel Discussion, Dallas, Texas. May 27, 1992.

"Antioxidants: Clearing the Confusion." *IDEA Today* (Sept. 1994): 67–73.

Balsam, P.D. "Creatine Supplementation Per Se Does Not Enhance Endurance Exercise Performance." *Acta Phys Scand* 149, no. 4 (1993): 521–523.

Blomstrand, E., et al. "Administration of Branched Chain Amino Acids during Sustained Exercise—Effects on Performance and on Plasma Concentrations of Some Amino Acids." *European Journal of Applied Physiology* 62 (1991): 83–88.

Cade, R., et al. "Effects of Phosphate Loading on 2,3-diphosphoglycerate and Maximal Oxygen Uptake." *Medicine and Science in Sports and Exercise* 16, no. 3 (1984): 263–268.

Cera, F.B., et al. "Branched-Chain Amino Acid Supplementation During Trekking at High Altitude." *European Journal of Applied Physiology* 65 (1992): 394–398.

Clement, D.B., et al. "Branched Chain Metabolic Support: A Prospective, Randomized Double-Blind Trial in Surgical Stress." *Annals of Surgery* 199 (1984): 286–291.

Cordain, L., Department of Exercise and Sport Science, Colorado State University, Fort Collins, CO. Personal communication.

Cordain, L. *The Paleo Diet*. New York: Wiley & Sons, 2002.

Doherty, M. "The Effects of Caffeine on the Maximal Accumulated Oxygen Deficit and Short-Term Running Performance." *International Journal of Sports Nutrition* 8, no. 2 (1998): 95–104.

Eaton, S.B., and D.A. Nelson. "Calcium in Evolutionary Perspective." *American Journal of Clinical Nutrition* 54 (1991): 281S–287S.

Eaton, S.B. "Humans, Lipids and Evolution." *Lipids* 27, no. 1 (1992): 814–820.

Eaton, S.B., and M. Konner. "Paleolithic Nutrition: A Consideration of its Nature and Current Implications." *The New England Journal of Medicine* 312, no. 5, 283–289.

"Elevation of Creatine in Resting and Exercised Muscle of Normal Subjects by Creatine Supplementation." *Clinical Science* 83 (1992): 367–374.

"An Evaluation of Dietary Intakes of Triathletes: Are RDAs Being Met?" *Brief Communications* (Nov. 1989): 1653–1654.

Evans, W., et al. "Protein Metabolism and Endurance Exercise." *The Physician and Sports Medicine* 11, no. 7 (1983): 63–72.

Goedecke, J.H., et al. "Effects of Medium-Chain Triaclyglycerol Ingested with Carbohydrate on Metabolism and Exercise Performance." *International Journal of Sports Nutrition* 9, no. 1 (1999): 35–47.

Graham, T.E., and L.L. Spriet. "Caffeine and Exercise Performance." *Sports Science Exchange* 9, no. 1 (1996): 1–6.

Graham, T.E., et al. "Metabolic and Exercise Endurance Effects of Coffee and Caffeine Ingestion." *Journal of Applied Physiology* 85, no. 3 (1998): 883–889.

Guilland, J.C., et al. "Vitamin Status of Young Athletes Including the Effects of Supplementation." *Medicine and Science in Sport and Exercise* 21 (1989): 441–449.

Horowitz, J.F., et al. "Pre-exercise Medium-Chain Triglyceride Ingestion Does Not Alter Muscle Glycogen Use during Exercise." *Journal of Applied Physiology* 88, no. 1 (2000): 219–225.

Kovacs, E.M.R., et al. "Effect of Caffeinated Drinks on Substrate Metabolism, Caffeine Excretion and Performance." *Journal of Applied Physiology* 85, no. 2 (1998): 709–715.

Kreider, R.B., et al. "Effects of Phosphate Loading on Metabolic and Myocardial Responses to Maximal and Endurance Exercise." *International Journal of Sports Nutrition* 2, no. 1 (1992): 20–47.

Kreider, R.B., et al. "Effects of Phosphate Loading on Oxygen Uptake, Ventilatory Anaerobic Threshold, and Run Performance." *Medicine and Science in Sports and Exercise* 22, no. 2 (1990): 250–256.

Massey, L.K., et al. "Interactions between Dietary Caffeine and Calcium on Calcium and Bone Metabolism in Older Women." *Journal of the American College of Nutrition* 13 (1994): 592–596.

McMurtrey, J.J., and R. Sherwin. "History, Pharmacology and Toxicology of Caffeine and Caffeine-Containing Beverages." *Clinical Nutrition* 6 (1987): 249–254.

Mujika, I., and S. Padilla. "Creatine Supplementation as an Ergogenic Aid for Sports Performance in Highly Trained Athletes: A Critical Review." *International Journal of Sports Medicine* 18, no. 7 (1997): 491–496.

Nelson, A.G., et al. "Muscle Glycogen Supercompensation Is Enhanced by Prior Creatine Supplementation." *Medicine and Science in Sports and Exercise* 33, no. 7 (2001): 1096–1100.

Peyrebrune, M.C., et al. "The Effects of Oral Creatine Supplementation on Performance in Single and Repeated Sprint Training." *Journal of Sports Science* 16, no. 3 (1998): 271–279.

Somer, E., and Health Medical of America. *The Essential Guide to Vitamins and Minerals.* New York: HarperPerennial, 1992.

Stahl, A.B. "Hominid Dietary Selection before Fire." *Current Anthropology* 25, no. 2 (1984): 151–168.

Stewart, I., et al. "Phosphate Loading and the Effects on VO_2max in Trained Cyclists." *Research Quarterly for Exercise and Sport* 61, no. 1 (1990): 80–84.

Vanzyl, C.G., et al. "Effects of Medium-Chain Triglycerides Ingestion on Fuel Metabolism and Cycling Performance." *Journal of Applied Physiology* 80, no. 6 (1996): 2217–2225.

Wemple, R.D., et al. "Caffeine vs. Caffeine-Free Sports Drinks: Effects on Urine Production at Rest and during Prolonged Exercise." *International Journal of Sports Medicine* 18 (1997): 40–46.

Wilcox, A.R. "Caffeine and Endurance Performance." *Sports Science Exchange* 3, no. 26 (1990).

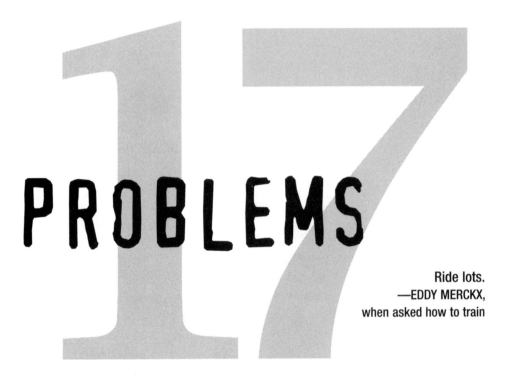

Ride lots.
—EDDY MERCKX,
when asked how to train

Cycling is an addiction. The addictive nature of racing on two wheels is usually a positive, but from time-to-time problems do appear.

We so desperately want to excel in racing, and yet things get in the way. Sometimes it seems that life just isn't fair. Or is it? Where do our problems come from? In our greed to become more fit in less time, we may overtrain. We work out despite the scratchy throat and lose ten days to illness rather than five. Or our bodies seem invincible, so we push big gears in the hills repeatedly and wind up nursing a sore knee while watching the next race from the curb.

With rare exception, the problems we face in training and racing are of our own making. Our motivation to excel is exceeded only by our inability to listen to our bodies. The result is often overtraining, burnout, illness, or injury. This chapter describes how to avoid these problems, or, if necessary, how to deal with them.

Overtraining

Overtraining is best described as a decreased work capacity resulting from an imbalance between training and rest. In the real world of cycling, this means decreasing performance is the best indicator of training gone awry. But when we have a bad race, what do most of us do? You guessed it—we train harder. We put in more miles, or do more intervals, or both. It is a rare athlete who rests more when things aren't going well.

Of course, poor races don't always result from too much training. You could be "overliving." A forty-hour-per-week job, two kids, a spouse, a mortgage, and other responsibilities all take their well-deserved toll on energy. Training just happens to be the thing most easily controlled. You sure aren't going to call the boss to ask for the day off since you're on the edge of overtraining. (Try to imagine how that conversation would go.) Nor will you tell the kids to get themselves to the scout meeting. Life goes on. Your smartest option is to train less and rest more.

Figure 17.1 shows what happens when we refuse to give in and insist on more, more, more. Notice that as the training load increases, fitness also increases, up to our personal limit. At that point, fitness declines despite an increasing load. Training beyond our limit causes a loss of fitness.

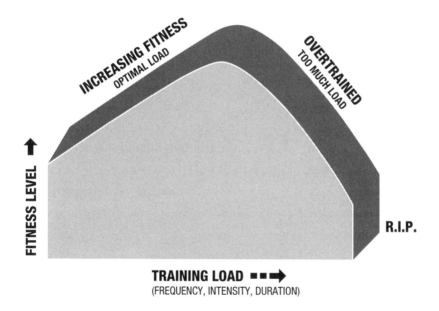

Figure 17.1
Overtraining curve

Increased training loads that eventually lead to overtraining stem from three common training excesses:

1. Workouts are too long (excess duration).
2. Exertion is too high too often (excess intensity).
3. Too many workouts are done in too little time (excess frequency).

The most common cause I see in competitive cyclists is excess intensity. Road racing is roughly 90-percent aerobic and 10-percent anaerobic. Training should reflect that relationship. Placing too much emphasis on anaerobic training for a few weeks is a sure way to overtrain. That's why the Build period is limited to six weeks of high intensity plus two recovery weeks.

Overtraining Indicators

Table 17.1
Overtraining Indicators in
Cyclists

The body responds to the overtrained state by issuing warnings in many forms (see Table 17.1). These reactions are the body's way of preventing death by making further increases in stress volume all but impossible.

BEHAVIORAL	PHYSICAL
Apathy	Reduced performance
Lethargy	Weight change
Depression	Morning heart rate change
Poor concentration	Muscle soreness
Sleep pattern changes	Swollen lymph glands
Irritability	Diarrhea
Decreased libido	Injury
Clumsiness	Infection
Increased thirst	Amenorrhea
Sluggishness	Decreased exercise heart rate
Craving for sugar	Slow-healing cuts

If you've had blood testing during the Preparation or Base periods of training, you have a healthy baseline for later comparison. When you suspect overtraining during other periods of the season, it's a good idea to have your blood tested again. Table 17.2 lists primary blood indicators of overtraining reported in a 1992 study of experienced middle- and long-distance runners. Realize that you are comparing your recent test results with the baseline established when you were known to be healthy, not with standards for the general population.

None of the items listed in Tables 17.1 and 17.2 are "sure" indicators. Many of these situations may even exist in perfectly healthy athletes who are in top shape. In dealing with overtraining, there are no absolutes. You're looking for a preponderance of evidence to confirm what you already suspect.

Table 17.2
Blood Marker Indicators of
Overtraining

SIGNIFICANT DECREASES FROM INDIVIDUAL BASELINE MARKERS MAY INDICATE OVERTRAINING:		
Albumin	Glycerin	Leukocytes
Ammonium	Hemoglobin	Magnesium
Ferritin Iron	Iron	Triglycerides
Free fatty acids	LDL cholesterol	VLDL cholesterol

Stages of Overtraining

There are three stages on the road to becoming overtrained. The first stage is "overload." This is a part of the normal process of increasing the training load beyond what you are used to in order to cause the body to adapt. If great enough, but controlled, it results in supercompensation as described in Chapter 10. During this stage it's typical to experience short-term fatigue, but generally you will feel great and may have outstanding race results. But also during this stage it's common to feel as if your body is invincible. You can do anything, if you want to. That belief brings on the next stage.

In the second stage, "overreaching," you continue to train at the same abnormally high load levels, or even increase them for a period of two weeks or so. Extending the Build period of training with its higher intensity is a common cause of overreaching. Now, for the first time, your performance noticeably decreases. Usually this happens in workouts before it shows up in races, where high motivation often pulls you through. Fatigue becomes longer lasting than in the overload stage, but with a few days of rest it is still reversible. The problem is that you decide what's needed is harder training, which brings on the third stage.

The third and final stage is a full-blown overtraining syndrome. Fatigue is now chronic—it stays with you like a shadow. You are tired on awaking and throughout the day, on the job, or in class, and yet have trouble sleeping normally at night. Your adrenal glands are exhausted.

The Geography of Overtraining

I tell the athletes I train that in order to get to the "peak of fitness" they must travel through the "valley of fatigue" dangerously close to the "precipice of overtraining." Figure 17.2 shows how increasing the training load causes a decline in fitness and brings you closer to the edge of the Precipice. The idea is to go the edge infrequently, and then back off. By "infrequently" I mean once every four weeks or so. After three weeks of load increases, you need to allow for recovery and adaptation. Some athletes, especially masters and novices, may need to recover more frequently, perhaps after only two weeks. To do more is to fall over the edge.

Figure 17.2
Valley of fatigue

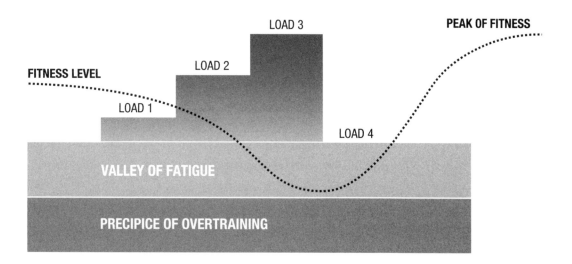

As the body enters the valley of fatigue, overtraining indicators rear their ugly heads. You may experience poor sleep quality, excessive fatigue, or muscle soreness on a continuing basis. Once in the valley, indicators may be minor in number and severity, but with too great an increase or too prolonged a period of stress, you're on the edge of overtraining. At this point, you wisely reduce training (Load 4 in Figure 17.2) and rest more. Rest brings adaptation marked by fitness increasing to a level exceeding the starting level four weeks before. By repeating this process several times, you are eventually ready to peak.

If you fall over the edge into overtraining, the only option is rest. At the first signs of overtraining, take forty-eight hours of complete rest, and then try a brief recovery workout. If you are still not feeling peppy, take another forty-eight hours off and repeat the test ride. It could take five to eight weeks of this to fully beat back overtraining, at a great loss of fitness.

The Art of Training

The art of training is knowing where the precipice of overtraining is for you. Highly motivated, young, or novice cyclists are less likely to recognize having crossed the line than are seasoned riders. That is why many cyclists are better off training under the guidance of an experienced coach.

Smart training requires constantly assessing your readiness to train. Chapter 15 provided a training diary format with suggested daily indicators to rate. Judiciously tracking these indicators will help you pay closer attention to the body's daily messages.

Unfortunately, there is no sure-fire formula for knowing when you have done too much and are starting to overreach. The best prevention is the judicious use of rest and recovery. Just as workouts must vary between hard and easy, so must weeks and months vary. It's far better to be undertrained, but eager, than to be overtrained. When in doubt—leave it out.

Burnout

By August every year, many riders begin to experience burnout. It is not overtraining—there are no physical symptoms, but more a state of mind marked by decreased interest in training and racing, sometimes even frustration and a feeling of overwhelming drudgery when it comes time to get on the bike.

A mentally fried athlete may have been experiencing a slump for a couple of weeks. Negative reactions to the slump lower self-esteem and motivation, making focused concentration a thing of the past. This downward spiral leads to burnout.

A medical condition such as mononucleosis or anemia may be masquerading as burnout, but this is rare. For most of us, it is just a matter of timing. This is still a good time to get a blood test, just in case.

Burnout Timing

That some cyclists become mental toast by August is not just bad luck or mere coincidence. About 220 to 250 days into heavy training without a break, athletes begin to experience burnout. If your serious workouts started in December or January, and there have been no breaks, August burnout fits right into that timeline.

Many riders race twice every weekend and do a hard club ride and BT workout at mid-week. That is a lot of intensity and emotional investment week after week. For this reason, Build periods should last no longer than eight weeks including recovery weeks. Serious racing without time off the bike for more than six weeks, less for some, may also lead to August burnout.

Those who experience burnout are usually zealous athletes who set high racing goals. By August, they have either attained the goals or have decided they are unattainable. Either situation may contribute to racing and training apathy.

Circumstances other than the two-wheeled variety may also contribute to you becoming mental toast. Emotional stresses such as job change, divorce, and moving definitely lead to burnout. Environmental factors including heat, humidity, high altitude, and pollution take a toll on enthusiasm. All of this may be compounded by a diet deficient in nutrients and water.

Burnout Potion

If there is no doubt that you are burned out and yet you still have an important race at the end of the season, there are only three things to do: rest, rest, and rest. Time off the bike is probably the hardest medicine to take for a usually enthusiastic rider. But a week to ten days of no training should have you ready to go again soon.

I can hear you now: "I'll lose all my fitness." No you won't, but even if you did, which would be better—fit but apathetic, or unfit and ready to go? It takes months to develop endurance, force, and speed. They won't slip away in a few days. After a short break, you'll be ready to race again with two weeks of Build 1 training, three weeks tops.

More important, you need to learn something from the experience: Don't let it happen again next year. The way to avoid burnout in August is to plan on a two-peak season by bringing yourself into race form in the spring and then taking a short break of five to seven days off the bike. After that, rebuild your base fitness and be ready to go with another late-season peak.

The key to racing well when you want to is foresight. Good races in August don't just happen—they are planned well in advance.

Illness

You would think that a lot of training would be healthy and help you avoid illness. That is not the case. Those who work out frequently are more likely to catch a bug than those who work out occasionally.

A study of runners in the Los Angeles Marathon found that those running more than 60 miles per week were twice as susceptible to respiratory illness as those who ran less than 20 miles each week. Runners who completed the marathon were six times as likely to be ill in the week following the race as those who trained hard for the race but for some reason did not run it.

Timing

The six hours following a hard workout or race has been shown as the most critical phase for remaining healthy, as the immune system is depressed and less capable of fighting off disease. This six-hour period is a good time to avoid public places. Washing your hands frequently if you have contact with others during this time is also a good idea for staying healthy.

Neck Check

But what should you do when a cold or flu bug gets you down? Should you continue to train as normal, cut back, or stop altogether? Doing a "neck check" will help you decide. If your symptoms are a runny nose, sneezing, or a scratchy throat (all symptoms above the neck), start your workout but reduce the intensity to zones 1 or 2 and keep the duration short. If you feel worse after the first few minutes, stop and head home. If the symptoms are below the neck, such as chest cold, chills, vomiting, achy muscles, or a fever, don't even start. You probably have an acute viral infection. Exercising intensely in this condition will increase the severity of the illness and can even cause extreme complications, including death.

These below-the-neck symptoms are likely to be accompanied by the Coxsackie virus that can invade the heart muscle, causing arrhythmia and other complications. I can speak from experience on this one. In November 1994 I caught a bad cold with several below-the-neck symptoms including fever, achy muscles, and coughing up mucous. Five months later, I had a full-blown Coxsackie virus in my heart. After a year of inactivity, I was finally able to start training again. No race or any amount of fitness is worth paying such a price. Don't take these symptoms lightly. Suspect Coxsackie virus is present whenever you have a respiratory infection with indicators below the neck.

Recuperating

After the illness has abated, you are likely to be run down for some time. There is a 15-percent reduction in muscle strength for up to a month following a bout of the flu. Aerobic capacity is also reduced for up to three months and muscles become acidic at lower levels of intensity during this time. This means you will feel weak when working out even though the acute stage is past. Following a below-the-neck illness, return to the Base period of training for two days for every day you had symptoms.

Trying to "push" past the flu will likely make your condition worse and cause it to last longer. It is best to get rid of the illness as soon as possible by allowing your limited energy reserves to go into fighting the disease rather than training.

Injuries

There is nothing worse than an injury. It is not bad enough that fitness is slipping away, but so much of an athlete's life is tied to being physical that depression often sets in. No one wants to be around a lame athlete.

Some people seem prone to injuries. They get them doing what others do routinely. It is more than a nuisance. Here are some prevention tips that help keep injury-prone people healthy—most of the time.

Equipment

Get equipment that fits correctly. Riding a bike that is too big or too small sets you up for an injury. This is especially a problem for women cyclists who all too often ride bikes designed for men and for juniors riding bikes they'll "grow into."

Bike Set-up

Having poor biomechanics can easily injure a joint, especially the knee, as it repeats the same movement pattern hundreds or thousands of times under a load. Once you have the right equipment, ask an experienced cyclist, bike shop, or coach to take a look at your position and offer suggestions for improvement. Be especially concerned with saddle fore-aft position and height.

Training

The most likely times to get injured are the two days after very long or very hard workouts and races. These days should be short and easy, reserved for crosstraining or days off altogether. In the same manner, two or three hard weeks of training should be followed by a week of reduced volume and intensity. This may be difficult to do when you know your cardiovascular and energy production systems are willing and able to handle it, but such restraint will keep you injury free.

Strength and Stretching

For most of us, our weakest link is the muscle-tendon junction. This is where tears and strains are likely to occur. Many muscle-tendon problems can be prevented early in the season by gradually improving the muscle's strength and range of motion. These are probably the most neglected areas for endurance athletes. Going for a ride is fun, but grunting through a combined strength and stretching session in the gym seems like drudgery. Hang in there, and you'll reap the benefits.

Listen

Learn to tell the difference between sore muscles that come from a high-quality effort and sore joints or tendons. Pinpoint any discomfort and try to put the sensation into words. Don't just say "my knee hurts." Is it above or below the kneecap? Front or back of the knee? Is it a sharp pain or a dull ache? Does it hurt only while riding or all of the time? Is the pain worse going up stairs or down? These are the sorts of questions you will be asked when you finally seek professional help. Be ready for them.

If the pain is not gone with five days of reduced activity, it is time to see a health-care provider. Don't put it off. Injuries are easier to turn around in the early stages than later on.

References

Brenner, I.K.M. "Infection in Athletes." *Sports Medicine* 17, no. 2 (1994): 86–107.

David, A.S., et al. "Post-viral Fatigue Syndrome: Time for a New Approach." *British Medical Journal* 296 (1988): 696–699.

Fitzgerald, L. "Exercise and the Immune System." *Immunology Today* 9, no. 11 (1988): 337–339.

Fry, R.W., and D. Keast. "Overtraining in Athletes." *Sports Medicine* 12, no. 1 (1991): 32–65.

Heath, G.W., et al. "Exercise and Upper Respiratory Tract Infections: Is there a Relationship?" *Sports Medicine* 14, no. 6 (1992): 353–365.

Hoffman-Goetz, L., and B.K. Peterson. "Exercise and the Immune System: A Model of the Stress Response?" *Immunology Today* 15, no. 8 (1994): 382–387.

Hooper, S.L., and L.T. MacKinnon. "Monitoring Overtraining in Athletes: Recommendations." *Sports Medicine* 20, no. 5 (1995): 321–327.

Hooper, S.L., et al. "Markers for Monitoring Overtraining and Recovery." *Medicine and Science in Sports and Exercise* 27, no. 1 (1995): 106–112.

Keast, D., et al. "Exercise and the Immune Response." *Sports Medicine* 5 (1988): 248–267.

Kuipers, H. and H.A. Keizer. "Overtraining in Elite Athletes: Review and Directions for the Future." *Sports Medicine* 6 (1988): 79–92.

Lehmann, M., et al. "Overtraining in Endurance Athletes: A Brief Review." *Medicine and Science in Sports and Exercise* 25, no. 7 (1993): 854–862.

Milne, C. "The Tired Athlete." *New Zealand Journal of Sports Medicine* 19, no. 3 (1991): 42–44.

Nieman, D.C., et al. "Infectious Episodes in Runners Before and After the Los Angeles Marathon." *Journal of Sports Medicine and Physical Fitness* 30 (1990): 316–238.

Sharp, N.C.C. and Y. Koutedakis. "Sport and the Overtraining Syndrome." *British Medical Journal* 48, no. 3 (1992): 518–533.

Stone, M., et al. "Overtraining: A Review of the Signs, Symptoms and Possible Causes." *Journal of Applied Sport Sciences* 5, no. 1 (1991): 35–50.

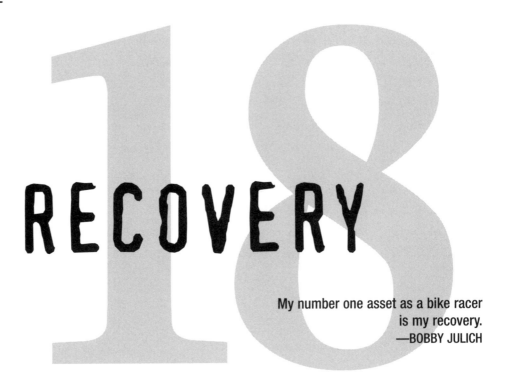

RECOVERY

My number one asset as a bike racer
is my recovery.
—BOBBY JULICH

Throughout this book, I have often referred to recovery and occasionally given some guidelines. This chapter will emphasize and more fully explain this important, and often underrated, aspect of training. Due to the nature of the sport, with its stage races and double-race weekends, cycling requires the athlete to be ready to go again within a few hours. In addition, the sooner a cyclist can do another breakthrough workout, the sooner his or her fitness will improve. Recovery holds the key to both of these situations.

The Need for Recovery

It is reasonably easy to get athletes to train hard. Give serious riders tough workouts and they are not only challenged, but most are even happy. Competitive cyclists are successful in part because they have a great capacity and affinity for hard work. Without such drive, they would never make it in the sport.

If daily, arduous training was the key to victory, everyone would be atop the winner's platform. The greater challenge for the self-coached cyclist is not formidable training sessions, but rather knowing how, when, and for how long to recover following tough workouts and races. Although that sounds like it should be easy, for most it is not. Recovery is the one area of training that athletes have the most difficulty getting right.

Recovery determines when you can go hard again, and ultimately, it determines your fitness level. Cut recovery short enough times and the specter of overtraining lurks ever nearer. Go beyond the time needed to recover, and you end up wasting time and may even be losing some components of your fitness. Most serious athletes err on the side of not allowing enough recovery. They believe that "training" only takes place on the bike. It is how many miles they ride, how hard the workouts are, and how often they ride that matter. To most, what they do off the bike has no relevance to fitness—it is viewed as "non-training" time and, therefore, of no consequence.

If you think that way, you are wrong. Off-the-bike-recovery time is critical to improving performance. Workouts provide the potential for increased fitness. But it's during recovery that the potential is realized. The time it takes for your body to realize this potential is also critical. The sooner you recover, the sooner you can do another quality workout. The sooner you can do another quality workout, the more fit you become. Another way of looking at it is as a formula:

Fitness = Workout + Recovery

In this formula, workout and recovery are of equal value. So the higher the intensity of the workout, the greater the depth of recovery must be, not only in terms of time, but also in terms of method. They must balance. If the balance is right, your fitness is bound to improve. Get the balance wrong often enough, and you are initially suffering, then off the back, and finally overtrained.

If you understand this relationship between workouts and recovery you will be as concerned about the quality of recovery as the difficulty of the preceding workout. The first question to answer in writing a weekly training schedule should be, "How quickly can I recover?" With the answer to that question, the week can be scheduled.

Recovery Time

What happens inside the muscles during a hard workout is not a pretty sight. If you could look into your legs with a microscope after a hard race or BT workout, what you would see looks like a battleground. The muscles appear as if a miniature bomb has exploded, with torn and jagged cell membranes evident. The damage can vary from slight to extreme, depending on how powerful the workout was. Under such conditions, it is unlikely the muscles and nervous system will be able to go hard again. Not until the cells are repaired, the energy stores rebuilt, and cellular chemistry returns to normal will another all-out effort be possible. Your racing performance depends on how long that process takes.

Much of the time needed for recovery has to do with creating new muscle protein to repair the damage. Research conducted at McMaster University in Hamilton, Ontario, and at the Washington University School of Medicine in St. Louis found that this protein resynthesis process takes several hours. The study used young, experienced weight lifters and maximal efforts followed by observation of the muscles' repair process.

Reconstruction work started almost immediately following the workout. Four hours after the weight session protein activity was increased about 50 percent. By twenty-four hours post-workout it reached a peak of 109 percent of normal. Protein resynthesis was back to normal, indicating that repair was complete, thirty-six hours after the hard workout.

While this study used exhaustive strength training to measure recovery time, the results are similar to what could be expected following a hard race or cycling workout.

Recovery Phases

The recovery process can be divided into three phases in relation to the workout— before and during, immediately following, and long term. If each is carefully planned, recovery will be quicker and the next quality session made more productive.

Recovery before and during the Workout

Recovery actually starts with a warm-up before the workout or race that will cause the damage, not after. A good warm-up before starting to ride hard helps limit damage by:

- Thinning body fluids to allow easier muscle contractions
- Opening capillaries to bring more oxygen to muscles
- Raising muscle temperature so that contractions take less effort
- Conserving carbohydrates and releasing fat for fuel

The recovery process should continue during the workout with the ongoing replacement of carbohydrate-based energy stores. By drinking 18 to 24 ounces of a sports drink every hour, the training session is less stressful on the body and the recovery of the energy production system later on is enhanced. There is some research indicating that the addition of protein to your sports drink may also be beneficial. Other research has supported the addition of caffeine to the sports drink. These bodies of research are still growing.

There are individual differences in how well carbohydrate drinks are tolerated and emptied from the stomach. Find a sports drink that tastes good and doesn't upset your stomach when riding hard. Before a race, make sure you have plenty of whatever works for you on your bike and are prepared for hand-ups at feed zones. Making the drink more concentrated than is recommended on the label may cause you to dehydrate during a fast race, especially on a hot and humid day. You most likely to benefit from a sports drink during races and workouts longer than one hour are . In races lasting longer than about four hours, solid food is also necessary.

Gels may be used in place of or in addition to sports drinks. By using a gel with water you are essentially mixing a sports drink in your gut. If you don't take in enough water with the gel the risk of dehydration increases, as fluid will be pulled from the blood plasma into the gut to help break down the sugar of the gel. Due to this same mechanism, it's also best to wash down the gel with water rather than a sports drink.

Recovery continues with a cool-down. If you complete the interval portion of a workout and hammer all the way back to the front door and then collapse in a heap, recovery will be prolonged. Instead, always use the last ten to twenty minutes of a hard ride to bring the body back to normal. The cool-down should be a mirror image of the warm-up, although it may be considerably shorter, ending with easy pedaling in zone 1 for several minutes.

Short-Term Recovery following the Workout

As soon as you are off the bike, the most important thing you can do to speed recovery is to replace the carbohydrates and protein just used for fuel. A long and hard workout or race can deplete nearly all of your stored glycogen, a carbohydrate-based energy source, and consume several grams of muscle-bound protein. In the thirty minutes after riding, your body is several times more capable of absorbing and replenishing those fuels than at any other time.

At this time, you don't want to use the same sports drink you used on the bike. It's not potent enough. You need something designed for recovery. There are several such products now on the market. As long as you like the taste and can get 15 to 20 grams of protein and about 80 grams of simple carbohydrates from one of them, it will meet your recovery needs. You can easily make a recovery "homebrew" by adding 5 tablespoons of table sugar to 16 ounces of skim milk. Whatever you use, drink all of it within the first thirty minutes after finishing.

Short-term recovery continues for as long as the preceding workout or race lasted. So if the race was three hours long, this recovery phase lasts three hours after getting off the bike. Once past the first thirty minutes the remaining portion should be focused on foods that are moderate- to high-glycemic index along with some protein. Following the short-term recovery phase return to eating foods that are dense in vitamins and minerals and are lower on the glycemic index scale. The best such foods for long-term recovery are vegetables, fruits, and lean meats including fish and poultry. See Chapter 16 for more information on the glycemic index and nutrient-dense foods.

Long-Term Recovery

In the six to nine hours after a BT workout or race, you must actively seek recovery by using one or more specific techniques. This is critical when stage racing, meaning the difference between finishing well in subsequent stages and failing to finish at all.

The most basic method is sleep. Nothing beats a nap for rejuvenation. In addition to a 30- to 60-minute, post-workout nap, seven to nine hours of sleep are needed each night. Other recovery methods are unique to each individual, so you will need to experiment with several of these to find the ones that work best for you.

Most of these methods speed recovery by slightly increasing the heart rate, increasing blood flow to the muscles, accelerating the inflow of nutrients, reducing soreness, lowering blood pressure, or relaxing the nervous system.

Hot Shower or Bath

Immediately following the cool-down and recovery drink, take a hot shower or bath for ten to fifteen minutes. Do not linger, especially in the bathtub, as you will dehydrate even more.

Active Recovery

For the experienced rider, one of the best recovery methods is to pedal easily for 15 to 30 minutes several hours after the workout and before going to bed. Pressure on the pedals should be extremely light and cadence comfortably high with very low power and heart rate low in zone 1.

Another effective active recovery technique is better for the novice, but also works well for seasoned riders. This technique is swimming, especially with a pull buoy between the legs, or simply moving in the water while floating.

Massage

Other than sleep, most riders find a massage by a professional therapist is the most effective recovery technique. A post-race massage should employ long, flushing strokes to speed the removal of the waste products of exercise. Deep massage at this time may actually increase muscle trauma. After thirty-six hours, the therapist can apply greater point pressure, working more deeply.

Due to the expense of massage, some athletes prefer self-massage. Following a hot bath or shower, stroke the leg muscles for 20 to 30 minutes working away from the feet and toward the heart.

Sauna

Several hours following a workout or race some athletes report that a dry sauna speeds recovery. Do not use a steam room for recovery as it will have the opposite effect. Stay in the sauna for no more than ten minutes and begin drinking fluids as soon as you are done.

Relax and Stretch

Be lazy for several hours. Your legs want quality rest. Give it to them by staying off your feet whenever possible. Never stand when you can lean against something. Sit down whenever possible. Better yet, lie on the floor with your feet elevated against a wall or furniture. Sit on the floor and stretch gently. Overused muscles tighten and can't seem to relax on their own. This is best right after a hot bath or sauna and just before going to bed.

Walk in a Park or Forest

A few hours after finishing the workout or race, a short, slow walk in a heavily vegetated area such as a park or forest seems to speed recovery for some. Abundant oxygen and the aroma of grass, trees, and other plants are soothing.

Other Methods

The sports program of the former Soviet Union made a science of recovery and employed several techniques with their athletes that may or may not be available to you. They included electro muscle stimulation, ultrasound, hyperbaric chambers, sport psychology, and pharmacological supplements such as vitamins, minerals, and adaptogens. These require expert guidance.

Figure 18.1
Recovery time with and without specific techniques

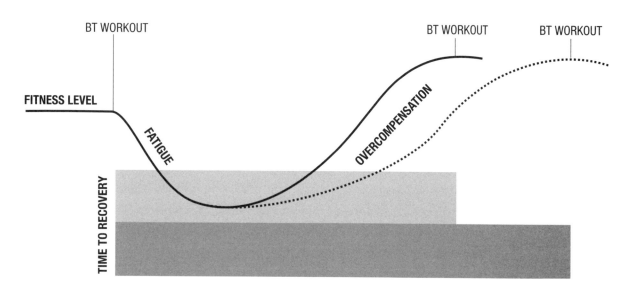

By employing some of the specific methods described here, you can accelerate the recovery process and return to action sooner. Figure 18.1 illustrates how this happens.

Individualization

While I have listed several possible methods to speed recovery, you will find that some work better for you than others. You may also discover that a teammate doing the same workouts as you and following the same recovery protocol springs back at a different rate—either slower or faster. This goes back to the principle of individualization discussed in Chapter 3. While there are many physiological similarities between athletes, we are each unique and respond in our own way to any given set of circumstances. You must experiment if you want to discover how best to recover. As always, do this in training rather than in the first important stage race of the season.

There are several individual factors affecting recovery. Younger athletes, especially those who are 18- to 22-years old, recover faster than older athletes. The more race-experienced an athlete is, the quicker he or she recovers. If fitness is high, recovery is speeded up. Females were shown in one study to recover faster than males. Other factors influencing the rate of recovery are climate, diet, and psychological stress.

How do you know if you are recovering? The best indicator is performance in races and hard workouts, but these are the worst times to find out that you're not ready. Typical signs that recovery is complete include a positive attitude, feelings of health, a desire to train hard again, high-quality sleep, normal resting and exercise heart rates, and balanced emotions. If any of these are lacking, continue the recovery process. By closely monitoring such signs, you should be able to determine not only the best procedure, but also the typical time needed to bounce back.

Recovery in the Real World

If you're following the periodization program suggested in this book, there will occasionally be periods of time when you experience an increasing load of fatigue. Despite your best recovery efforts, you will not unload all of the fatigue between planned workouts and will go into some BT workouts a bit heavy legged and lacking snap. Don't expect to be fully recovered for every workout, all the time. In fact, a little workout fatigue sometimes can bring benefits in the form of supercompensation, which was discussed in earlier chapters. This can better prepare you for stage races and peak performances. You just don't want this to happen too often. Every three or four weeks, depending on your ability to avoid overtraining, a recovery week should be included to allow for the unloading of fatigue before starting a new three- or four-week block of training.

References

Bompa, T. *Periodization, Theory and Methodology of Training: The Key to Athletic Performance*. Dubuque, IA: Kendall/Hunt Publishing, 1994.

Brunner, R., and B. Tabachnik. *Soviet Training and Recovery Methods*. Sport Focus Publishing, 1990.

Cade, J.R., et al. "Dietary Intervention and Training in Swimmers." *European Journal of Applied Physiology* 63 (1991): 210–215.

Dragan, I., and I. Stonescu. *Organism Recovery Following Training*. Bucharest: Sport-Turism, 1978.

Ernst, E. "Does Post-Exercise Massage Treatment Reduce Delayed Onset Muscle Soreness? A Systematic Review." *British Journal of Sports Medicine* 32, no. 3 (1998): 212–214.

Greiwe, J.S., et al. "Effects of Endurance Exercise Training on Muscle Glycogen Accumulation in Humans." *Journal of Applied Physiology* 87, no. 1 (1999): 222–226.

Newham, D.J., et al. "Muscle Pain and Tenderness after Exercise." *Australian Journal of Sports Medicine and Exercise Science* 14 (1982): 129–131.

Phillips, S.M., et al. "Mixed Muscle Protein Synthesis and Breakdown after Resistance Exercise in Humans." *American Journal of Physiology* 273, no. 1 (1997): E99–E107.

Rasmussen, B.B., et al. "An Oral Essential Amino Acid–Carbohydrate Supplement Enhances Muscle Protein Anabolism after Resistance Exercise." *Journal of Applied Physiology* 88, no. 2 (2000): 386–392.

Ready, S.L., et al. "Effect of Two Sports Drinks on Muscle Tissue Stress and Performance." *Medicine and Science in Sports and Exercise* 31, no. 5 (1999): S119.

Roy, B.D., et al. "Effect of Glucose Supplement Timing on Protein Metabolism after Resistance Training." *Journal of Applied Physiology* 82 (1997): 1882–1888.

Roy, B.D., et al. "The Influence of Post-Exercise Macronutrient Intake on Energy Balance and Protein Metabolism in Active Females Participating in Endurance Training." *International Journal of Sport Nutrition, Exercise and Metabolism* 12, no. 2 (2002): 172–188.

Smith, L.L., et al. "The Effects of Athletic Massage on Delayed Onset Muscle Soreness, Creatine Kinase, and Neutrophil Count: A Preliminary Report." *Journal of Orthopedic Sports Physical Thearpy* 19, no. 2 (1994): 93–99.

Tiidus, P.M., and J.K. Shoemaker. "Effleurage Massage, Muscle Blood Flow and Long-Term Post-Exercise Strength Recovery." *International Journal of Sports Medicine* 16, no. 7 (1995): 478–483.

Tiidus, P.M. "Massage and Ultrasound as Therapeutic Modalities in Exercise-Induced Muscle Damage. *Canadian Journal of Physiology* 24, no. 3 (1999): 267–278.

VanHall, G., et al. "Muscle Glycogen Resynthesis during Recovery from Cycle Exercise: No Effect of Additional Protein Ingestion." *Journal of Applied Physiology* 88, no. 5 (2000): 1631–1636.

VanNieuwenhoven, M.A., et al. "Gastrointestinal Function during Exercise: Comparison of Water, Sports Drink, and Sports Drink with Caffeine." *Journal of Applied Physiology* 89, no. 3 (2000): 1079–1085.

Viitsalo, J.T., et al. "Warm Underwater Water-Jet Massage Improves Recovery from Intense Physical Exercise." *European Journal of Applied Physiology* 71, no. 5 (1995): 431–438.

EPILOGUE

A couple of hundred pages back I explained that my purpose in writing this book was to help you become a better cyclist. By now I hope you know what that means: work out with a purpose, listen to your body, train with a scientific method, and place a high value on rest and recovery. I have had so many cyclists tell me that the changes they made in these areas with their own training was successful in producing better racing that I feel confident you will benefit, also.

Sometimes the hardest part of training is doing what you know is right rather than what others want you to do. Cycling is unique in many ways, beginning with the plethora of group rides available to most cyclists. Be careful of these rides as they will divert you from the path of improved performance. The number of racing "opportunities" throughout the race season also makes cycling unique. Frequent racing means infrequent training. Be conservative with how often you race regardless of whether it is an organized event or weekday group ride. In the final analysis, you'll be better off because of it.

In the seven years since I first wrote this book there have been many changes in the world of cycling. Some have been technological. The most promising of these is the trend toward training with power. In 1995 powermeters were almost unheard of. Practically no one had one. I had to import one from Germany just to see what they were all about. Now there are three companies making them, with more in the wings preparing their offerings. If you aren't doing so now, within five years you will consider training with power a necessity. There will still be some who don't fully grasp the value of such equipment, but they will be in the minority.

Expect other technological advances in training. Someday we may opt to have a small biometrics chip implanted that monitors heart rate, reports lactate levels, and helps us regulate blood glucose. Our friends and spouses may be able to track the geographic progress of our daily ride or race from home or car. All of this data and more will be easily uploaded from a single source to your pocket computer where a virtual coach will analyze it and alter your training schedule appropriately. And you will remember the days when your self-coaching was incredibly basic and naïve.

We aren't fully to this technological training nirvana yet, although we are inching closer every year. In the meantime, if you want to succeed as a road racer, you need to understand the many subtle nuances of training. Or, you need to hire a coach. In 1995 there was only a handful of knowledgeable coaches available. I knew most of them by name. Now USA Cycling has trained hundreds of coaches, and the career field is becoming more professional every year. If you have doubts about your capacity for self-coaching or the time to devote to it, I'd highly recommend seeking out a professional coach to work with. It's truly amazing what a good coach can do for a rider.

I'd like to close this book with one guiding thought that summarizes much of what is included here as you begin to plan for the best race performances of your career: Train hard—rest harder!

APPENDIX A

Maximum Weight Chart

To determine one repetition max (1RM) from a submaximal lift of 2 to 10 repetitions:

1. Select from the top row of the chart the number of reps completed (for example, 5).
2. In the reps completed column find the weight used for the exercise (for example, 100).
3. From the weight used, look to the far lefthand "Max" column to determine predicted 1RM (in example, 115 pounds).

Reprinted with permission of Strength Tech, Inc., P.O. Box 1381, Stillwater, OK 74076.

Max	10	9	8	7	6	5	4	3	2
45	35	35	35	35	40	40	40	40	45
50	40	40	40	40	45	45	45	45	50
55	40	45	45	45	45	50	50	50	50
60	45	45	50	50	50	55	55	55	55
65	50	50	50	55	55	55	60	60	60
70	55	55	55	60	60	60	65	65	65
75	55	60	60	60	65	65	70	70	70
80	60	60	65	65	70	70	70	75	75
85	65	65	70	70	70	75	75	80	80
90	70	70	70	75	75	80	80	85	85
95	70	75	75	80	80	85	85	90	90
100	75	80	80	85	85	90	90	95	95
105	80	80	85	85	90	90	95	95	100
110	85	85	90	90	95	95	100	100	105
115	85	90	90	95	100	100	105	105	110
120	90	95	95	100	100	105	110	110	115
125	95	95	100	105	105	110	115	115	120
130	100	100	105	105	110	115	115	120	125
135	100	105	110	110	115	120	120	125	130
140	105	110	110	115	120	125	125	130	135
145	110	110	115	120	125	125	130	135	140
150	115	115	120	125	130	130	135	140	145
155	115	120	125	130	130	135	140	145	145
160	120	125	130	130	135	140	145	150	150
165	125	130	130	135	140	145	150	155	155
170	130	130	135	140	145	150	155	155	160
175	130	135	140	145	150	155	160	160	165
180	135	140	145	150	155	160	160	165	170

Max	10	9	8	7	6	5	4	3	2
185	140	145	150	155	155	160	165	170	175
190	145	145	150	155	160	165	170	175	180
195	145	150	155	160	165	170	175	180	185
200	150	155	160	165	170	175	180	185	190
205	155	160	165	170	175	180	185	190	195
210	160	165	170	175	180	185	190	195	200
215	160	165	170	175	185	190	195	200	205
220	165	170	175	180	185	195	200	205	210
225	170	175	180	185	190	195	205	210	215
230	175	180	185	190	195	200	205	215	220
235	175	180	190	195	200	205	210	215	225
240	180	185	190	200	205	210	215	220	230
245	185	190	195	200	210	215	220	225	235
250	190	195	200	205	215	220	225	230	240
255	190	200	205	210	215	225	230	235	240
260	195	200	210	215	220	230	235	240	245
265	200	205	210	220	225	230	240	245	250
270	205	210	215	225	230	235	245	250	255
275	205	215	220	225	235	240	250	255	260
280	210	215	225	230	240	245	250	260	265
285	215	220	230	235	240	250	255	265	270
290	220	225	230	240	245	255	260	270	275
295	220	230	235	245	250	260	265	275	280
300	225	235	240	250	255	265	270	280	285
305	230	235	245	250	260	265	275	280	290
310	235	240	250	255	265	270	280	285	295
315	235	245	250	260	270	275	285	290	300
320	240	250	255	265	270	280	290	295	305
325	245	250	260	270	275	285	295	300	310
330	250	255	265	270	280	290	295	305	315
335	250	260	270	275	285	295	300	310	320
340	255	265	270	280	290	300	305	315	325
345	260	265	275	285	295	300	310	320	330
350	265	270	280	290	300	305	315	325	335
355	265	275	285	295	300	310	320	330	335
360	270	280	290	295	305	315	325	335	340
365	275	285	290	300	310	320	330	340	345
370	280	285	295	305	315	325	335	340	350
375	280	290	300	310	320	330	340	345	355
380	285	295	305	315	325	335	340	350	360
385	290	300	310	320	325	335	345	355	365
390	295	300	310	320	330	340	350	360	370

Max	10	9	8	7	6	5	4	3	2
395	295	305	315	325	335	345	355	365	375
400	300	310	320	330	340	350	360	370	380
405	305	315	325	335	345	355	365	375	385
410	310	320	330	340	350	360	370	380	390
415	310	320	330	340	355	365	375	385	395
420	315	325	335	345	355	370	380	390	400
425	320	330	340	350	360	370	385	395	405
430	325	335	345	355	365	375	385	400	410
435	325	335	350	360	370	380	390	400	415
440	330	340	350	365	375	385	395	405	420
445	335	345	355	365	380	390	400	410	425
450	340	350	360	370	385	395	405	415	430
455	340	355	365	375	385	400	410	420	430
460	345	355	370	380	390	405	415	425	435
465	350	360	370	385	395	405	420	430	440
470	355	365	375	390	400	410	425	435	445
475	355	370	380	390	405	415	430	440	450
480	360	370	385	395	410	420	430	445	455
485	365	375	390	400	410	425	435	450	460
490	370	380	390	405	415	430	440	455	465
495	370	385	395	410	420	435	445	460	470
500	375	390	400	415	425	440	450	465	475
510	385	395	410	420	435	445	460	470	485
520	390	405	415	430	440	455	470	480	495
530	400	410	425	435	450	465	475	490	505
540	405	420	430	445	460	475	485	500	515
550	415	425	440	455	470	480	495	510	525
560	420	435	450	460	475	490	505	520	530
570	430	440	455	470	485	500	515	525	540
580	435	450	465	480	495	510	520	535	550
590	445	455	470	485	500	515	530	545	560
600	450	465	480	495	510	525	540	555	570
610	460	475	490	505	520	535	550	565	580
620	465	480	495	510	525	545	560	575	590
630	475	490	505	520	535	550	565	585	600
640	480	495	510	530	545	560	575	590	610
650	490	505	520	535	555	570	585	600	620
660	495	510	530	545	560	580	595	610	625
670	505	520	535	555	570	585	605	620	635
680	510	525	545	560	580	595	610	630	645
690	520	535	550	570	585	605	620	640	655
700	525	545	560	580	595	615	630	650	665

APPENDIX B

Annual Training Plan Template

ANNUAL TRAINING PLAN

Annual Hours:
Seasonal Goals:
1.
2.
3.
Training Objectives:
1.
2.
3.
4.
5.

WORKOUTS

WK#	MON	RACE	PRI	PERIOD	HOURS	DETAILS	WEIGHTS	ENDURANCE	FORCE	SPEED SKILL	MUSCULAR ENDUR.	ANAEROBIC ENDUR.	POWER	TESTING	
01	/														
02	/														
03	/														
04	/														
05	/														
06	/														
07	/														
08	/														
09	/														
10	/														
11	/														
12	/														
13	/														
14	/														
15	/														
16	/														
17	/														
18	/														
19	/														
20	/														
21	/														
22	/														
23	/														
24	/														
25	/														
26	/														
27	/														
28	/														
29	/														
30	/														
31	/														
32	/														
33	/														
34	/														
35	/														
36	/														
37	/														
38	/														
39	/														
40	/														
41	/														
42	/														
43	/														
44	/														
45	/														
46	/														
47	/														
48	/														
49	/														
50	/														
51	/														
52	/														

APPENDIX C

Workout Menu

These workouts are listed by ability area, which are also included in the Annual Training Plan (Figure 8.1). Following the description of each workout is the suggested training period or periods in which to incorporate it. The workouts are listed in a progressive manner, meaning that the easiest, or least stressful, come first and they progressively get harder. It's best to follow this sequence as you continue to refine the ability.

This menu is hardly an exhaustive list of workouts. You can do many more simply by modifying some of the characteristics. You may also create others from scratch, based on conditions known to be in a given race. Combining workouts often provides a comprehensive race simulation, but be careful not to try to accomplish so much in a single session that the benefits are diluted. It's best to limit a multiple-benefit workout to two combinations.

Each workout is preceded by an alpha-numeric code that may be used as a scheduling shorthand. Chapter 15 discussed training diaries and provided a weekly scheduling format where such shorthand will come in handy.

The intensity levels of the workouts listed are based on Figure 9.1. Individual indicators of intensity are discussed in greater detail in Chapter 4.

Endurance Workouts

E1: Recovery

Done in zone 1 using the small chainring on a flat course. Do these the day after a BT workout. Best if done alone. May also be done on an indoor trainer or rollers, especially if flat courses are not available. Crosstraining is appropriate for recovery in Preparation, Base 1, and Base 2 periods. An excellent time to do a recovery spin is in the evening on a day when you've done intervals, sprints, a hard group ride, hills, or a race. Spinning for 15 to 30 minutes on rollers or a trainer hastens recovery for most experienced riders. Novices will typically benefit more from taking the time off. These workouts are not scheduled on the Annual Training Plan, but they are an integral part of training throughout the season. (Periods: All)

E2: Aerobic

Used for aerobic maintenance and endurance training. Stay primarily in zones 1 and 2 on a rolling course up to 4 percent grades. Remain seated on the uphill portions to build greater strength while maintaining a comfortably high cadence. Can be done with a disciplined group or on an indoor trainer by shifting through the gears to simulate rolling hills. Crosstraining is effective during Preparation and Base 1. (Periods: All)

E3: Fixed Gear

Set up your bike with a gear that is appropriate for your strength level using a small chainring (39–42) and a large cog (15–19). If you are in your first two years of training, don't do this workout. Start by riding flat courses and gradually add rolling hills. Intensity should be mostly in zones 2 and 3. This is a multi-ability workout including endurance, strength, and speed—all elements required in Base training. (Periods: Base 2, Base 3)

Strength (Force) Workouts

F1: Moderate Hills

Select a course that includes several hills of up to 6 percent grade that take up to three minutes to ascend. Stay seated on all climbs pedaling from the hips. Cadence should be at 70 rpm or higher. Stay in zones 1–4 on this ride. (Periods: Base 3)

F2: Long Hills

Ride a course including long grades of up to 8 percent that take six or more minutes to climb. Remain mostly seated on the hills and keep your cadence at 60 rpm or higher. Go no higher than zone 5a. Concentrate on bike position and smooth pedaling. (Periods: Base 3, Build 1)

F3: Steep Hills

Ride a course that includes 8 percent or steeper hills requiring less than two minutes to climb. You can do repeats on the same hill with three to five minutes of recovery between climbs. Be sure to warm up thoroughly. Intensity may climb to zone 5b several times with recoveries into zone 1. Climb in and out of the saddle. Maintain a cadence of 50–60 rpm. Stop the workout if you cannot maintain at least 50 rpm. Do this workout no more than twice per week. Do not do this workout if you have knee problems. (Periods: Build 1, Build 2, Peak, Race)

Speed Workouts

S1: Spin-ups

On a downhill or on an indoor trainer set to light resistance, for one minute gradually increase cadence to maximum—this is the cadence that you can maintain without bouncing. As the cadence increases, allow your lower legs and feet to relax, especially the toes. Hold your maximum for as long as possible. Recover for at least three minutes and repeat several times. These are best done with a handlebar computer that displays cadence. Heart rate and power ratings have no significance for this workout. (Periods: Preparation, Base 1, Base 2, Base 3)

S2: Isolated Leg

With a light resistance on trainer or downhill, do 90 percent of the work with one leg while the other is "along for the ride." Spin with a higher than normal cadence. Change legs when fatigue begins to set in. This can also be done on a trainer with one foot out of the pedal and resting on a stool while the other works. Focus on eliminating "dead" spots at top and bottom of stroke. Heart rate and power ratings have no bearing on this workout. (Periods: Base 1, Base 2)

S3: Cornering

On a curbed street with a clean surface and 90-degree turns, practice cornering techniques: lean both bike and body into turn, lean body while keeping bike upright, and keep body upright while leaning bike. Avoid streets with heavy traffic. Practice several speeds with different angles of approach. Include two or three sprint efforts into the turn. Heart rate and power ratings are not important for this workout. (Periods: Base 3, Build 1, Build 2)

S4: Bumping

On a firm, grassy field, practice making body contact with a partner while riding slowly. Increase speed as skill improves. Also include touching overlapped wheels. (Periods: Base 3, Build 1, Build 2)

S5: Form Sprints

Early in a ride, do 6 to 10 sprints on a slight downhill or with a tail wind. Each sprint should last about 15 seconds, followed by a 5-minute recovery. These sprints are done for form, so hold back a bit on intensity. Heart rate is not an accurate gauge. Power/RPE should be in zone 5b. Stand for the first 10 seconds while running smoothly on the pedals, building leg speed. Then sit for 5 seconds and maintain a high cadence. This workout is best done alone to avoid "competing." (Periods: Base 3, Build 1, Build 2, Peak, Race)

S6: Sprints

Within an aerobic ride, include several 10- to 15-second, race-effort sprints. These can be done with another rider or with a group. Designate sprint primes such as signs. Employ all of the techniques of form sprints, only now at a higher intensity. Power/RPE should be zone 5c. Heart rate is not a good indicator. There should be at least 5-minute recoveries between sprints. (Periods: Build 1, Build 2, Peak, Race)

Muscular-Endurance Workouts

M1: Tempo

On a mostly flat course, or on an indoor trainer, ride continually in zone 3 without recovery at time trial cadence. Avoid roads with heavy traffic and stop signs. Stay in an aerodynamic position throughout. Start with 20 to 30 minutes and build to 75 to 90 minutes by adding 10 to 15 minutes each week. This workout may be done two or three times weekly. (Periods: Base 2, Base 3)

M2: Cruise Intervals

On a relatively flat course, or an indoor trainer, complete three to five work intervals that are 6 to 12 minutes long. Build to zones 4 and 5a on each work interval. If training with a heart rate monitor, the work interval starts as soon as you begin pedaling hard—not when you reach zone 4. Recover for 2 or 3 minutes after each interval. Rest intervals should be 2 to 3 minutes and your heart rate should drop into zone 2. The first workout should total 20 to 30 minutes of combined work interval time. Stay relaxed, aerodynamic, and listen closely to your breathing while pedaling at time trial cadence. (Periods: Base 3, Build 1, Build 2, Peak, Race)

M3: Hill Cruise Intervals

Same as M2 cruise intervals, except that you do them on a long 2–4 percent grade. These are good if strength is a limiter. (Periods: Build 1, Build 2, Peak, Race)

M4: Motor-Paced Cruise Intervals

Same as M2 cruise intervals, except that you do this as a motor-paced workout. Whenever doing motor-pace use only a motorcycle for pacing. Do not use a car or truck. Not only do they make the workout too fast, they also make it more dangerous. Be sure the driver of the motorcycle has experience with motor-paced workouts and will always be thinking about your safety. Discuss the workout details with the driver before starting. (Periods: Build 1, Build 2, Peak)

M5: Crisscross Threshold

On a mostly flat course with little traffic and no stops, ride 20 to 40 minutes in zones 4 and 5a. Once you have reached zone 4, gradually build effort to the top of zone 5a, taking about 2 minutes to do so. Then begin backing off slightly and slowly drop back to the bottom of zone 4, taking about 2 minutes again. Continue this pattern throughout the ride. Cadence will vary. Complete three or four cruise interval workouts before attempting this workout. (Periods: Build 2, Peak)

M6: Threshold

On a mostly flat course with little traffic and no stops, ride 20 to 40 minutes non-stop in zones 4 and 5a. Stay relaxed, aerodynamic, and listen closely to your breathing throughout the workout. Don't attempt a threshold ride until you've completed at least four cruise interval workouts. This workout definitely should be included in your training, preferably on your time trial bike. (Periods: Build 2, Peak)

M7: Motor-paced Threshold

Same as M6 threshold, except this is done as a motor-paced workout. (Periods: Build 2, Peak, Race)

Anaerobic-Endurance Workouts

A1: Group Ride

Ride how you feel. If tired, sit in or break off and ride by yourself. If fresh, ride hard, going into zones 5a–5c several times. (Periods: Build 1, Build 2, Peak, Race)

A2: SE Intervals

After a good warm-up, on a mostly flat course with no stop signs and light traffic, do five work intervals of 3- to 6-minutes duration each. Build to zone 5b on each with a cadence of 90 rpm or higher. If unable to achieve zone 5b by the end of the third work interval, stop the workout. You aren't ready. Recover to zone 1, with the duration of the rest interval matching the preceding work interval. (Periods: Build 1, Build 2, Peak, Race)

A3: Pyramid Intervals

The same as SE intervals, except the work intervals are 1-, 2-, 3-, 4-, 4-, 3-, 2-, 1-minutes, building to zone 5b. The recovery after each should be equal to the preceding work interval. (Periods: Build 1, Build 2, Peak, Race)

A4: Hill Intervals

Following a thorough warm-up, go to a 6–8 percent hill that takes 3 to 4 minutes to complete and do five climbs. Stay seated with cadence at 60 or higher rpm. Build to zone 5b on each. Recover to zone 1 by spinning down the hill and riding at the bottom for a total of 3 to 4 minutes depending on the duration of the climb. (Periods: Build 2, Peak)

A5: Lactate Tolerance Reps

This is to be done on a flat or slightly uphill course or into the wind. After a long warm-up and several jumps, do four to eight repetitions of 90 seconds to 2 minutes each. Intensity is zone 5c. Cadence is high. The total of all work intervals must not exceed 12 minutes. Recovery intervals are 2.5 times as long as the preceding work interval. For example, after a 2-minute rep, recover for 5 minutes. Build to this workout conservatively starting with 6 minutes total and adding no more than 2 minutes weekly. Do this workout no more than once a week and recover for at least 48 hours after. If you are unable to achieve zone 5c after three attempts, stop the workout. Do not do this workout if you are in the first two years of training for cycling. (Periods: Build 2, Peak)

A6: Hill Reps

After a good warm-up, go to a 6–8 percent hill and do four to eight reps of 90 seconds each. Stay seated for the first 60 seconds as you build to zone 5b at 60–70 rpm. In the last 30 seconds, shift to a higher gear, stand, and sprint to the top, attaining zone 5c. Recover completely for four minutes after each rep. If you are unable to achieve zone 5c after three attempts, stop the workout. Do not do this workout if you are in the first two years of training for cycling. (Periods: Build 2, Peak)

Power Workouts

P1: Jumps

Warm up well. Then early in a workout, on an indoor trainer or the road, do 15–25 jumps to improve explosive power. Complete three to five sets of five jumps each. Each jump is 10 to 12 revolutions of the cranks (each leg) at high cadence. Recover for 1 minute between efforts and 5 minutes between sets. Power/RPE should be zone 5c. Heart rate is not a good indicator of exertion for this workout. (Periods: Build 1, Build 2, Peak, Race)

P2: Hill Sprints

Early in the workout, after a good warm-up, go to a hill with a 4–6 percent grade. Do six to nine sprints of 20 seconds each. Use a flying start for each sprint taking 10 seconds to build speed on the flat approach while standing. Climb the hill for 10 seconds applying maximal force standing on the pedals with a high cadence. Recover for five minutes after each sprint. Power/RPE should be zone 5c. Heart rate is not a good indicator of exertion for this workout. (Periods: Build 1, Build 2, Peak)

P3: Crit Sprints

Warm up and then go to a course with curbed corners, clean turns, and little traffic. Do six to nine sprints of 25–35 seconds duration including corners just as in a criterium. Recover to zone 1 for five minutes after each. Can be done with another rider, taking turns leading the sprints. (Periods: Build 2, Peak, Race)

Test Workouts

T1: Aerobic Time Trial

This is best on an indoor trainer with a rear-wheel computer pick-up, or on a CompuTrainer. May also be done on a flat section of road, but weather conditions will have an effect. After a warm-up, ride five miles with heart rate 9–11 beats below lactate threshold heart rate. Use a standard gear without shifting. Record time. The conditions of this workout must be as similar as possible from one test to the next. This includes the amount of rest since the last BT workout, the length and intensity of the warm-up, the weather if on the road, and the gear used during the test. As aerobic fitness improves, the time should decrease. (Periods: Base 1, Base 2)

T2: Time Trial

After a 15- to 30-minute warm-up, complete an eight-mile time trial on a flat course. Go four miles out, turn around, and return to the start-line. Mark your start and turn for later reference. Look for faster times as your anaerobic endurance and muscular endurance improve. In addition to time, record average power/heart rate and peak power/heart rate. Keep the conditions the same from one time trial to the next as in the aerobic time trial. Use any gear and feel free to shift during the test. (Periods: Build 1, Build 2)

APPENDIX D

Weekly Training Diary Template

WEEK BEGINNING: **PLANNED WEEKLY HOURS/MILES:**

NOTES _____

_____
_____
_____
_____
_____
_____
_____
_____
_____
_____
_____
_____
_____
_____

MONDAY	/ /

☐ Sleep ☐ Fatigue ☐ Stress ☐ Soreness

Resting heart rate   Weight

WORKOUT 1

Weather

Route

Distance

Time   Total

Time by zone **1**   **2**

3   **4**   **5**

WORKOUT 2

Weather

Route

Distance

Time   Total

Time by zone **1**   **2**

3   **4**   **5**

TUESDAY	/ /

☐ Sleep ☐ Fatigue ☐ Stress ☐ Soreness

Resting heart rate   Weight

WORKOUT 1

Weather

Route

Distance

Time   Total

Time by zone **1**   **2**

3   **4**   **5**

WORKOUT 2

Weather

Route

Distance

Time   Total

Time by zone **1**   **2**

3   **4**   **5**

NOTES _____

_____
_____
_____
_____
_____
_____
_____
_____
_____
_____
_____
_____
_____
_____

WEDNESDAY	/ /

☐ Sleep ☐ Fatigue ☐ Stress ☐ Soreness

Resting heart rate   Weight

WORKOUT 1

Weather

Route

Distance

Time   Total

Time by zone **1**   **2**

3   **4**   **5**

WORKOUT 2

Weather

Route

Distance

Time   Total

Time by zone **1**   **2**

3   **4**   **5**

THURSDAY	/ /

☐ Sleep ☐ Fatigue ☐ Stress ☐ Soreness

Resting heart rate   Weight

WORKOUT 1

Weather

Route

Distance

Time   Total

Time by zone **1**   **2**

3   **4**   **5**

WORKOUT 2

Weather

Route

Distance

Time   Total

Time by zone **1**   **2**

3   **4**   **5**

WEEK'S GOALS (Check off as achieved)

- _____
- _____
- _____

FRIDAY	/ /

☐ Sleep ☐ Fatigue ☐ Stress ☐ Soreness

Resting heart rate _____ Weight _____

WORKOUT 1

Weather _____

Route _____

Distance _____

Time _____ Total _____

Time by zone **1** _____ **2** _____

3 _____ **4** _____ **5** _____

WORKOUT 2

Weather _____

Route _____

Distance _____

Time _____ Total _____

Time by zone **1** _____ **2** _____

3 _____ **4** _____ **5** _____

SATURDAY	/ /

☐ Sleep ☐ Fatigue ☐ Stress ☐ Soreness

Resting heart rate _____ Weight _____

WORKOUT 1

Weather _____

Route _____

Distance _____

Time _____ Total _____

Time by zone **1** _____ **2** _____

3 _____ **4** _____ **5** _____

WORKOUT 2

Weather _____

Route _____

Distance _____

Time _____ Total _____

Time by zone **1** _____ **2** _____

3 _____ **4** _____ **5** _____

NOTES _____

_____

_____

_____

_____

_____

_____

_____

_____

_____

SUNDAY	/ /

☐ Sleep ☐ Fatigue ☐ Stress ☐ Soreness

Resting heart rate _____ Weight _____

WORKOUT 1

Weather _____

Route _____

Distance _____

Time _____ Total _____

Time by zone **1** _____ **2** _____

3 _____ **4** _____ **5** _____

WORKOUT 2

Weather _____

Route _____

Distance _____

Time _____ Total _____

Time by zone **1** _____ **2** _____

3 _____ **4** _____ **5** _____

WEEKLY SUMMARY

	Weekly total	Year to date
Bike miles		
Bike time		
Strength time		
Total		

Soreness _____

_____

Notes _____

_____

_____

_____

_____

_____

NOTES _____

_____

_____

_____

_____

_____

_____

_____

_____

_____

_____

_____

_____

_____

GLOSSARY

aerobic In the presence of oxygen; aerobic metabolism utilizes oxygen.

aerobic capacity The body's maximal capacity for using oxygen to produce energy during maximal exertion. Also known as VO_2max.

agonistic muscles Muscles directly engaged in a muscular contraction.

anaerobic In the absence of oxygen; nonoxidation metabolism.

anaerobic endurance (AE) The ability resulting from the combination of speed skills and endurance allowing the athlete to maintain a high cadence for an extended period of time.

anaerobic threshold (AT) When aerobic metabolism no longer supplies all the need for energy, energy is produced anaerobically; indicated by an increase in lactic acid. Also known as lactate threshold.

antagonistic muscles Muscles that have an opposite effect on movers (see "agonistic muscles"), or against muscles, by opposing their contraction. For example, the triceps is an antagonistic muscle for the biceps.

Base period The period during which the basic abilities of endurance, speed skills, and force are emphasized.

bonk A state of extreme exhaustion during a workout caused mainly by the depletion of glycogen in the muscles.

breakaway A rider or group of riders that rides away from the main pack.

BT Breakthrough workouts that provide the stress to start the adaptive process.

Build period The specific preparation mesocycle during which high-intensity training in the form of muscular endurance, anaerobic endurance, and power are emphasized and endurance, force, and speed skills are maintained.

capillary A fine network of small vessels located between arteries and veins where exchanges between tissue and blood occur.

carbohydrate loading (glycogen loading) A dietary procedure that elevates muscle glycogen stores.

cardiorespiratory system Cardiovascular system and lungs.

cardiovascular system Heart, blood, and blood vessels.

chase The attempt to catch a breakaway.

circuit training Selected exercises or activities performed rapidly in sequence; used in weight training.

criterium A road race that is generally held on city streets or parks; a course usually one mile or less and marked by short straights and tight turns.

crosstraining Participating in one sport to train for another.

duration The length of time of a given workout.

endurance The ability to persist despite the onset of fatigue.

ergogenic aid A substance or phenomenon that can improve athletic performance.

fast-twitch fiber (FT) A muscle fiber characterized by fast contraction time, high anaerobic capacity, and low aerobic capacity, all making the fiber suited for high power output activities.

force The ability of a muscle or muscle group to overcome a resistance.

free weights Weights not part of an exercise machine (i.e., barbells and dumbbells).

frequency The number of times per week that one trains.

glucose Simple sugar.

glycogen The form in which glucose (sugar) is stored in the muscles and the liver.

growth hormone A hormone secreted by the anterior lobe of the pituitary gland that stimulates growth and development.

hamstring Muscle on the back of the thigh that flexes the knee and extends the hip.

individuality, principle of The theory that any training program must consider the specific needs and abilities of the individual for whom it is designed.

intensity The qualitative element of training such as speed skills, maximum force, and power.

interval training A system of high-intensity work marked by short but regularly repeated periods of work stress interspersed with periods of recovery.

jump A sudden burst of speed that provides the initial acceleration for a sprint.

lactate Formed when lactic acid from the muscles gives off a hydrogen atom on entering the blood stream.

lactate threshold (LT) The point during exercise of increasing intensity at which blood lactate begins to accumulate above resting levels. Also known as anaerobic threshold.

lactic acid A by-product of the lactic acid system resulting from the incomplete breakdown of glucose (sugar) in the production of energy.

limiter A race-specific weakness.

long, slow distance (LSD) training A form of continuous training in which the athlete performs at a relatively low intensity.

macrocycle A period of training including several mesocycles; usually an entire season.

mesocycle A period of training generally two to six weeks long.

microcycle A period of training of approximately one week.

motor-pace Riding behind a motorcycle or other vehicle that breaks the wind.

muscular endurance (ME) The ability of a muscle or muscle group to perform repeated contractions for a long period of time while bearing a load. The combination of force and endurance abilities.

overload, principle of A training load that challenges the body's current level of fitness.

overtraining Extreme fatigue, both physical and mental, caused by training at a volume/intensity higher than that to which the body can adapt.

Peak period The mesocycle during which volume of training is reduced and intensity is proportionally increased, allowing the athlete to reach high levels of fitness.

periodization Represents a process of structuring training into periods.

power The ability to apply maximum force in the shortest time possible.

Preparation period The mesocycle during which the athlete begins to train for the coming season; usually marked by the use of crosstraining.

progression, principle of The theory that workload must be gradually increased, accompanied by intermittent periods of recovery.

quadriceps The large muscle in front of the thigh.

Race period The mesocycle during which workload is decreased, allowing the athlete to compete in high-priority races.

Rating of Perceived Exertion (RPE) A subjective assessment of how hard one is working.

recovery interval The relief period between work intervals within an interval workout.

repetition The number of work intervals within one set.

repetition maximum (RM) The maximum load that a muscle group can lift in one attempt. Also called "one-repetition maximum" (1RM).

road race A mass-start race that goes from point to point, covers one large loop or is held on a circuit longer than those used for criteriums.

set The total number of repetitions performed before an extensive recovery interval is taken.

slow-twitch fiber (ST) A muscle fiber characterized by slow contraction time, low anaerobic capacity, and high aerobic capacity, all making the fiber suited for low-power, endurance activities.

specificity, principle of The theory that training must stress the systems critical for optimal performance in order to achieve the desired training adaptations.

speed skills In cycling, the ability to turn the cranks quickly and efficiently.

stage race A multi-day event consisting of road races, time trials, and often criteriums.

tapering A reduction in training intensity and volume prior to a major competition.

time trial (TT) A race against the clock in which individual riders start at set intervals.

Transition period The mesocycle during which the workload and structure of training are greatly reduced, allowing physical and psychological recovery from training and racing.

ventilatory threshold (VT) The point during increasing exertion at which breathing first becomes labored. Roughly corresponds with lactate threshold.

VO$_2$max The maximal capacity for oxygen consumption by the body during maximal exertion, also known as aerobic power and maximal oxygen consumption.

volume A quantitative element of training, such as miles or hours of training within a given time.

work interval High-intensity efforts separated by recovery intervals.

workload Measured stress applied in training through the combination of frequency, intensity, and duration.

INDEX

ABOUT THE AUTHOR

Joe Friel has trained endurance athletes since 1980. His clients have included amateur and professional road cyclists, mountain bikers, triathletes, duathletes, swimmers, and runners. They have been from all corners of the globe and included American and foreign national champions, world championship competitors, and an Olympian.

In addition to *The Cyclist's Training Bible*, Joe is the author of *Cycling Past 50*, *Precision Heart Rate Training* (co-author), *The Triathlete's Training Bible*, *The Mountain Biker's Training Bible*, and *Going Long: Training for Ironman-Distance Triathlons* (co-author). He holds a master's degree in exercise science and is a USA Triathlon and USA Cycling certified coach.

He is a featured columnist for *Inside Triathlon* and *VeloNews* magazines, and writes feature stories for other international publications and Web sites.

Joe speaks at seminars and camps around the world on training and racing for endurance athletes, and provides consulting services for corporations in the fitness industry. Every year he selects a group of the brightest coaches with the greatest potential and closely oversees their progress as they advance into the ranks of elite-level coaches.

For more information on personal coaching, seminars, camps, developmental coach mentoring, certification of coaches in the Training Bible methodology, coaching symposia, and consulting go on-line to www.Ultrafit.com. There you will also find *e-Tips*, a free newsletter that provides monthly updates to the Training Bible methodology. For all of the tools necessary for effective self-coaching using the concepts of this book, including a "virtual coach," go to www.TrainingBible.com.